likeable
SOCIAL MEDIA

likeable
SOCIAL MEDIA

HOW TO DELIGHT YOUR CUSTOMERS,
CREATE AN IRRESISTIBLE BRAND,
AND BE GENERALLY AMAZING ON ALL
SOCIAL NETWORKS THAT MATTER

{ **Revised and Expanded
Third Edition** }

DAVE KERPEN

with Michelle Greenbaum
and Robert Berk

New Foreword by Carrie Kerpen

Mc
Graw
Hill
Education

New York   Chicago   San Francisco   Athens   London   Madrid
Mexico City   Milan   New Delhi   Singapore   Sydney   Toronto

1 2 3 4 5 6 7 8 9 LCR 24 23 22 21 20 19

ISBN   978-1-260-45328-7
MHID   1-260-45328-6

e-ISBN   978-1-260-45329-4
e-MHID   1-260-45329-4

Library of Congress Cataloging-in-Publication Data

Names: Kerpen, Dave, author.
Title: Likeable social media : how to delight your customers, create an irresistible brand, and be generally amazing on all social networks that matter / by Dave Kerpen.
Description: Third edition. | New York : McGraw-Hill, [2019] | Includes bibliographical references and index.
Identifiers: LCCN 2018050130| ISBN 9781260453287 (alk. paper) | ISBN 1260453286
Subjects: LCSH: Internet marketing. | Online social networks. | Social media--Economic aspects. | Customer relations. | Branding (Marketing)
Classification: LCC HF5415.1265 .K425 2019 | DDC 658.8/72--dc23 LC record available at https://lccn.loc.gov/2018050130

Interior design by THINK Book Works

McGraw-Hill Education books are available at special quantity discounts to use as premiums and sales promotions or for use in corporate training programs. To contact a representative, please visit the Contact Us pages at www.mhprofessional.com.

Thank you so much for
purchasing the third edition of
Likeable Social Media!

As a special bonus just for you, please visit
http://www.LikeableEngagement.com
to download a free white paper:
The Meaning of Meaningful:
Content for the New Facebook News Feed

For my amazing children,
Charlotte, Kate, and Seth.
May you grow up in a more likeable world.

And for my amazing wife, Carrie,
my partner in all things.

I love you all to infinity and beyond.

Contents

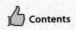

The world was a different place in 2011.

There were only 1.2 billion people using social media. Now there are nearly three billion.

Politicians were only beginning to experiment with social media. Now it's their primary method of communication.

Brands were building fan bases on social. Now they're building their businesses there.

In 2011, social media was a tool. In 2019, it's a utility.

I wrote the Foreword for this book in 2015—four years after the first edition and four years before this one. Social media has changed a lot over the past eight years, and it will change again over the next. But I'm going to fill you in on a secret—one that I've learned being married to the author of this book and running a social media agency with him for the past decade.

The networks may change. The rules may change. The tactics may change. But the principles never will.

In looking at this new edition, I was excited to see all of the new networks incorporated. I was inspired by the innovative approaches to social media advertising. I remain thrilled by how smart, scrappy brands use the latest and greatest changes to the landscape to their advantage. But mostly? I was heartened to see that Dave's original principles like listening, engaging, and being authentic are still not only relevant but imperative to success—regardless of the network or content type.

Neither Mark Zuckerberg, nor Jack Dorsey, nor Evan Spiegel, nor any network CEO could have imagined what social media would one day become. In its transformation to a utility, it's created a lot of complications—including affecting our interpersonal skills and even our elections. But with every challenge that social media brings about, there is equal opportunity—opportunity to spread messages of hope, kindness, and good. And brands, just as they did in 2011, have a platform to tell likeable stories. Except now, the tools and technologies afforded to them allow them to share those likeable stories more quickly and more easily sell their products and services.

As I write this Foreword, I'm imagining what social media, and my own life, will look like for future editions. I'm certain there will be more users and surely some new networks (and some that will have faded into the distance). I have no doubt that reporting will evolve to yield a deeper correlation between brand affinity and purchase. And I believe wholeheartedly that the world will come together to fix some of the privacy challenges we've seen in recent years.

As for me? I'll be celebrating being married to the author of this book for even longer—with many of our memories publicly documented across every social channel.

I wouldn't have it any other way.

—Carrie Kerpen
Cofounder and CEO, Likeable Media
Author, *Work It: Secrets for Success from the Boldest Women in Business*

Acknowledgments

Those of you who know me (and know the giant social media universe) know that there are literally thousands of people I'd like to thank here. But since that wouldn't make for very good reading material, I'll summarize by key categories. If your name isn't listed but you're among my extended group of friends, family, colleagues, and supporters, please know how appreciative I am of you and your impact on my life.

MY LIKEABLE PUBLISHING FAMILY

Thanks to all of the editors and staff at McGraw-Hill Professional who worked on the original book as well as the second and the third editions, and showed me there is still room for traditional publishers today. Thanks especially to Julia Baxter, my marketing rep and the first person at McGraw-Hill to accept my Facebook friendship—it meant a lot. To Zach Gajewski, my developmental editor and BU brother, thank you for being my ambassador of book quan. Thanks to Mary Glenn, Jane Palmieri, and Cheryl Ringer, who helped to make the second and third editions a reality, and special thanks to Cheryl, who championed this third edition as well as any editor I've ever worked with.

Thanks to my amazing agent, Celeste Fine, who for the first edition of this book helped me navigate the crazy new waters of publishing, and who to this day endlessly supports me, and to her associates John Maas and Jaidree Braddix, excellent additions to the team.

There would be no book whatsoever had my acquisitions editor Niki Papadopoulos not emailed me, encouraged me, signed me, and challenged me. Thanks Niki!

MY LIKEABLE WORK FAMILY

I am so incredibly fortunate to be surrounded by an amazing team at our companies, Likeable Media, Likeable Local, and UMA Health. Thanks most to Michelle Greenbaum and Robert Berk, two of our most likeable team members and the two people who worked harder than anyone to get this third edition into the incredible, most-improved, valuable shape that it's in today. Michelle and Rob, you are both rock stars, and I can't wait to see how your careers grow from here, and to help you get there.

From Likeable Local: Thanks to Meg Riedinger, my amazing longtime chief of staff, and my coauthor on the second edition. I appreciate you more than you know. Thanks to Hugh Morgenbesser, my partner at Likeable Local and one of the smartest, more likeable people I've ever known. Thanks to all of you for your support, you're the best team, past and present: Gaby Piazza, Nicole Kroese, Shane Donnelly, Sam Sudakoff, Alexa Pfeffer, Josh Langtry, Mark Brooks, Ryan Balfe, Daniel Campbell, Brittany Martin, David Jolly, Julian Wyzykowski, Lisa Markuson, Ricky Ryan, Ryan Malone, Stefanie Peterson, and Jonathan Logan.

To my incredible Likeable Media family: Thanks to Mallorie Rosenbluth, my coauthor on the second edition. Thanks also to key Likeable Media employees, past and present: Candie Harris, Brian Murray, Megan McMahon, Jenna Lebel, Michele Weisman, Rachel Hadley, Jo Hague, Tim Bosch, Theresa Braun, and all the rest of the team. Special thanks to Valerie Tirella, Fer Wang, Honey Comer, Olivia Ellis, Alyssa Vitali, Jamie Deschamps, James Reichert, and Brian Leigh, who contributed to this edition.

You—and the whole Likeable team—rule!

Thanks to our investors and advisors as well—without you, we wouldn't have had three companies and hundreds of clients to write about. You're all awesome: Dave McClure and the team at 500 Startups, Tom DiBenedetto, Maurice Reznik, Roy Rodenstein, Verne Harnish, Mark Roberge, Milind Mehere, Nihal Mehta, Peg Jackson, Craig Gibson, Robb High, Christian McMahan, Jeff Hayzlett, Chris McCann, Michael Lasky, Julie Fenster, and Ed Zuckerberg. Thanks to all of our Likeable customers as well. Your faith and trust in us is invaluable.

Thanks to my most Likeable EO Forum, past and present—
Andy Cohen, Ben Rosner, Vinny Cannariato, Kevin Gilbert,
Dana Haddad, Addy Malhotra, Nora Herting, CeCe Chin, and
Jeff Bernstein—and the rest of my friends from Entrepreneurs'
Organization (EO), who have changed my life in so many ways.

MY LIKEABLE ONLINE FAMILY

There are dozens of social media thought leaders who have influenced me, taught me, shared with me, and inspired me. Some
I'm close friends with, others I've never met, but all of you on this
list (and beyond) have had a profound impact on my view of the
world. (They should all be followed on Twitter, too!) So thanks
to Mari Smith, John Bell, Jason Keath, Peter Shankman, Sarah
Evans, Jeremiah Owyang, Chris Brogan, Scott Stratten, Jay Baer,
Guy Kawasaki, Clara Shih, David Kirkpatrick, Scott Monty, David
Armano, Erik Qualman, Brian Solis, Aaron Lee, Tony Hsieh,
Josh Bernoff, Nick O'Neill, Justin Smith, Amber Naslund, Liz
Strauss, Sarah Evans, Todd Defren, Charlene Li, David Berkow-
itz, Geno Church, Jeff Pulver, Jeffrey Hayzlett, Philip Hotchkiss,
Stacey Monk, Leslie Bradshaw, Jesse Thomas, John Jantsch, David
Meerman Scott, Brian Carter, Shiv Singh, Ashton Kutcher, Greg
Verdino, Ann Handley, Bonin Bough, Andy Sernovitz, Pete
Blackshaw, Robert Scoble, Michael Stelzner, B. J. Emerson, Seth
Godin, Julien Smith, Mark Zuckerberg, Ev Williams, Biz Stone,
Dennis Crowley, Chris Treadaway, Jim Tobin, David Spinks, and
B. L. Ochman. Thank you, and keep up the amazing work.

MY LOVEABLE FRIENDS AND FAMILY

Thanks to my World Tour friends, Steve Evangelista, Kevin
Annanab, Tad Bruneau, Matt Sichel, Sean Fleischman, Kevin
Aeschlimann, and Andy Kaufmann, for allowing me to take a
break and have some fun during the crazy writing process. To
Havurah friends the Ruskins, Packers, Schiffers, and Richards
families for providing so many great memories. Thanks to my

colleagues from the Board of Education in Port Washington for challenging me to think of new use cases in social media: Karen Sloan, Nora Johnson, Rachel Gilliar, Larry Greenstein, Emily Beys, and Beth Weisburd. Thanks to all of my awesome friends in Port Washington!

Thanks to Aunt Lisa and Uncle Mark for being a steady, positive family influence, to my Da for her unconditional love and support, my brother Phil, the smartest person I've ever met, my brother Dan, the other smartest person I've ever met and now the most brilliant Facebook ads guy I know, and my brother Danny, a source of unending strength. Thanks to my mom, who taught me how to write, and my dad, who taught me how to think. Last but not least, thanks to my women and man at home. To my girls, Charlotte and Kate, thanks for putting up with Daddy being so busy when this book was written. I am so proud of you both and love you so much. To Seth, I love you SO MUCH! And to Joyce, thanks for making it so easy for the Kerpens to do what we do.

To Carrie, my partner in marriage, business, parenthood, and life, for you I am most thankful. You believed in me when I didn't. You left me alone when I needed it and were right beside me when I needed it. You made sacrifices to allow this book to be written, and I will forever remember and appreciate that. ILYSMNAF.

Thanks to all of the amazing, likeable people who helped get the third edition of *Likeable Social Media* into your hands.

FROM MICHELLE GREENBAUM

First and foremost, thank you to the Kerpens. Dave, it has been incredible to work with you on this book, and I am truly grateful for the experience. Carrie, you inspire me every single day—as a leader, as a mother, as a woman. To my family, thank you for the continued love and support. You've all made me who I am! I love you, Mom, Dad, Jeff, Rinah, Danny, and Nana. Terez and Steve, thank you for taking me in upon my move to New York and introducing me to the world of advertising (and "Josh" wine!).

Amanda DiAntonio, Candie Harris, and Rachel Hadley, you are the best mentors—thank you for believing in me. And to all my friends from Vegas to Oregon to New York, but especially Jenn Burgess, Skylar Ojeda, and Natalie Chan, I don't know what I'd do without you.

FROM ROBERT BERK

To Dave, thank you for giving me a life-changing opportunity and for being the best mentor!

To Carrie, Brian, Jo, Michelle, and the rest of the Likeable Team, thank you for the constant support!

To my friends, whether from Hunter, Hamilton, or Empire, thank you for always making me smile, laugh, and be genuinely happy. I love you all.

To Didy and Devorah Waks, thank you for welcoming me into your house and really giving me a home away from home.

To Neil Potter and Jordan Baltimore, I would be a completely different person if it weren't for learning so much from the both of you. You both taught me way beyond the playing field and really shaped who I am as a person.

To Nana, Papa Shel, Grandma Ruth, and Grandpa Frank, I love you all so much. Papa Shel and Grandpa Frank, I miss you. Nana and Grandma Ruth, thank you for always being just a phone call away.

Mom and Dad, you are the most supportive parents, and I know I don't say this enough, but thank you! Whether it's a FaceTime late at night, or calling you in the middle of the day, I know you're going to be there. It means so much, thank you!

likeable
SOCIAL MEDIA

I was standing in line to check in at Las Vegas's then-trendiest hotel in town, the Aria, for nearly an hour. It was June 2010, and I had just arrived after a twice-delayed six-hour flight from New York. I was tired and annoyed, and the last thing I wanted to do was waste an hour of my life waiting in line. Frustrated, I pulled out my smartphone and tweeted, "No Vegas hotel could be worth this long wait. Over an hour to check in at the Aria. #Fail."

Interestingly enough, the Aria didn't tweet back to me, but a competitor did. I got a private tweet from the Rio Hotel just two minutes later. If you're anything like most people with whom I've shared this story, you're probably thinking, "What did the Rio tweet, 'Come on over, we have no line'?" Indeed, many a small business owner and corporate senior executive who has heard this story has thought that this was the Rio's ROI moment, and that was surely what the Rio tweeted back.

Had the Rio tweeted such a message, I would have likely felt annoyed by two things: "First, why are they stalking me like a creepy character looking to manipulate me and benefit from my bad experience? Second, why is it jam-packed and happening at the Aria while it's wide open at the Rio?" On the contrary, however, the Rio Las Vegas tweeted the following to me: "Sorry about the bad experience, Dave. Hope the rest of your stay in Vegas goes well."

Guess where I ended up staying the next time I went to Las Vegas? And the time after that, and the time after that?

The hotel used social media to listen and to be responsive, showing a little empathy to the right person at the right time. An ad or a push-marketing message simply wouldn't have worked. But its ability to listen, to respond, and to be empathic did.

The Rio essentially earned a $600 sale from one tweet, one message that got my attention and ended up being integral in my decision as to where to stay next time I was in the city. Not a single person reading this could argue that the tweet was a marketing or sales message from the Rio either—because it wasn't. That would be considered an excellent return on investment (ROI) by anyone's standards. But the story doesn't end there.

Before even arriving at the Rio, I *liked* it on Facebook by clicking the Like button at Facebook.com/RioVegas, thereby letting my 3,500 friends, and the world at large, know of my endorsement of its customer-friendly practices. A few months later, my friend Erin was looking for a hotel to stay at in Las Vegas over the New Year's holiday, and I received the following message from her on Facebook: "Hey, Dave, I noticed you liked the Rio's page. Thinking about staying there for New Year's. What do you think?"

A friend's recommendation is more powerful than any advertisement, and Erin ended up staying at the Rio as well, along with 10 family members. Dozens of other friends have surely noticed my tweets and Facebook *likes* about the Rio and have been influenced since. So, one tweet led to one *like* on Facebook and, in fact, many *thousands of dollars' worth of business*.

It used to be said that happy customers tell three people about their good experiences and unhappy customers tell ten about their bad ones. But as my experiences with the Aria and Rio hotels demonstrate, today, thanks to social media, happy customers *and* unhappy customers can tell thousands of people their feelings about a company's service or products with just a few clicks, relying on the Like button as a virtual endorsement. The Rio leveraged this fact to its advantage, while the Aria did not.

FROM ADAM AND EVE TO MASS MEDIA TO THE DAWN OF A NEW ERA IN COMMUNICATIONS

In the beginning, there was Adam and Eve. Eve said to Adam, "You've got to try this apple," and the first marketing interaction in the history of the world had taken place. It was simple and effective, from one trusted person's lips to another's ears, and it resulted in a successful, if free, "transaction."

Word-of-mouth marketing had begun, and it would remain the best, purest, most efficient form of marketing for thousands of years (see the timeline in Figure I.1). Then, in the year 1440, the printing press ushered in a new era of mass marketing and media. Direct mail, followed by newspapers and magazines, and radio and television, allowed marketers and advertisers to target huge groups of people at once.

But today there are literally thousands of radio stations you can listen to—or free ways to listen to music—so why would you ever listen to a radio ad, when you can just change the station? There are literally thousands of television channels you can watch at any given moment and—better yet—technology that allows you to record your favorite shows and fast-forward through the commercials. So why on earth would you watch the commercials, unless you work in the industry and have professional interest?

No, people are not watching and listening to commercials the way they used to, and the marketing and media industries are changing faster than ever before. So what's a marketer to do? How can you get the word out about your product, drive trials, drive sales, and accomplish all of the other marketing objectives you've got? How do you get people talking about you without being so disruptive, and, well, unlikeable? The good news is, people are already talking about brands like yours more than ever before, and thanks to social media, word can spread faster than ever before—so all you have to do is listen, respond, and harness that word to allow consumers to drive the action.

THE SOCIAL MEDIA AND *LIKE* REVOLUTIONS

The social media revolution has given consumers around the world the most powerful voice they've ever had. It's also forced companies to think about how they can be more transparent and responsive. Social media has led companies, organizations, and governments to figure out how to accomplish more with less money—to get their messages out there and talked about

FIGURE 1.1 **History of Marketing Timeline**

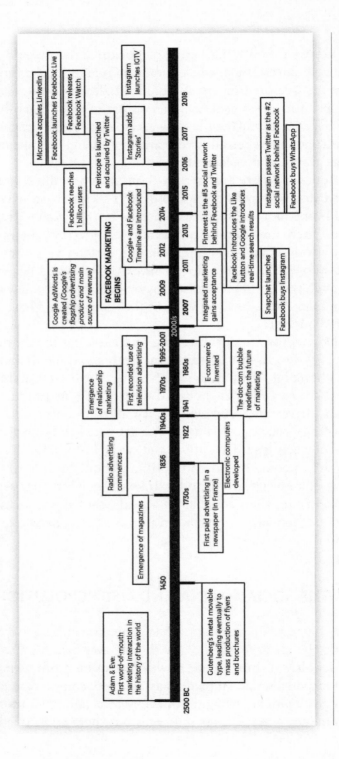

without spending as many dollars on declining media like television, radio, and print.

Word-of-mouth marketing has always been considered the purest and best form of marketing, and social media has continued to prove this fact in many ways. People like to share with and feel connected to each other, brands, organizations, and even governments they like and trust.

Facebook's Like button (Figure I.2), introduced in April 2010, has already been added by more than 150 million distinct websites. The Like button allows Facebook's more than one billion users, with one click, to express approval of companies, organizations, articles, or ideas. Whether it's a friend's picture of her baby you *like*, an article shared from the *New York Times*, a video from a local organization, or a contest from a global brand, the Like button gets more than two billion clicks per day.

FIGURE I.2 **Facebook's Like Button**

Yet as astounding as these numbers are, it's the new personalization of the Web that matters most in the social media revolution, both to companies and consumers. It's Facebook's ability to show you exactly what your friends and friends of friends *like* that makes the *like* function such a powerful tool. If you have a new baby, for example, you don't care what stroller is advertised on television, and in fact, you probably don't care if 50, 500, or 5,000 people *like* a new stroller on Facebook. But if a friend of yours *likes* that stroller, you are more apt to feel that you can trust the company that made the item, and you will be more comfortable buying a stroller from that company.

Facebook isn't the only social network to adopt a *like* feature either. Twitter, YouTube, LinkedIn, Pinterest, Instagram, and Snapchat have all added their own functionality that allows users to express approval of content. Content, companies, products, and ideas judged likeable by people you know and trust can be easily found throughout today's Internet. Companies and professionals who are worthy of people clicking their Like button will, in the short term, build trust and, in the long term, win the new Web in their respective categories.

As the cofounder and chairman of social media and word-of-mouth marketing firm Likeable Media, I've had the privilege of being an early adopter of social media technology and an eyewitness to the social media and *like* revolution. Likeable's mission is to help build more transparent and responsive companies, nonprofit organizations, and governments. We believe that social media, used well, is nothing short of transformational, not only in marketing but also in public relations, sales, customer service, and operations. We believe it has the potential to break down silos to better connect companies internally and externally.

We've worked to improve social media branding for more than 3,000 companies and organizations, such as 1-800-Flowers .com, Verizon, Neutrogena, the New York City Department of Health, and the National Multiple Sclerosis Society, and, through Likeable Local, thousands of small businesses such as dentists, jewelers, and real estate firms. There are organizations of all sizes that have learned to really listen, deliver value, and respond to customers—brands that share and inspire social content that's worthy of being shared online and offline, and *liked*, literally and figuratively.

JOIN THE COCKTAIL PARTY

Social media is like the world's largest cocktail party, where people can listen to others talking and join the conversations with other people about any topic of their choice. Just as in real-life cocktail parties, in the giant social media cocktail party, there are some participants who are a lot more influential than others (so-called "influencers"). There are two main distinctions, though, between a real cocktail party and an online one: First, there's no drinking online, of course. Second, but more important, whereas at an actual, in-person cocktail party, you can only have a few conversations with a handful of people in one night, online, and through social networks, you can have numerous conversations with potentially thousands or millions of people at once.

In both "parties," you will find a mix of likeable people and not-so-likeable people. At a cocktail party, you might encounter people who won't stop talking about themselves, but you'll also run into those who are great listeners and show you they're interested in what you're discussing. You'll find people who tell great stories and people who bore you to death. Who do you want to see again or maybe even do business with at a cocktail party: the sales guy who talks incessantly about how great his company and products are or the person who listens to the problems you face, has an open discussion with you, and maybe even makes you laugh?

We all intuitively know what makes some people at cocktail parties interesting and enjoyable to interact with. Yet most companies have not figured out how to be likeable in the cocktail party known as social media. Many companies still act like the sales guy who won't shut up about his products, or someone who tries too hard to dazzle people, or the person who bores everybody to death talking without listening and not asking other people what they want to have a conversation about.

The good news is, you, as a company, have an opportunity to do better, to be the organization that isn't "that guy" at the cocktail party. By applying the same set of rules you'd apply to be the person everyone wants to be involved with at the party, you can become the most likeable company or organization in your category—and end up the most profitable as well.

Listen carefully, be transparent, be responsive, be authentic, tell great stories—the qualities that would make you the hotshot at the party—and your organization will become more likeable on social networks.

LIKE IS THE NEW LINK: HOW FACEBOOK IS REORGANIZING GOOGLE'S WEB

You wake up one morning, and your back really hurts. You've been putting off finding a new doctor ever since you moved to town, it's been forever since you've had a checkup, and now you're paying the price. The pain is too much to wait any longer, and you've got to find a chiropractor now. So you grab your computer, go to Google.com, and enter "back doctor" and your town's name. You see a list of 10 chiropractors who have paid Google to be listed there and dozens of others who come up in organic search results. But do you really want to trust your throbbing back to a complete stranger in an emergency?

Then you think of another idea, and you head to Facebook and again search "back doctor." At the top of the results is a doctor's listing with a sidebar telling you that three of your friends *like* this doctor. Beneath the top listing is a chiropractor, next to which you see two friends who *like* him. "Sweet," you think. "Someone I can trust because my friends *like* him." You make a quick call, and you're off to get your backache taken care of by a recommended doctor, a professional your friends *like*.

This scenario and scenarios like it are happening every day now, and the use of Facebook and the social graph (global mapping of people and how they're connected) for search and commerce isn't far off. Think about it: Why would you possibly make a decision about a doctor, an attorney, a mechanic, or any important product or service for that matter based on advertising or Google search placement when you can make this decision based on the preference and recommendations of trusted friends? Facebook and social media have made it infinitely easier to do the latter. *It's nothing short of a game changer for marketers and businesses of all sizes.*

The great news about the new world of communications we live in today is that everybody has a shot. Build a great product, get the word out to a few people, make it easy for people to share with their friends, and you can win without spending a boatload. Just five years ago, for instance, if you went to a new restaurant that you loved, you might have shared the experience with a few of your friends, family members, or neighbors. Perhaps if you really loved the restaurant, you might have raved about it for a week to as many as 10 or 15 friends. Today, you can share these thoughts with 350 Facebook friends, 300 Twitter followers, or 150 LinkedIn connections, all with one click on your computer or phone. Or you can post a picture of that appetizing, or unappetizing, meal and share it with hundreds of people on Pinterest, Instagram, or Snapchat.

No matter what the size of your business, organization, or your client's business, you too have the ability to follow the simple rules of social media outlined in this book to reap the rewards. Senior management, and anyone in a communications position for that matter, needs to know that marketing in a social media world is not about broadcasting your message and getting the largest reach and frequency. It's about tapping into the conversation, listening, engaging, and empowering. The loudest, biggest spenders don't win anymore. The smartest, most flexible listeners do.

WHAT SOCIAL MEDIA CAN AND CAN'T DO

Before we move on, I'd like to share three key points about social media to dispel any myths you may have heard and make sure I manage your expectations from the start:

1. **Social media cannot make up for a bad product, company, or organization.** If you're marketing a bad service or widget, not only will social media not help you but it will actually *hurt* your cause because word will spread quickly. The good news is, if you're using social media well, you'll quickly know when you have bad products, employees, or processes. As a good businessperson or marketer, you can fix these problems before they cause any serious damage.
2. **Social media won't lead to overnight sales success.** Success will take time, and it will come in increased buzz, referrals, traffic, and eventually, sales. I wish I could tell you that after you read this book you'll have all of the tools to instantly turn

on the social media revenue engine and watch the money pour in. I can't, of course. I'll demonstrate the return on investment of "likeable social media" in lots of case studies, but no matter what, social media is not an instant win. We're talking about *building relationships with people*, and that invariably takes time.

3. **Social media is not free.** It will take time and/or money to achieve sustained growth. Since it's free to join any social network worth talking about, many marketers think social media is free, or at least cheap. Well, the good news is, no matter how large your company is, it's nearly impossible to spend the kind of money on social media that large companies regularly have spent on network television in the last 20 years. But building and executing a likeable social media plan will take lots of time and work. Ultimately, such a plan can't be the sole effort of any one marketing or public relations department. Instead, it must be integrated across your entire company, its agencies, and its vendors. And as for dollars, since this book was first published in 2012, the biggest change we've seen in the social media landscape is the growth of paid social media, or advertising. In 2019, in order to have your organization's social media content seen, you're going to have to spend money with the social networks on ads.

BOOKS CAN BE SOCIAL TOO

I write a lot in this book about the two-way interactive nature of social media and the importance of leveraging that potential. Of course, a book is typically as one-directional as a medium can be: author writes, and reader reads and digests. As a social media author, I simply won't allow that to be the case. So here's my promise to you: as you read this book, if you have any questions, you need clarification, you are uncertain about content, or you want to challenge me on the points or strategies within, *please do let me know*, using social media.

Ask me questions through Twitter.com/DaveKerpen, Instagram @DaveKerpen, or LinkedIn.com/in/DaveKerpen. For a speedier answer, if perhaps not one directly from me, post on our company page at Facebook.com/LikeableMedia or through Twitter.com/LikeableMedia. If you have a question, even if you think it applies only to you, there are probably many others out there with similar questions. So I truly hope you'll take me up on that offer, and ask away.

LET'S GET LIKEABLE

Facebook, Twitter, Instagram, YouTube, LinkedIn, Pinterest, and other social media sites and tools are innovating and changing faster than any other communications technologies in history. It's important to understand the basics behind how each major network works and how marketers and businesses can best leverage each site. Before we delve into the following 18 strategies to help you create an irresistible brand through online social media networks, I urge you take a look at the recently updated Appendix first. This section provides a brief refresher course on Facebook, Twitter, Pinterest, Instagram, LinkedIn, and other social networks, blogs, and tools that matter most. It contains insight on how to best think about them and use them in marketing and advertising. If you feel as if you don't need a refresher, read on, but strongly consider using the Appendix as a guide at any time and to provide further context.

While social media sites and tools will continue to change with every week that goes by, the 18 strategies discussed in this book will remain the same and help you utilize social media to become more transparent, responsive, engaging, and profitable.

Thanks for choosing to go on this journey with me. Let's get likeable.

CHAPTER 1

Listen First, and Never Stop Listening

You are angry.

You just got a letter in the mail from your car insurance company explaining that it will cover only half the cost of the recent work you did on your car following an accident. You're out $700, which stinks, but more important, you're wondering why you pay these high monthly premiums if not to cover situations just like this. So you call the company, and you're placed on hold for 30 minutes. Finally you get a representative who says, "I'm sorry, there's nothing I can do. This is the policy." As you sit there, frustrated and dejected, the telephone representative feeds you the next line in the script: "Is there anything else I can help you with today?"

"Of course not," you think. "How about paying for my car repairs? Maybe you should spend a little less money on your stupid TV ads I see all day and a little more time on your customer service." It's so frustrating not feeling listened to.

Then you post on Facebook or Twitter: "My car insurance company _____ sucks. Same old story." A few minutes later, you get a notification that someone responded to your post. Surprisingly, you click to find a written response from your car insurance company: "We hear you. Please send us a quick email about the particular issue, and we'll get to the bottom of it as quickly as we can." Somehow, you already feel a little bit better about the situation.

Did the company respond so positively only because you posted publicly? Maybe. The point is, a representative realized your frustration with the company's services and was forced to take notice of your post. Companies can no longer afford to ignore their customers' specific needs or complaints when the conversation can so easily be made public. Instead, they must listen, understand the issue, and respond appropriately.

EVERYBODY LOVES TO FEEL HEARD

Communication is 50 percent listening and 50 percent talking. Yet for many years, companies large and small have done a disproportionate amount of talking, shouting even. Customer service representatives, marketing researchers, and focus group organizers may listen, but budgets for these "listening" activities amount to little compared to the money spent on mass media "talking." Now, for the first time in our history, companies can listen, through social media, to conversations about them and their competitors. Social media is a 24/7/365 focus group!

You have a front row seat to spontaneous chatter of interest to your business. You have the ability to check in on prospective customers discussing problems your company solves. You can listen to existing customers talk about unrelated issues just to get to know them better. Checking in on your vendors, partners, or even your competitors' customers has never been easier. The amount of data you can gather and the number of conversations you can tap into through social media are nothing short of mind-boggling.

As tempting as it may be to "join the conversation," Facebook, Instagram, Twitter, and other social networks aren't simply broadcast media. They're engagement media—that is, they are listening networks. Letting you listen to the conversation before you try to join in is an opportunity: How can you possibly know what to talk about in any conversation until you listen, at least a little bit?

Ask anyone who has ever dated or who has been in a successful relationship how important it is not only to listen to your partner but also to show him or her that you are truly listening. The guy on that first date who talks incessantly and does not listen—he strikes out every time. So does the woman at the cocktail party who talks only about herself. Increasingly, the same goes for the company that spends most of its marketing dollars talking and little time or money listening. Social media is the first communications channel that allows for such listening in large scale, and no matter what you sell or market, your customers are definitely talking.

Listen first before you talk back. You *can* join the conversation as a listener.

THE BENEFITS OF LISTENING: WHY DOES IT REALLY MATTER?

If and when customers or prospects acknowledge that you're listening, you immediately strengthen your relationships with them. We'll talk more about responding later, but clearly the ability to not only listen but also to acknowledge others makes them feel heard, which makes them happier, which is always a good thing. Even if you can't acknowledge customers (as is the case for highly regulated industries such as pharmaceutical and financial services companies in which only professionals can legally supply appropriate responses, if they can legally respond at all), there are other benefits to listening. A better understanding of how your customers use your products (or don't use them) can help you make critical changes in your offerings and in your communications with your customers. You can also uncover new opportunities you hadn't thought of, or you'll find out that some of the features you thought would be big hits have ended up not mattering to customers or failing altogether.

Knowing what's important to your customers can help you better plan your offers, promotions, and contests to further drive buzz and sales. Instead of expensive product launches, you can test new ideas carefully and receive feedback quickly, keeping your finger on the pulse of your customers. You'll be able to avoid pricey ad campaigns that champion things you *think* people will love about your product or service by listening to what people *actually want* before you spend a single dollar. Consider social listening the ultimate surveying and focus group tool—practically free, and running 24/7/365 for you. In fact, we used social media to crowdsource the cover of this third edition of *Likeable Social Media*—we listened to feedback on four possible covers across Facebook, Twitter, LinkedIn, and Instagram, and this was the most popular one. So, thank you!

LISTENING VERSUS MONITORING

Let's briefly compare the word *listening* to the word *monitoring*. A lot of companies and people use these words interchangeably to describe the process of seeing what people are saying about you, your products, and your competitors. Some may believe it is only a matter of semantics, but there is, in fact, an important distinction between the two.

Monitoring has an impersonal feel to it, imparting a certain amount of creepiness. When you hear "monitoring," you most likely think of the FBI or surveillance cameras. You think of negative situations: "Monitor that cough; it might get worse." *Listening*, on the other hand, is an important human process, and I've yet to meet someone who didn't like being listened to. Do you like being monitored? Do you like being listened to and heard?

How to Listen

There are lots of free ways to listen to what customers and prospects are saying online, and there are many paid enterprise systems available as well, with costs ranging from a few dollars to thousands of dollars per month. If you're new to listening, try these free ways first:

- Google Alerts
- Social Mention
- Twitter search
- Facebook search
- Mention
- Hootsuite

If you go to any social network and type a phrase or keyword into its search function, you will see what people are saying using that keyword in real time. National and global brands might search the entire Web, while local and regional organizations will want to use geographical filtering to find posts only in your coverage area. Remember, don't search just for your brand name but also for your competitors', and more important, for terms and words that your customers would use.

For instance, if you're a real estate broker, sure, you can search social networks for the name of your agency. But wouldn't it be more helpful to search for the phrase "want to buy a house" in conversations on social networks in your town so you can find real people in real time sharing their needs with others? If you're an attorney, you can search for your firm's name, but it might be more helpful to search for the phrase "need to hire a lawyer" to listen to potential future clients talk about what they are looking for in the way of legal services.

More advanced listeners, or brands with higher volumes of conversations to listen to, should consider a paid enterprise software solution. There are dozens of listening platforms available, but below are several good ones to start with:

- Meltwater
- Tagboard
- Cision
- BuzzSumo
- Brand24

Such products allow you to tap into large volumes of conversations across the social Web in a systematic, easy-to-follow way. You can generate real-time, daily, or weekly reports on mentions, competitive analysis, sentiment, and more. While solutions such as these are much more expensive than "free," they're a lot less expensive (and a lot more valuable) than traditional marketing research, such as surveying and working with focus groups.

I'm Listening; Now What?

It's important to keep an open mind about what data you'll find when you listen and, more important, what you can do with it. If your brand or product is being talked about in a negative way, it's urgent to fix the problems being discussed as efficiently as possible. If people are asking for something new, figure out a way to create that for them.

For instance, maybe your customers love a product but wish it came in a different flavor, color, or design. Or maybe they'd be willing to pay more for your service if you offered a new tool they need. If customers are revealing their favorite features about your product that you didn't realize were popular, consider accentuating these features in future marketing and communications materials. And of course, once you've begun to formally listen to what customers and prospects are saying, you'll want to formulate a plan to respond appropriately whenever possible (as will be discussed in detail in following chapters).

THE COST OF NOT LISTENING

At best, by not listening, you're not leveraging potential opportunities for growth, damage control, or both. At worst, you're causing your customers and prospects to turn to your competitors—those who *are* listening and will respond to customer needs. You're also allowing your brand reputation to be significantly hurt because by the time you get around to learning what people are saying, it may be too late to respond efficiently and make necessary changes to keep your company growing. Even if you're in a highly regulated industry and you're unable to fully join the conversation, it simply doesn't make sense not to leverage the resources available to find out what your customers and prospects are saying and to use that information to create better products, services, and processes.

I talked with Shel Horowitz, expert on ethical marketing, author, and longtime social media user, about the importance of listening, and he confessed that, at first, he didn't always take the concept to heart as he does today:

> The first discussion list I joined, I didn't listen first. I went in with keyboard blazing, did not take the time to understand the group, and ended up slinking off with my tail between my legs and leaving entirely. Since then, I've been in many groups, and I usually read all the posts for about two weeks before posting, and then I start with an introduction. I've developed a reputation as a friendly, caring, helpful, knowledgeable, and very transparent individual whose advice carries some weight.

Shel told me he can now safely attribute 15 to 20 percent of his book sales directly to his time spent listening and responding across social networks and online communities. So many marketers have taken to using new marketing channels to talk before listening, essentially filling each new channel that comes along with noise. Think about email and most other forms of so-called interactive marketing. Is it really interactive, or is it mostly marketers talking? Social networks provide marketers with a massive opportunity to leverage the listening half of their communications.

NEVER STOP LISTENING

Remember, it's not about listening for a while and then talking to all of your new prospects and converting them into customers. Listening will always be 50 percent of the communication process, so you'll want to continue to refine your listening skills and processes throughout your work in social media. Always listen to the conversations in real time. In fact, sometimes the best daters, friends, businesspeople, and companies are the ones who do even more listening than talking, hearing what everyone has to say and speaking only when they have something really worthwhile to express.

In dating lore, there's always the guy who *thinks* he knows how important listening is, so he starts the date by saying, "Tell me about yourself." After his date talks for a minute or so about herself, she says, "How about you?" and he proceeds to talk her ear off for the rest of the date, telling her all about himself. The guy may claim he listened to what she said, but the truth is, he was just going through the motions, not really carrying it through in a meaningful way.

That's not listening. In order to be a likeable organization that effectively listens to its customers and prospects, you've got to fully integrate listening into your job or agency's functions.

When You Can Only Listen: Allergan Facial Aesthetics

Allergan, a Fortune 500 pharmaceutical organization, is like many pharma brands when it comes to social media. Because of the highly regulated nature of the industry and its products and offerings, the brand needs to be extremely careful about what it says and doesn't say online, especially when it comes to interactive social media sites. While some pharmaceutical organizations decided to ignore the conversations entirely, Allergan Medical Aesthetics (the division behind popular brands such as BOTOX Cosmetic, Latisse, Juvéderm, and others) recognized social conversations were happening about its brands, and believed it could glean a significant understanding about patients and the perception of its products if it paid attention to what was being said.

With the assistance of Likeable Media and the listening platform Sysomos, Allergan Medical Aesthetics identified a variety of keywords and categories that would allow the brand to capture key information (Figure 1.1). It now mines through tens of thousands of mentions of its brands every week. From this data, the company is able to report and follow up on off-label uses of the brand (an important part of meeting FDA regulations for pharmaceutical brands) as well as track and measure the overall sentiment toward their brands. Key trends and themes can be identified and used to inform future marketing plans. Because a strong listening process is in place, the brand can be made quickly aware when any out-of-the-norm situations arise.

By keeping a finger on the pulse of and recognizing the importance of social media in understanding its patients, Allergan Medical Aesthetics can make more informed and better-educated decisions, which in turn positions its brands for success.

FIGURE 1.1   **Allergan Listens to Latisse Mentions on Twitter**

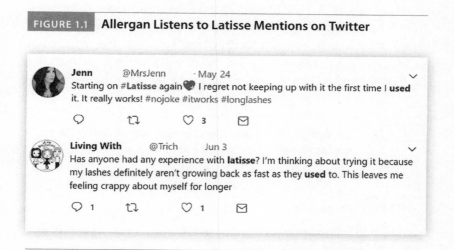

By listening and responding, greater sentiment comes from customers, whose loyalty grows. They, in turn, become better advocates for your products. It's as simple as this: the customer talks, the company listens and acknowledges, and the customer is happier (as is anyone else watching since the conversation is public). Would *you* rather buy a product from a company that obviously, publicly listens to its customers, or a company that seemingly ignores them by not utilizing social networks to directly interact with the public?

The ROI of Listening for One Small Business: Stoneybrook Dental

Dr. Wendi Wardlaw of Stoneybrook Dental, a Likeable Local customer, had practiced dentistry for nearly 20 years before diving into social media. Today, as a dentist, missionary, and public speaker, Dr. Wardlaw understands the importance of listening on social media. Despite her hectic schedule, she manages to listen on Facebook every day. "Everything happens really fast there. You have to listen," Dr. Wardlaw said.

In August 2014, Dr. Wardlaw was monitoring her Facebook News Feed one night when she searched dental keywords and saw that one of her patients was posting about discomfort and pain (Figure 1.2). The patient in question had undergone a routine outpatient procedure earlier that week, so her abnormal symptoms were concerning. Dr. Wardlaw private messaged the patient and asked her to send a picture of her mouth.

FIGURE 1.2 **Dr. Wardlaw's Patient Complaining About Tooth Pain on Facebook**

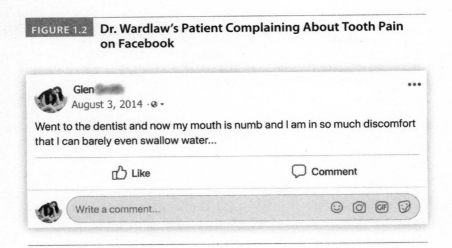

Upon seeing the photo, Dr. Wardlaw immediately sent the patient to the hospital where she received antibiotics to treat the start of a serious infection. After a few nights in the hospital, the patient was healthy enough to be released. Had Dr. Wardlaw not been listening on Facebook, the patient's health could have been much further compromised. By listening on social media, you can gain knowledge of your customers' needs and desires—and you can identify and address major problems.

ACTION ITEMS

1. Write down a list of five phrases people might use that would identify themselves as potential customers of yours. Conduct Facebook, Instagram, LinkedIn, and Twitter searches for each of these phrases.
2. Conduct Facebook, Instagram, Twitter, and YouTube searches for your brand, competitors, products, and services. Take inventory of what people are saying.
3. Develop a plan and system to formally or informally listen on a regular basis throughout the social Web, and determine ways your organization can benefit from the insight and knowledge gained by listening.

LISTENING SHOULD ALWAYS BE 50 PERCENT OF THE CONVERSATION

Listening is the single most important skill in social media, and it's one that's easy to forget once you get started with all of the sexier, more exciting things you can do. So whatever you do, once you start, never stop listening. Even once you start talking, it doesn't mean you stop listening—it's quite the opposite actually. If you feel like you're running out of conversation to listen to, broaden your search terms and find new audiences—people who don't even know you exist yet but, based on what they're saying, probably should. Results will follow, and it won't be long until your company is the "coolest person" at the social media cocktail party—and more important, the most successful!

CHAPTER 2

Way Beyond "Women 25 to 54"

Define Your Target Audience Better Than Ever

I was talking with friends at the South by Southwest Interactive conference in March 2009 about a concept I call *hypertargeting*, by which a company gears a marketing and advertising effort toward a specific group through individuals' social media profiles, activities, and networks. At the time, and even more so now, Facebook, Twitter, and LinkedIn held an unbelievable amount of data on hundreds of millions of people. From users' profiles and comments, you could advertise and market toward groups more efficiently than ever before. On Facebook alone, you could target people based on their age, gender, education, marital status, interests, job title, and employer.

For example, instead of a beer company randomly searching for men aged 21 to 23, the company could easily find 21- to 23-year-old males in key geographic markets who list "drinking," "partying," or "bars" as interests on their profiles. My friend Leslie Bradshaw overheard the conversation on hypertargeting and chimed in with her thoughts on what she called *nanotargeting*—a concept similar to hypertargeting but with search criteria so narrow that you can target just one individual among hundreds of millions.

"Cool," I thought. I raced back to my hotel room that night, jumped onto the Facebook ad platform, played around with targeting options, and took out an ad for 31-year-old, married, female employees of Likeable Media living in New York City. The ad copy read, "I love you and miss you Carrie. Be home from Texas soon."

That advertisement had a target audience of one (Figure 2.1). One person, out of hundreds of millions of people on Facebook, could see it. Of course, when my wife and business partner, Carrie, saw the ad, she immediately loved it, freaked out, and did what any social media marketing firm partner would do. She took out a Facebook ad targeting 31-year-old, married, *male* employees of Likeable Media living in New York: "Thanks, Dave. Love you too. This is pretty cool."

FIGURE 2.1   **Nanotargeted Ad**

I Love You Carrie

I love you and miss you Carrie. Be home from Texas soon.

Today, the smallest audience size you can target is 20 people, and unless you just want to impress your spouse or friend, or you're a social media dork like this author, you probably don't have a target audience of one. But whether your perfect target audience is 100, 1,000, or one million people, you can now engage them in a way that was virtually impossible several years ago.

Once you find your target audience, listen to them (see Chapter 1), find out what they are looking for, and provide your product or service to meet their needs. You can build a relationship with your audience and even allow them to directly buy your goods or services, all using social media.

In the past, newspapers, magazines, television, and radio allowed marketers to tap into wide audiences of people based on broad demographic criteria: 18- to 34-year-olds, 25- to 54-year-old females, or males 55 and older in New York, for example. But in hindsight, in almost every case, these categories were too sweeping. Specifics will help you hone in on your target audience, connecting you directly with the consumer. For instance, are you targeting parents or singles? Sports fans? Hockey fans only? Are you in every major market or only certain markets?

Traditional marketers may be naysayers here with regard to the advent of social media and its relation to reaching the right customers. They will argue that currently with cable TV networks, you can target people with specific interests, such as home decorating or cooking. They might believe that trade publications and conferences are the best way to find your niche audience in the business-to-business (B2B) space.

While clearly you can target your audience *better* using niche trade publications and cable television shows than you previously could with just network television or radio, magazines and specialized publications are quickly perishing. Also, everyone I know either fast-forwards through TV commercials using DVR technology or subscribes to an ad-free streaming service like Netflix. With the introduction of commercial-free, audience-targeted podcasts, music and news blogs, and online user-friendly music listening sites, such as Spotify and Pandora, fewer and fewer people are tuning into traditional radio broadcasts. Besides, just because targeting through traditional media is *better* than it used to be doesn't mean it is *the best*. And why settle for anything but the best in your search for the perfect audience for your product or service? Let's take a look at a few examples of how to find this ideal audience on Facebook/Instagram (they have the same targeting capabilities), LinkedIn, and Twitter.

FACEBOOK AND INSTAGRAM: REACH AS MANY USERS AS YOU WANT (OR AS FEW!)

In the movie *The Social Network*, the Sean Parker character played by Justin Timberlake has a famous line: "You know what's cooler than a million dollars? A billion dollars." My line on Facebook marketing is the opposite: "You know what's cooler than reaching a billion people on Facebook? Reaching the perfect 100 prospects." Facebook's and Instagram's ads aren't free to run, of course. Facebook earned more than $11 billion in ad revenue in the first quarter of 2018,[1] but its self-serve ad platform *is* free to explore. (We'll talk a lot more about Facebook ads in Chapter 3.) This means that anyone who wants to can easily research exactly how many people on Facebook fit into whatever targeting criteria he or she desires, free of charge. In other words, without even running any ads, you can find your target population among hundreds of millions of people simply by feeding Facebook the exact attributes you're looking for in an audience.

I've included a screenshot (Figure 2.2) of various targeting criteria available to advertisers. The basics—gender, age, and location—allow you to quickly target millions of people at scale the way you would using traditional media. (And before you tell me Facebook is solely for young people, note that in the United States alone, there are more than 57 million users over the age of 55.)

FIGURE 2.2 **Basic Targeting Criteria**

So, even though it's very general, if you're looking for your audience based only on age, gender, or location, you can certainly find it easily. It's the other categories, however, that allow you to drill deep down to identify your perfect audience. Let's focus on the two key targeting categories in this process: interests and demographics (Figure 2.3).

FIGURE 2.3   Targeting by Interests and Demographics

In the "Interests" category, you can input literally any interest held by at least 100 people on their profiles. Note: There are *hundreds of thousands of options* here. Type in "cooking," for instance, then more specifically "Italian cooking," "Chinese cooking," or "French cooking." You could also go with "baking," and then make the target more specific by layering on "pies" or "cakes." There are of course many possibilities and dozens of other cooking-related keywords. If you work in the food industry, these keywords are powerful search criteria in helping you find your target audience. The cooking-related words you decide to pick will depend on whether your products are meant for Italian cooking or Chinese cooking or baking.

If you're a yoga studio, consider targeting people nearby with "yoga" as an interest or who have shown interest based on activity. Perhaps you'd like to be more specific and target people who engage with "Bikram yoga" or "Reiki," depending on the services you offer or are researching offering in the future. If you represent a nonprofit, consider targeting the thousands of people who are interested in "philanthropy." Then take it a step further, and check for specific causes that are relevant or reach out to other nonprofit workers who share a similar mission, locally or even globally.

In the "More Demographics" section, you can also select a job title. Perhaps you want to target retail buyers, distributors, HR managers, journalists, doctors, dentists, or maybe CEOs. This search function is especially helpful in the B2B space.

Remember, even in the B2B space, you're not marketing to businesses. You're marketing to people who happen to be decision makers for businesses—this is an important distinction. As I like to say, there's no such thing online as B2B. It's all P2P, or person to person. We've grown our B2B businesses at Likeable Media and Likeable Local significantly by targeting brand managers, CMOs, and senior marketing directors (Likeable Media) and dentists, real estate agents, doctors, jewelers, and other small business owners (Likeable Local). For example, when Likeable Media wanted to land an account with Neutrogena, we targeted marketing directors and managers at their company using Facebook ads. After we got their attention, they called us and became clients within a month.

In the "Work" category, you can input any workplace that people on Facebook have identified as their employer. This function can actually be a helpful guide for local businesses that are geographically close to similar, larger companies. We had a chiropractor client in San Francisco, for instance, who targets employees of nearby offices. You can also use this function for internal marketing and communications. Imagine telling the whole staff, "You're doing a great job, keep up the good work," just by sending out a Facebook message. Get creative with this function, and you'll figure out how to best utilize it for your organization.

When you combine the "Job Title" category with "Work," as well as other specifications like "Industry" or "Office Type," then you can pinpoint your key audience with precision. Imagine, for instance, searching for only CIOs at Fortune 500 companies in the medical industry, or targeting real estate agents at the top five firms in town.

Whether you're a small business, huge brand, nonprofit, or government agency, your perfect target audience will be found on Facebook. Frankly, I've yet to find an organization anywhere whose target audience *isn't* on Facebook. Be sure to listen, and then find and engage your share of the hundreds of millions of people across the world who communicate via Facebook—the share that makes sense for *your* organization.

LINKEDIN: FOR MAXIMUM IMPACT, TARGET PROFESSIONALS ONLY

While Facebook may boast 2.23 billion monthly users, LinkedIn boasts over 500 million professionals and business users. If you're in the business-to-business space, it's well worth looking at specific targeting options on LinkedIn. Such information provided includes the obvious, again—age, gender, and location—but LinkedIn also utilizes criteria that allow you to determine exactly who your audience should be, based on job title, school or degree, skills, group affiliations, industry, seniority, and company size.

Software marketers might target information technology professionals. Financial planners might target C-level senior management in markets where the financial planners have offices. We use LinkedIn to target senior marketing professionals in New York, Boston, and Chicago. Also, the reality is that there are still many professionals who aren't on Facebook, and if you're going to find these folks at all online, LinkedIn is a great place to start.

FORGET DEMOGRAPHICS: TARGETING ON TWITTER

We've been talking about the amazing demographic targeting capabilities of Facebook's and LinkedIn's ad platforms. But what about targeting people *based on actual needs they have expressly shared*? In other words, who cares about people's age or their job title or interests if you know that they are looking for a service or product you provide? You can find such people using Google, but the current leading platform for finding conversation is Twitter. All tweets are, by default, public. There is an immensely high volume of tweets every day—more than 500 million![2] By utilizing Twitter, your target audience becomes based on what people are actually saying, not simply on what you glean from demographic research.

Say, for instance, you're an entertainment lawyer, or you're in the marketing department for an entertainment law firm. You can target movie producers or actors or others you *think* might need your services. Or you can do a Twitter search, such as the one featured in Figure 2.4. In this example, a search for the keywords "need entertainment lawyer" yields three people who in the last 18 hours actually asked for an entertainment lawyer!

FIGURE 2.4 **Entertainment Law Firm Twitter Search**

How much potential revenue would three inbound leads mean to most law firms?

If you haven't done one before, take a moment to try a Twitter search on your smartphone. Just go to Search.Twitter.com, and type in the search bar "need [your product, service, or category]" or "I want [something you have to offer]." You may be happily surprised with how large a perfect target audience you find out there practically begging for you. This method of targeting is not going to scale for low-priced, high-frequency products, but for anyone selling or marketing a high-end product or service (jewelry, real estate, or financial or other professional services, to name a few), it's the ultimate in targeting. Imagine communicating only with the people who want to hear from you or who are sharing problems you can solve. The time spent targeting on Twitter may quickly pay off. Stop guessing what your audience wants and start searching—and listen to what they are saying.

HOW DO *YOU* LIKE TO BE TARGETED AS A CONSUMER?

Take off your marketing hat and put on your consumer cap for a moment. Do *you* like being targeted broadly by marketers and advertisers? Do you enjoy watching incessant car commercials interrupting your favorite TV shows? Or would you rather see ads and marketing materials from car companies when you are actually looking to buy a new car and have expressed interest in doing so? Similarly, if you're single, it doesn't necessarily mean you want to see ads for dating sites, and the fact that you're a woman doesn't mean you want to hear about department store sales.

And for goodness sake, just because you're a man doesn't mean you want to be bombarded by men's sexual health companies. No, you likely want to hear from companies and organizations based on your specific stated needs and interests. Now that it's possible to more narrowly target people using social networks, put your marketing hat back on and leverage the opportunity.

HOW WELL DO YOU KNOW YOUR TARGET AUDIENCE?

The last few decades have brought numerous improvements in marketing intelligence and research. But until you had today's ability to target such specific groups of people, you may have had no need to identify your target audience so narrowly. For example, you might have known your audience loved playing sports, but perhaps they preferred one sport to another. Or maybe young women loved your product, but you didn't know that 21- to 22-year-olds were far more likely to buy it than 23- to 24-year-olds. Today you can run the appropriate Facebook or Twitter searches to target your audience precisely and find out who the consumers for your products and services actually are.

While some businesses have narrower and more well-defined target audiences than others, you can always refine the notion of who is part of your ideal audience. You will likely find that there is more than just one group of people looking for your goods or services. Huge global brands, for example, have certain categories of customers that are more common than others. Perhaps female lawyers spend more on your product than stay-at-home moms, for instance. If you don't know the specifics, you can always ask, too: if you have 1,000 Facebook fans, ask what their favorite sport is. If you find out for some reason that 9 out of 10 of them prefer baseball, you might consider sponsoring a local Little League team. Social media will help you find your target audience and provide you with further insight about these groups.

Put an End to Wasteful Marketing Spending

There's a common axiom about advertising among key marketing executives: "Fifty percent of my advertising works. I just don't know which half."

Search marketing and social media have rendered it possible to target exactly the people you know are your customers and best prospects, not the people you *think* are in those groups based on your intuition and vague understanding of market research. You can continue to spend your marketing and advertising dollars on less targeted media in the name of greater reach and awareness, or you can focus on a narrower but much more potent audience. When you tap into that unique target audience, you'll never again want to waste precious marketing dollars on less accountable, out-of-focus media.

Targeting Is Just the Beginning of the Conversation

Remember, we're not talking about advertising repeatedly in the hopes of eventually finding the right person at the right time who may happen to need to buy your product or service. We're talking about defining and finding the narrowly targeted, correct audience and then beginning to engage them in a conversation, so that *when they are ready to buy*, you're the obvious, logical choice. If you've targeted them correctly and then engaged with them along the way, when it comes time to buy, they won't even need to search, and they certainly won't need to respond to a television or radio ad. They'll already know you, trust you, and like you, so they'll turn right to you. And of course, you don't need to be peddling a physical product. Take, for example, Likeable's work with the Fibromyalgia & Fatigue Centers (FFC) and the steps we took in helping people afflicted with fibromyalgia and chronic fatigue syndrome connect with the organization.

Fibromyalgia and Fatigue Centers Target Just the People in Need

Millions of Americans suffer from fibromyalgia and chronic fatigue syndrome. The Fibromyalgia & Fatigue Centers of America is one of the leading treatment facilities in the country. The centers provide help in the form of doctors, nurses, counselors, and group support with 12 physical locations throughout the country. The typical broad profile of someone who suffers from one of these illnesses is a female between the ages of 35 and 60, and in the past, FFC has used mass targeting initiatives in the form of television ads, radio commercials, and print ads in the hope of reaching these and other people who can benefit from its services.

That kind of advertising is expensive and wasteful, however, so we developed a narrower targeting initiative. We used Facebook to target people who actually listed "fibromyalgia" in their profiles as an interest because we assumed that, aside from a few doctors and researchers, most people who list it as an interest suffer from the illness or have a close family member who does. We also listened on Twitter for people actually talking about one of the illnesses, regularly searching for keywords such as "fibromyalgia," "tired all of the time," "chronic fatigue," and "why am I so tired?"

Equally important, we set up a community on Facebook called Fibro 360, where anyone who had been affected by fibromyalgia or chronic fatigue syndrome could share stories, support one another, and get news, tips, research, and information on the illnesses. We didn't link online ads and marketing messages to FFC's website or to its phone number. Instead, we linked all communications to the community on Facebook. Nine months later, the results were astounding: tens of thousands of people had joined the community on Facebook.

Hundreds of people connected and talked with one another each and every day, and if and when people in the community wanted additional help, they turned to Fibromyalgia & Fatigue Centers and often hired our client. Hundreds have done this, resulting in a greater than 20 percent sales lift, attributed to Facebook.

LIKEABLE'S OWN TARGETING

The best B2B targeting we've done using social media is for our own companies, Likeable Media and Likeable Local. We may be smaller than lots of big agencies, but with more than 41,800 *likes* on Facebook, we've grown one of the largest fan bases of any marketing agency our size in the world. More important than the number of fans we have, though, is who they are. From the start, we've targeted people on Facebook with job titles such as "chief marketing officer," "vice president of marketing," "brand manager," and "marketing director." These key decision makers are our perfect customers, so we've focused our efforts on them and geared our ads toward them. They've become fans, they've interacted with us over time, and many of them have called or emailed asking to do business with us. No matter whom your organization is looking to reach, you can find them on Facebook, Instagram, LinkedIn, and Twitter. There are several more examples in Table 2.1 of types of companies and the narrow audience targeted for them using both social media sites.

So, who are *your* perfect customers? How narrowly can you define your target audience?

TABLE 2.1   **Targeted Audience for Various Companies**

CLIENT	TARGETED AUDIENCE
Real estate coach	Real estate agents and brokers across the country
Beachside hotel in south Florida	Engaged women living in colder, northern states
Telecommunications provider	Users complaining on Twitter about problems with the client's competitors
New shopping center	People within a 10-mile radius of the center who list "shopping" or "buying new things" as an interest in their profiles
Cat accessory company	Users who list "cat lover," "cat," and "I have a cat" in their profiles
Author	Fans of authors with similar writing styles and book types
Public relations firm	Publicity managers and public relations directors at the 100 biggest companies in the client's city

ACTION ITEMS

1. Write down a description of your perfect target audience. Define your customers and prospects as narrowly as you can. What is their age and gender? Are they married, engaged, or single? Where do they live? What are their interests? What are their job titles? Where do they work? What do they talk about? If the answer to some of these questions is, "That doesn't matter," then that's OK. But try to paint as detailed a picture of who your customers are, and who you want them to be, as you can.

2. Once you've defined this audience, look for and find them on social networks. Dive into the Facebook/Instagram advertising platform, and see if you can determine how many people fit all of the criteria that you've written down. Search LinkedIn by job title or industry if you're in the B2B space. Search Twitter and Facebook for people talking about whatever it is that you think your customers talk about.

3. Write down a list of places in your marketing budget where you're spending too much money targeting too wide an audience. How can you cut back from other marketing and advertising expenses that are reaching a broader group in favor of more narrow targeting using social networks?

HASTE MAKES WASTE; SO DOES TRADITIONAL MARKETING AND ADVERTISING

I understand that after reading this chapter, you won't go out and immediately cut your entire advertising budget because you're targeting too wide an audience. You don't have to. But surely you can think of somewhere to cut back in order to start targeting the right people through social networks, those who will become your customers, advocates even, in the future. Find them, bring them into the conversation, and when they're ready, you'll be their first choice.

CHAPTER 3

Use Social Network Ads for Much Greater Impact

You're relaxing one night at home after work, on the couch, watching some television. Your favorite show cuts to a commercial, and you're about to hit fast-forward on your DVR to skip the downtime, as you usually do, when you notice something strange. On the upper-right corner of your television screen, you see your friend's name! You hold off on fast-forwarding, examine closer, and read the words, "Your friend Megan Miller likes this ad."

"Wow," you think. "How crazy." You watch the ad and actually find it pretty entertaining. You're glad you paid attention to your friend Megan's approval and didn't skip the commercial.

The next morning, on your way to work, you're listening to the radio, and just before the DJ goes to the commercial break, you hear, "Three of your friends, including Megan Miller, like this next company you'll hear an ad from." Since three of your friends like the company, the ad must be worth paying attention to, so you decide to listen.

You arrive at work, and since you're in charge of scanning the local newspaper for articles of importance to your company, you open up the first page and begin reading. You can't help but notice an advertisement on page three, because right underneath this ad is printed: "Five of your friends, including Megan Miller, like this company."

None of these advertising examples are possible through traditional, linear media, of course. In fact, they probably seem downright absurd. But can you imagine how incredible it would be if they were possible? The ability to build word-of-mouth endorsements from your friends into personalized advertising units is more powerful than any form of linear advertising ever created, and it's currently possible using Facebook's ad unit.

Because social ads relate people to their own friends and to other real people, they're inherently more powerful than nonsocial ads. In the past, advertisements were about product features and benefits. Today, the content of a social network advertisement can be personalized to have the greatest impact on each user. Which copy do you think would have a greater effect: "Our widgets are the best because they're the fastest" or "Your friends Johnny and Susie like our widgets"?

FACEBOOK AND INSTAGRAM ADVERTISING

Furthermore, the targeting criteria that are available to marketers through Facebook and Instagram are so much greater than any previous model that you can literally eliminate all waste. Facebook has *lots* of data, shared by over two billion users, so you can target *exactly* the people you want to reach.

The Amazing "Friends of Connections" Ads

Once you have customers who have *liked* your page on Facebook, the best way to grow your fan base and to leverage the organic power of word of mouth is to use Facebook ads that target Friends of Connections among your targeting criteria (Figure 3.1). Done right, you essentially use these ads to market your company through your existing customers' and fans' connections and *likes*, gaining their friends' attention instead of simply marketing to a mass audience or an untargeted group of people.

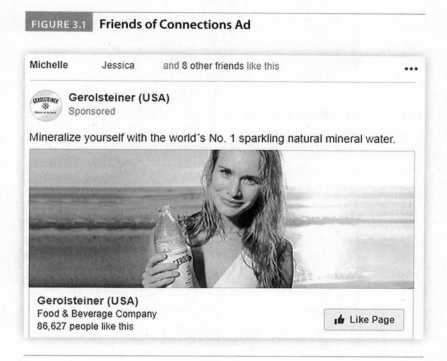

FIGURE 3.1   **Friends of Connections Ad**

The average person on Facebook has around 350 friends. So even if you have only 100 people who *like* your page to begin with, an ad seen only by friends of connections *has a target audience of roughly 35,000 people.* If you have 1,000 fans, *that's an average target audience of 350,000 people.* The numbers can be astounding, but much more compelling is the fact that every ad served is personalized to tell your prospects which of his or her friends already *like* you inside the ad itself. You cannot receive a better endorsement!

Four Important Types of Facebook Ads

Over the years, Facebook extended Friends of Connections targeting to its different types of ads. Gone are the days of solely advertising to drive page *likes*. Unlike other advertising media, Facebook allows you to target your precise demographic with the exact call to action to fit the campaign needs. From driving users to download your app to boosting engagement on your content, Facebook allows you to seamlessly advertise on mobile and desktop. Though there are more than a dozen different types of ads, these are four of my favorites:

1. **Driving traffic and leads.** Driving website traffic is the most common use of Facebook advertising. Oftentimes companies use these to drive customers to specific landing pages such as a blog or a "Buy Now" page. In the past, domain ads (which appeared on the right-hand side of your Facebook News Feed) were extremely popular. Nowadays, ads using images and videos in the News Feed are much more successful, and you can even drive traffic through a series of images or videos in one post, known as a carousel ad. In addition to driving clicks to a website, Facebook has made it possible to capture leads without taking users away from the platform at all. Want to get customer sign-ups or grow your email list? A simple click will open a "lead form," already prepopulated with the contact information your target has shared with Facebook, ready to be sent directly to you. Now let's look at the block of ads from my News Feed shown in Figure 3.2. The *Huffington Post* ad with a picture of a wedding (and my friend Tessa's recommendation) is way more powerful than Poland Spring's sidebar ad. When you're marketing, remember to think like a consumer. Ask yourself, "Would this catch my attention? Would I click on that link?"

2. **Post engagement and awareness.** Post *boosts* have become increasingly important since early 2014. As Facebook's News Feed algorithm continues to evolve (more on that in the following chapter) and Facebook works to bring in more ad revenue, it's become much more difficult to get your business page's content viewed organically. This has huge implications for businesses, both big and small. You've worked hard to build your audience, and it would be a shame for them to miss out on your posts. Facebook allows you to boost content right from the post, and what's more is it will actually serve your ad to different people based on your ad optimization. For example, if you optimize your ad for engagement,

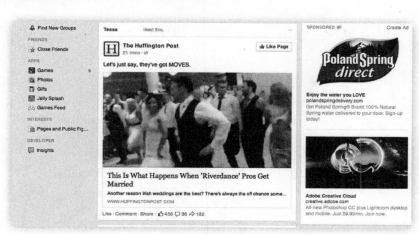

FIGURE 3.2   **Which Ad Is More Powerful?**

Facebook will show your ad to those who, based on previous behavior, are more likely to *like*, comment, or share, ensuring you don't waste your ad dollars on someone who hasn't *liked* a post since joining Facebook. On the other hand, if you optimize your post for brand awareness, Facebook will show your ads to people who are more likely to recall them. With just a few clicks, you can have your Facebook post in front of thousands of your fans—and their friends. Figure 3.3 is an ad for a Likeable Media augmented reality game that reached thousands of people for just $40.

3. **App install ads.** App installation ads have become increasingly more important for brands with mobile apps. Americans alone download millions of apps every day. In fact, Apple reported nearly 200 billion app downloads in 2017. App installation ads allow for users to download applications directly from Facebook on mobile phones. Through *call-to-action buttons*, users are redirected to the app store to complete the download.

4. **Dynamic ads.** Have you ever added an item to your cart but not bought it, then the next day you see that same product on Facebook? Dynamic ads use the Facebook pixel to build audiences based on your website's activity. If you use a service like Shopify or Magento, you can easily link your product catalog

FIGURE 3.3 **A Post Boost**

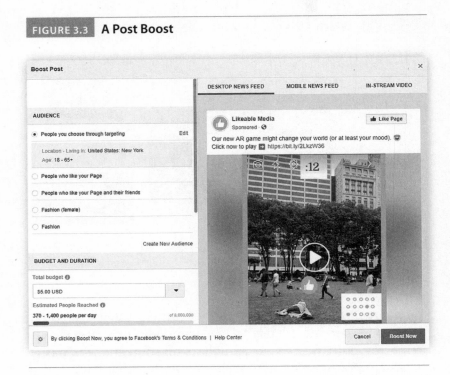

to your business's Facebook account so the ads served are up-to-date with the latest pricing and availability.

Advertising on Instagram

Because Instagram is owned by Facebook, the platforms have the same targeting and optimization capabilities, but there are a few additional things to consider when adding Instagram ads into your mix:

1. **Mixed placement ads.** Let's say you're running an ad on Facebook, but you want to see how it does on Instagram. Without having to create a new ad, you can choose to run your campaign across both networks, letting the algorithm decide which platform is the best fit for that specific ad. The ads won't show up in your Instagram profile grid; instead, they'll appear in between other photos and videos in the feed.

2. **Stories ads.** Instagram Stories are full-screen vertical photos and videos that typically feature "in the moment" content (like Snapchat). Aside from posting Stories organically on your profile, you can create an ad that will run in between users' friends' Stories. If done right, users won't even notice the interruption. Instead, they'll be informed and entertained. Of the 400 million accounts using Instagram Stories, one-third of the most viewed Stories come from businesses, and they can be optimized by reach, video views, traffic, conversions, app installs, and brand awareness. New features and capabilities are constantly being added to the network, and you can stay informed on the latest with Facebook's marketing courses on Blueprint (facebook.com/blueprint).

Choosing Targeting Criteria

It's great targeting friends of existing *likers*, and chances are many of your customers' friends have a lot in common with your customers. But remember, you can choose exactly what targeting criteria you want to apply to each ad you take out on Facebook. Not all of these will necessarily apply to you, but they're all worth a look.

- **Demographics.** This is where you input age, gender, and language. (There are more than 100 different languages spoken on Facebook!) Ideally, you have an understanding of who your customers are so that you can target here, as in 23- to 25-year-old women, or 56- to 65-year-old men.
- **Location.** Target people by country, state, city, zip code, or town. For local businesses, you can input a specific address and target people in your town, or within a 10-, 25-, or 50-mile radius around it to help create more walk-ins.
- **Education and work.** Target people by their education status or their company. This is incredibly valuable in the business-to-business space. Perhaps you want to reach people at five specific companies in your town or land a new client from one particular company or industry. Maybe you want to get someone's attention to land a new job.

- **Relationship status and interested in.** Target just singles, married people, people in relationships, or engaged people here. You can also target people who list "it's complicated" or "in an open relationship," among others. For obvious reasons, this category is particularly valuable to companies in the wedding industry or dating industry.
- **Life events.** Facebook lets users update their profiles based on major life events, such as "expecting a child" or "newly engaged," and, naturally, Facebook lets advertisers leverage these updates. For instance, if you're a jewelry store, try targeting a necklace ad to men with upcoming anniversaries. Just like that, they have inspiration for that gift they've been putting off.
- **Interests.** Arguably the most important category of ad targeting, this is where you can identify people by their interests. With data on over two billion people, Facebook allows marketers to target by interests like cooking, biking, running, jazz, going to church, or reading fiction. There are over one million possible *likes* and interests to choose from!
- **Behaviors.** Before March 2018, advertisers were able to target users based on data provided by third-party companies, for example, "in the market for a new vehicle" or "likely to relocate." After the Cambridge Analytica data scandal (more on that later), those capabilities were removed, but you can still target by behaviors like device usage (mobile device brand, tablet owner, etc.), digital activities (Internet browser, operating system, etc.), and travel (frequent travelers, international travelers, etc.).

The more specific your target audience, the better. Personalized ads based on these criteria will go so much further in promoting your organization than any traditional mass-media outlet. Use your current fans to create ads that apply to their friends and will therefore attract new customers.

Custom and Lookalike Audiences

Another capability of Facebook ad targeting is creating custom audiences. With the ability to upload email lists or import data from your website's conversion pixels, companies can target more precisely. Say, for example, you're an e-commerce brand looking to advertise to women who have purchased from you in the past six months. Using custom audience targeting, reaching those women is easier than ever. You can also create custom audiences based on Facebook activity, such as the set of people who have liked your page, engaged with your posts, or viewed your videos.

Lookalike audiences let companies advertise to people who resemble current fans or people who would be interested in your business. All you need is a custom audience list for Facebook to match with other users with similar interests, behaviors, or demographics. For example, if you're a fitness club that wants to target people who "look like" your current members, just upload your member email list. If you're a retail brand that saw tons of clicks on a particular T-shirt ad, you'll want to create a lookalike audience of those who clicked on it.

Six Cool Things You Can Do with Facebook Ads

Just to get you thinking about all of the potential that's out there, consider these six possibilities for using Facebook ads:

1. **Target people with upcoming birthdays!** Reach your customers or prospects when they have upcoming birthdays. You can offer them a coupon code or a special prize like a free appetizer, or simply surprise them by saying "happy birthday" from your company.
2. **Target your fans with reminders about cool events and promotions, or just to say thank you.** Once you generate *likers*, you can talk to them for free through the information stream on Facebook. But if you have a particular message or offer you want to reinforce to people who you know already *like* you, this is a great, inexpensive way to guarantee that message will be seen.
3. **Target your employees!** Has it been a tough week? Congratulate them for getting through it, or thank them for their hard work! You can do this using the "companies" targeting feature, or you can upload an email list to create a custom audience.

4. **Introduce yourself to a new company.** Just landed a job as a social media specialist at a new firm? Show the company just how cool and social-media-nerdy you are by introducing yourself to your new coworkers in an ad.

5. **Build potential relationships with key partners.** Target people with "CEO" or "president" and other similar job titles in their profiles at the companies you're interested in building relationships with.

6. **Target specific job titles.** Get connected with the exact employees you want to reach. If you're a marketing software company, then targeting the CMO or marketing director will be more beneficial than targeting everyone at the company.

All six of these practices will help you further build relationships with your customers, prospects, coworkers, employees, and partners online and offline, but these are just a start. What other ways could you target your specific audience through Facebook ads?

Make the Ad Likeable

Once you've selected all of the targeting criteria, you have to actually create the ad, using a few lines of copy and a photo or video. The visual is by far the most important element of a Facebook ad, so you'll want to select a bright, size-optimized image or video that gets people's attention. You can run a virtually unlimited number of ads under the same budget, so you'll have the opportunity to test out dozens of different visuals and copy to see what's most effective in driving *likes*, clicks, comments, leads, or purchases.

You'll need to set a daily budget, which can be as low as $5 per day and as high as you'd like. You can buy ads through CPM (cost per thousand impressions), CPC (cost per click), or CPA (cost per action). With CPM, your ad may appear many thousands of times, but if nobody clicks on the ad, you'll have nothing to show for your money. With CPC or CPA, you pay only when people click on your ads or take your desired action—so you're only paying for results. Over the years, however, Facebook has developed methods to optimize CPM that can lead to very efficient results.

Keep Your Social Ads Social

A lot of companies have failed at using Facebook ads to drive direct sales because people spend time on Facebook to socialize and connect with others, not to buy stuff. The formula for ad success is not just to link ads to your website or shopping cart but to build a rapport with customers first. If you serve users an engaging video, you can later retarget those who viewed a substantial portion of that video. Direct them to your fan page and encourage them to engage with you. They might enter a contest or ask you some questions about products, services, or your industry. They have the opportunity to connect with other people in your community. The object is to engage with your customers or prospects. You'll have ample time to make a great impression on them later—you've just got to get them to *like* you first.

ADVERTISING IN OTHER SOCIAL NETWORKS

Facebook and Instagram advertisements are the most used and most effective form of social network ads, but they are not the only kind. Both LinkedIn and Twitter, for example, provide direct advertising opportunities as well, with the abilities to target specific audiences and help companies continue to build their online presence.

Use LinkedIn Ads to Reach Professionals

LinkedIn hosts more than 500 million user profiles, and the users are often more business focused than Facebook's users. While not quite as extensive as Facebook's criteria, LinkedIn offers great targeting criteria to reach professionals, including industry, job title, seniority, age, gender, location, skills, and group affiliation. It also offers CPC, CPM, and CPV (cost per view) models, and it allows for ad budgets as small as $10. LinkedIn ads are often more expensive than Facebook ads, but then again, you're reaching senior professionals. How valuable is that to your business?

In addition to its standard ad capabilities, LinkedIn recently rolled out a "Dynamic Ad" format featuring professionals' own LinkedIn profile data, like photo, company name, job title, and more. LinkedIn is dedicated to helping marketers create personalized experiences; in fact, one cool *social* LinkedIn ad format is Sponsored InMail, which sends personalized messages to active LinkedIn members from the profile of the person who took out the ad. This transparency and subtle invitation to connect is refreshing. Instead of an advertisement coming from a giant faceless organization, it's literally shown as coming from one individual, who's on LinkedIn, just like the person who is viewing the ad. Can you imagine if every ad you saw on television or read in a newspaper had the personal information of the person who took out the ad? That would lead to greater transparency and accountability and likely to better ads being made. Plus, as I mentioned earlier, B2B decision making is still person-to-person, and this ad format really brings that reality to life.

Twitter Ads Allow You to Join the Stream

Twitter has tinkered with a number of different advertising models, but at the moment, Promoted Tweets, Promoted Trends, and Promoted Twitter Accounts all allow advertisers to get their company's most recent tweets in front of people who are using particular keywords on Twitter. Similar to Facebook, Twitter has also increased its objective-based campaigns. This process is most similar to Google's AdWords model, wherein people who search on Google using specific keywords find sponsored listings from advertisers who have preselected (and bought) those keywords. With Twitter, though, it's more about the *conversation* than the search. For instance, try searching on Twitter for doctors in Brooklyn to see what people are saying about their doctors in that area. If a doctor in Brooklyn has purchased specific keywords (such as "Brooklyn," "doctor," "patient," or "care"), her last tweet will show up at the top of your stream.

Twitter ads are particularly useful for joining the conversation and engaging your audience, driving traffic to your website, and driving app installs for your mobile app.

THE LIFETIME VALUE OF A SOCIAL NETWORK AD

Advertisements have traditionally sought to raise awareness, to increase purchase intent, and to convert passive recipients into customers. At the end of a linear ad, the recipient has become more aware and has decided whether to purchase something or not. Social networks have incorporated those traditional objectives, but have added new ones that are extremely valuable in their own right. All that an ad on Facebook, Instagram, or Twitter really needs to do is generate a *like* or a follower, respectively, for your company. After that point, you have the ability to talk to (and engage with, and eventually sell to!) those fans or followers for the rest of their lives. Of course, if you become too marketing or sales heavy in your social network messaging, people can and will "unlike" you or "unfollow" you. To a great extent, that situation has happened with email marketing: email lists aren't usually used to engage or provide value. They're used to sell—and consequently, people who were once fans of a company often grow to be annoyed by, or even hate, that same company, and eventually they unsubscribe from its email list.

You have an amazing opportunity to target your ideal customer, and for the price of one click (this can range from $0.04 to $6.00, depending on your targeting criteria), you convert someone to *like* you or follow you and join the conversation. Once the person is in your community, you can have his attention literally for the rest of his life, as long as you engage appropriately. What is the lifetime value, then, of that initial ad, *like*, follow, or click?

Likeable's Ads Stumble but Then Build a Business or Two

At Likeable Media and Likeable Local, we've purchased Facebook ads for thousands of clients, and we've used the targeting criteria and Friends of Connections opportunities to grow many communities. But the number one example I'd like to share of how to use Facebook ads comes from our own firm's experience. Facebook ads were the first form of paid advertising we used, resulting in the growth of a company from literally nothing into over $25 million of revenue in nine years. We didn't target correctly at first, but we learned our lesson. And we only spent about $30 per day to do it.

Here's what we did first: We targeted keywords in the Interests category, such as "marketing," "promotions," and "social media." While this generated a lot of fans who were interested in these areas, they may not have been our actual prospects because they likely included students and other people who were interested in these topics but had no decision-making authority at companies. So we shifted gears.

We knew that the decision to hire a marketing agency is made by multiple people at a company, and we could reasonably identify most of them by job title. So we consistently created ads targeting these people: chief marketing officers, vice presidents of marketing, marketing directors, and brand managers. We didn't ask people to call us or even check out our website in ads. Instead, we asked them only to connect to our page on Facebook and join our community. Then, every day, we shared the best content we could find, and we wrote about social media and provided advice about how to best leverage it. The ultimate pull-marketing model eventually worked, and today, dozens of these people have called or emailed us asking for our help. Out of the 56,000 fans in our two Facebook communities, more will certainly reach out. But they'll reach out when they're ready to buy, not when we're ready to sell them.

Q Squared Sells Unbreakable Plates (Without Breaking the Bank)

Q Squared is a luxury brand that sells melamine plates and other dinnerware. The company had tested e-commerce campaigns on digital and social, but it came to Likeable hoping to crack the code for driving ROI on social.

We began with a test-and-learn mindset, using initial spend to identify the most receptive audiences and strongest calls to action. At the same time, we ran a detailed analysis of the e-commerce flow and page drop off. Once initial media testing was complete and e-commerce kinks were fixed, we implemented full-fledged creative testing, employing a mix of dynamic ad units such as video link posts, photo link posts, cinemagraphs, and carousels, each paired with carefully crafted A/B messaging sets. To speed up the pace of testing and optimization, we even helped develop unique promo offers for social (Figure 3.4). All ads were optimized daily, and the team pivoted as needed to take advantage of real-time insights. Overall, Q Squared saw an increase in direct site revenue from the prior year, and the ads helped the brand reach its ROI goals.

FIGURE 3.4   **Q Squared's Facebook Ad with Social Discount**

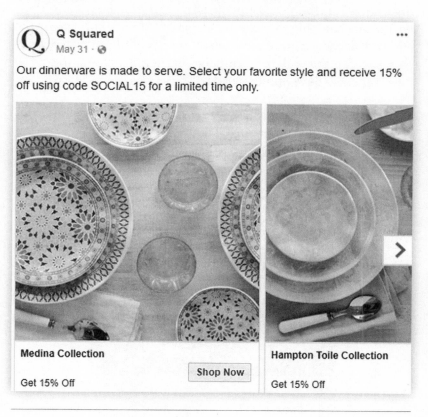

Pure Barre Turns Its Customers into Franchise Owners

Pure Barre is a fitness company that combines aspects of ballet, Pilates, and weights, and is said to be the "fastest, most effective way to change your body." The company wanted to expand locations across North America, but the requirements to become a franchise owner posed a significant barrier: Along with the traditional savings requirement, applicants needed either personal experience with Pure Barre or ballet training.

Using only Facebook, Likeable developed a lead-generation campaign that started by driving link clicks (Figure 3.5), then kicked in with remarketing to convert site visitors to leads. The team implemented sophisticated targeting built off of interests, lookalikes, and geo data. Knowing that Pure Barre customers were the most passionate about the brand, we focused prospecting efforts on that pool of people and tailored creative to their needs. The campaign reached over one million people across the country, driving 33,000 people to Pure Barre's franchise ownership page. In the end, the campaign garnered a whopping 1,400 new franchise development leads.

FIGURE 3.5 **Pure Barre's Facebook Ad Targeting Potential Franchise Owners**

ACTION ITEMS

1. Define your perfect target audience using Facebook's advertising categories to guide you. Determine exactly how big your audience is on Facebook once you've inputted all of the demographic and interests criteria.

2. Test various different creative ideas in advertising. Start with a very small budget and with several different pictures and headlines to determine what works best. (You can begin as low as $5, a budget that anyone can afford.)

3. Determine whether your organization could benefit from Instagram ads, LinkedIn ads, or Twitter ads. It's probably not worth it if your organization doesn't yet have a presence on Instagram, LinkedIn, or Twitter—but arguably you should, and it's likely worth testing.

CREATE LIKEABLE SOCIAL ADS

In a world dominated today by disruptive and unwanted advertising in so many forms, social media ads allow you to be more likeable, literally and figuratively. These ads give you the ability to find and connect to your perfect target audience and to leverage built-in word-of-mouth endorsements. Instead of creating transaction opportunities, these ads establish lifetime connections with potential customers—and their friends. In a challenging economy, when it's worth considering cutting back on your traditional advertisements (which may or may not be effective), it's time to look closely at social media ads to boost your fan base and generate new customers.

CHAPTER 4

Think—and Act—
Like Your Consumer

Do you like being disrupted? Do you enjoy when you're reading something online and a pop-up banner ad gets in the way of the next paragraph? What about when you're working on a project at the office, the phone rings, and you answer to find a sales guy on the other end of the line trying to pitch his wares?

When I speak at conferences, I often tell my audiences, many of whom are marketers, to place themselves in the role of the consumer. I then ask, "How many of you listen to and enjoy radio commercials?"

No hands.

"How many of you watch and enjoy television commercials?"

A couple of hands usually come up at this point, and normally, upon further review, these people are, in fact, ad guys.

"How many of you use and enjoy Instagram or another social network?"

Here, hands shoot up in the air, anywhere between 60 and 90 percent of the room.

Is this because social media is the newest, shiniest product in town? I don't think so. I believe it's because people fundamentally want to use media to relax, enjoy themselves, and connect with others—*not* to be interrupted. Here are a few marketing and advertising tools and methods that are available today. Placing yourself in the role of the consumer, think about how you feel when you receive or experience the following:

- Direct mail
- Magazine ads
- TV ads
- Radio ads
- Packaging (that is, "Free Toy Inside" on the cereal box)
- Flyers handed to you on the street
- Billboards off the highway
- Automated messages when you're on hold, telling you to visit the company website

- Mobile and/or text-messaging ads
- Ten minutes of ads before the trailers even start at the movie theater
- Emails constantly arriving in your inbox from marketing lists you don't remember signing up for
- Telemarketing and cold-calling to your home and office

Advertisements and marketing ploys are found just about everywhere we go. From the television in our living room to the stall in the public bathroom, from a drive down the interstate to a walk through the city's streets, from your phone line at work to your personal cell number: nowhere is safe from ads! And while some ads are funny, interesting, and even compelling—if you consider the consumer's viewpoint, you'll agree that most are simply disruptive and unwanted.

So what's a marketer to do? How can you possibly avoid joining the endless parade of marketing and advertising disruptions in the quest to find your consumers?

All you have to do is stop thinking like a marketer and start thinking like your consumer.

RULE OF THUMB: WHAT DO YOUR CUSTOMERS REALLY WANT?

Laura Fitton of HubSpot has a saying: "Your entire social media strategy can be summed up in two words: Be useful." With every

Facebook message you send out, with every Instagram Story or tweet you post, even with every email or radio and television advertisement you write, ask yourself the following:

- Will the recipients of this message truly find it of value, or will they find it annoying and disruptive?
- Would I want to receive this message as a consumer?

If you respond that yes, as *a consumer*, this message is of value and you would indeed want to receive it, then it is a message worth communicating to your customers and the world. On the other hand, if you cannot see any *true* value to the consumer or you believe the message will be only an annoyance, then it's simply not worth sending. Why spend money, time, and effort only to contribute to mass advertising, marketing, and information noise that the consumer does not want or need in the first place?

Sure, even a poorly conceived message can generate some Web traffic, phone calls, awareness, or even sales, but it can also erode your brand. In the long run, the organizations that will win are the organizations that engage in positive, useful communications with their customers and prospects. Today, the most effective way to do so is to utilize the tools offered by social media.

The Brilliance of the Facebook News Feed

On Facebook, when you log in as a user, you are brought to a home page that displays your News Feed. The News Feed is a stream of information from your Facebook social connections, including your Facebook friends, Facebook groups you've joined, and Facebook pages that you've *liked*. Not every piece of information posted by every one of your friends is included, but since the Top Stories pop up as the default for users when they log on, that's one of the first things you see, and it is your main source of information.

Facebook's News Feed algorithm is nothing short of revolutionary. Imagine if television commercials that people didn't want to watch disappeared or if direct mail that the first few recipients didn't open stopped being sent out, never making it to anyone else's door. Consider how much you would pay to have emails other people hadn't responded to positively remain out of your inbox. Facebook has effectively created a system that filters out all the junk the user couldn't care less about or, worse yet, will respond to negatively. This situation forces companies, and individuals, to think very carefully about the content they share: it's a great thing for users and a powerful tool for marketers and advertisers who understand what their consumers want and don't want.

Figure 4.1 shows a formula describing the original News Feed Optimization algorithm, also known as EdgeRank, from a presentation given by Facebook engineers Ruchi Sanghvi and Ari Steinberg at Facebook's 2010 F8 developer conference. The Facebook News Feed originally served users individualized content based on three factors:

1. How recently the content occurred or was created
2. The strength of the user's relationship with the person or organization who shared the content
3. How much engagement it received

FIGURE 4.1   News Feed Optimization

$$\sum_{edges\ e} u_e W_e d_e$$

u_e affinity score between viewing user and edge creator

W_e weight for this edge type (create, comment, like, tag, etc.)

d_e time for decay factor based on how long ago the edge was created

---

In 2013, Facebook abandoned the original EdgeRank formula, and in January 2018, CEO Mark Zuckerberg announced that the goal of the News Feed algorithm was shifting from serving "relevant content" to generating "meaningful social interactions."

On the surface, that sounds like semantics, but the scope of the change was tremendous. For years, Facebook told advertisers to ignore organic engagement, but Zuckerberg was now returning Facebook to an era where organic reactions (like, love, wow, etc.), comments, and shares were key. In doing so, Facebook hopes to restore the quality of time spent on the network. For brands and businesses, the question then becomes obvious. What is the best approach for driving meaningful engagement?

Facebook doesn't offer a definition for "meaningful engagement," but it does provide several clues. In January 2018, the network's Head of News Feed, Adam Mosseri, explained that posts will show higher in the News Feed if they "inspire back-and-forth discussion in the comments" or if they are things people "want to share and react to," and when Zuckerberg first announced the update, he also stressed the idea of connection. To paraphrase slightly, he said that the goal of the update is to "help people connect with each other." Reactions are strong endorsements, but they don't connect users to communities like comments and shares do. Let's look at an example.

Conglomerate A is a global sneaker brand that has spent millions of dollars in advertising to grow a Facebook fan base of one million fans. Your similar, though much smaller, organization has far fewer resources and currently has only 5,000 fans, half of whom happen to also be fans of Conglomerate A.

Conglomerate A shares a traditional marketing message with its fans: "Check out our new running shoes on our website and buy them now!" Only a handful of people click the Like button or comment on the content. Since the company has failed to engage its audience, only a few hundred people will end up seeing the update because it will not be moved up into users' Top Stories.

Your company, however, posts a beautiful photo with the following update at the same time as Conglomerate A's: "Happy Friday! Where's everyone going running this weekend?" Here, you attempt to engage the users with a more personalized, friendly, and less demanding message. You are not just telling them to "go buy shoes." Your update then generates *likes* and comments, enough to stay at the top of thousands of people's News Feeds for a day. This placement, in turn, generates greater awareness and, in turn, higher sales. More important, the comments left lead to a conversation that will aid your success in the *next* update you share. You've outdone Conglomerate A. While it was busy marketing, you were thinking like your consumers. You were engaging them and building an invaluable audience.

WHAT DO YOUR CONSUMERS LIKE?

The important question is: What do your consumers truly like? Consider what they care about. What do they value? What content will get them to authentically comment and share and increase your visibility among users? Keep in mind that you can't just keep sharing updates that ask people to *like* the content because that would quickly get as annoying and disruptive as many of the traditional marketing tactics you've grown to know and hate. In fact, in December 2017, Facebook announced it would begin demoting posts in the News Feed that use "engagement bait," or calls to action that seek to take advantage of the algorithm by boosting engagement in order to get greater reach. For example, "LIKE this if you're an Aries!" or "Tag a friend who NEEDS to see this!"

So instead of telling your fans what *to* like, ask them *what* they like! For instance, say you have a male-focused customer base. You suspect these consumers are big sports fans, but you're not sure what sports or teams they are most interested in. You could simply ask on Facebook, "What's your favorite major sporting event of the year? Who did you root for this past season?" If your fans overwhelmingly say the Super Bowl and provide their favorite football teams, you'll want to share content about that sport in the future, even if your product has nothing to do with football.

If *you* were your consumer, what would make *you* click Like or leave a comment? An appetizing photo? A funny video? A fact nobody knew about you?

One thing users are sure *not* to respond to positively is a press release about your latest earnings statement, new hire, or new product. There may be an audience who cares enough about this information to warrant sharing it elsewhere, but that audience is not the group to target on Facebook. The Facebook audience doesn't care. Social media networks such as Facebook, Instagram, Twitter, and LinkedIn are not broadcast media. I can't stress this enough. Engage. Don't broadcast!

IT'S ABOUT YOUR CUSTOMERS, NOT YOUR BRAND

In the past, traditional marketers didn't have the luxury of having a two-way conversation with customers, but they did have a captive audience. Consequently, traditional marketers pounded consumers over the head with marketing messages until the public bought from them. If you're over the age of 40, for example, you probably know the Jolly Green Giant jingle—not because it's a great song but because you were exposed to it so many times through television and radio ads that you couldn't help but learn it.

In a crowded marketing and advertising world, *mindshare* is how much your customers are thinking about your product or service. In order to win your customers' mindshare now, your marketing can't be *solely* about your brand, or products, or features and benefits anymore. More than anything, you have to get your customers talking, or you have to get involved in their already ongoing conversation. If they're talking and you're at the top of their News Feeds on Facebook, you've got some mindshare. Messaging has to be about *your customers*. What are their hopes and dreams? What do they want to do, hear about, talk about, and share? What's actually relevant to *them*?

This lesson is a hard one for companies to learn because it involves unlearning much of what they know about marketing, promotion, and publicity. They'll ask, "What about our brand? How can we spend precious marketing dollars and time on messaging that has nothing to do with our brand or company?"

But it's the results that matter, so remind yourself about the News Feed, for example. If the message is all about your brand and people don't find that message interesting or relevant, then they won't even see it. On the bright side, even if the message isn't about your brand at all, if it's being commented on and *liked*, your Facebook page name will still be seen by your fans, and it will garner attention from others. Your brand will not only be at the top of people's News Feeds but also at the top of their minds. Let's take a look at a couple of real-life examples of the power of thinking like your customers and appropriately using social media to engage them.

The Pampered Chef: Cooking Up Content Its Fans *Like*

The Pampered Chef (TPC) is one of the largest and best-known direct sales organizations in the country. Based in Chicago, it has a huge sales force of independent consultants who sell cooking and dining products through house parties and other events. The Pampered Chef joined Facebook as an organization after most of its direct-selling competition had already established their own pages and generated thousands of fans. TPC wanted to build an effective Facebook presence quickly for its overall brand and salespeople. It didn't have a budget for Facebook ads, which its competitors, and many other companies, were using to drive initial *likes* to their fan pages.

The Pampered Chef's team members thought carefully about the kinds of content TPC's customers would like, and what they wouldn't like, and they worked together to build a fan page, applications, and a daily content calendar that would be about neither the brand nor selling but instead all about the consumers. The result was that the team members shared useful content such as recipes and recipe contests, and they encouraged visitors to their fan page to share stories about their own great meals and pictures of their own culinary masterpieces. A virtual gift application allowed fans to share a picture of a scrumptious cake on their friends' Facebook walls on their birthdays or to celebrate other occasions. All of this content is loosely related to the brand and its mission, of course, but it isn't *about* the brand. It's about the *consumers*, and it is designed to be as intriguing as possible. By generating hundreds of comments and *likes* through consumer interaction (Figure 4.2), The

Pampered Chef remains at the top of its fans' News Feeds for as long as possible, generating more eyeballs, mindshare, clicks, and sales.

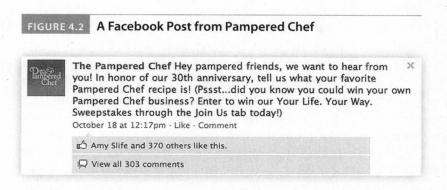

FIGURE 4.2   A Facebook Post from Pampered Chef

> **The Pampered Chef** Hey pampered friends, we want to hear from you! In honor of our 30th anniversary, tell us what your favorite Pampered Chef recipe is! (Pssst...did you know you could win your own Pampered Chef business? Enter to win our Your Life. Your Way. Sweepstakes through the Join Us tab today!)
>
> October 18 at 12:17pm · Like · Comment
>
> 👍 Amy Slife and 370 others like this.
>
> 💬 View all 303 comments

More than a hundred thousand people *liked* the page in the first two months, *without any paid advertising*, and hundreds of people comment on every daily update. The rich content shared by The Pampered Chef each day generates not only *likes* but lots of sharing as well, which in turn drives more and more people back to the page. While the company did not reveal revenue numbers generated by the initial Facebook engagement, rest assured that sales figures were very likeable too.

Stop & Shop Gamifies the Grocery Store

Like any grocery chain, Stop & Shop's main challenge is to get customers in-store. In the past, this was done by simply owning a location, but there have never been more options for buying groceries—including those that don't involve stores at all. To compete with online retailers, Stop & Shop started looking for ways to focus on the experience of in-store shopping vs. the transactional one taking place online.

Instead of creating social media posts that focused solely on product features and deals, Stop & Shop decided to listen to its customers and take advantage of a trend they were already passionate about: Pokémon GO. The day the wildly popular augmented reality app launched, community managers noticed shoppers tweeting pictures of the Pokémon they caught in-store. It was some of the most creative, engaging content they had ever seen users share.

Within days, Stop & Shop launched a campaign that encouraged fans to stop in, shop for groceries, and catch some wild Pokémon (Figure 4.3). On a microsite, a live "Pokémap" showed users which Pokémon had appeared in local stores and social posts compared bagging groceries to bagging Pokémon, but most of all, Stop & Shop invited shoppers to visit the store and keep sharing their amazing Pokémon photos.

In two weeks, the campaign generated more than 25,000 social actions. And despite not offering a prize, it encouraged shoppers to submit . . . and submit . . . and submit their in-store photos. As it stands, this was Stop & Shop's most successful user-generated content (UGC) campaign ever.

FIGURE 4.3   **A Facebook Post from Stop & Shop**

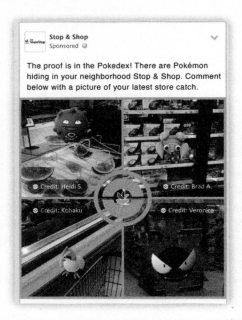

ACTION ITEMS

1. Write down what your typical customers like. Try to avoid writing things your customers like about your company, organization, or products, and instead focus on their interests. Then imagine what specific content would make you click the Like button if you saw it as a consumer. Write down 10 examples of such likeable content.

2. Take messaging that your organization has used in written marketing materials in the past, and rewrite it for social media, making the material more valuable or interesting to the audience. It should be short and sweet, and it should be something you'd want to receive as the consumer, not something you would have wanted to send as the marketer.

3. Develop a plan for how you might create valuable content not just for social networks but for all marketing and communications content. What would you change in your email marketing, direct mail, Web content, and ad copy if you thought like a consumer instead of a marketer? Can you create better content in all of your communication?

BE LIKEABLE, NOT DISRUPTIVE

We are all bombarded by more marketing messages every day than we can even count. You have an opportunity to rise to the top of the clutter, not by coming up with a more creative disruption but by producing content that people actually want to receive. Facebook's News Feed forces you to think like a consumer and challenges you to share content that will be truly valued or enjoyed by your consumers. If you don't want to be invisible, you'll have to be likeable, at least in social media. Remember, on Facebook, you're not competing with your competitors for the consumers' attention. You're competing with pictures of my best friend's baby!

CHAPTER 5

Invite Your Customers to Be Your First Fans

You've started an Instagram and a Twitter account for your company. You've put up a YouTube channel, started a blog, sharpened your LinkedIn profile, and you've even added a button on your website promoting your Facebook page. You're doing everything you're supposed to do to "join the conversation" with social media.

Yet up until now, the results have been dismal. You have a ridiculously low number of fans, considering the size of your business, and the only person you're having a conversation with is yourself. (OK, maybe the guy in the cubicle next to you has joined in too.) But the promise of social media that you've heard so much about is far from being fulfilled. You don't know what you've done wrong or what you need to do to get on the right track to social network success. Where are all of your Facebook fans? Why isn't everyone giving you the *like* stamp of approval?

There's no reason to worry. No matter the size of your organization, gaining lots of fans on Facebook, followers on Instagram, and subscribers on your blog and YouTube is far from automatic. The bad news is that you're going to have to work for fans, friends, and followers, but the good news is that everyone else has to as well. There are international brands that spend millions of dollars in marketing each year with fewer than a thousand fans on Facebook and no official Twitter presence at all—so whatever situation you're in right now, you're in good company and still have time for improvement.

The Internet is nothing like it was 15 years ago, when people endlessly surfed the Web. Many people just don't access information on the Web in that way anymore. If anything, users surf the Web using their own personalized Facebook, Twitter, and LinkedIn filters to look for relevant and recommended content. Moreover, people are increasingly accessing the Web through their smartphones and favorite mobile apps. What that means for you, as a company, is that whether you're a huge brand or brand-new, people who don't know your product or service already are unlikely to be your first Facebook fans or Instagram followers.

So who will become your first social media brand advocates? Your strongest assets are customers, staff, partners, and vendors. However, to leverage this goodwill, you have to ask them to support the company through social networking *and* tell them why they should. Explain the benefits of social networking to your current supporters. Tell them why it is imperative that your company move forward with social media initiatives. Describe the ways their actions will help your company in your marketing and advertising efforts, and make sure they understand how valuable their participation is in this process.

THE *LIKE* IS MORE IMPORTANT THAN THE LINK

Fifteen years ago, if you built a website for your company, you didn't expect thousands of strangers to just visit it, did you? Instead, you used other marketing initiatives and assets to direct people to your website and to publicize the website address or link wherever you could. Sometimes people checked it out, and if they were interested in your content and trusted you enough, maybe they even stayed a while or purchased your products and services. Or if other related companies found your content useful, it was possible that they would link your website to theirs, in exchange for you linking their website to yours. This linking took place in the hope of creating more "link value," greater search engine optimization, and more website traffic. Today, however, the *like* is more important than the "link." Getting people to your website may help them learn about your company and maybe even buy something, but getting them to *like* you on Facebook does two additional things that will contribute to your company's long-term success.

First, when people use the *like* function, they subscribe to your updates, allowing you to have a conversation with them on Facebook forever, unless you erode their trust and they unsubscribe. Second, it introduces and endorses you *to every one of the users' friends*. The average person on Facebook has around 350 friends, so with every *like*, you're exposing your brand to another 350 potential customers, or more. Can you imagine if every time one individual visited your website, she shared that fact with 350 of her friends? ("Hey ladies, I just visited this site. Check it out. It's so great!") The same phenomenon is true for followers on Instagram, subscribers on YouTube or your blog, and other social networking outlets, but the numbers aren't as big as those on Facebook.

Simply put, the more *likes*, comments, and shares your content receives, the more often it will be viewed, and the number of people seeing and accessing the content will grow over time. There are long-lasting effects of the *like* in Facebook search optimization: once you acquire a *like* on your page, any of that person's friends will see this during future searches. So if you're an attorney and one of your clients has *liked* you on Facebook, any time one of his friends searches for an attorney in the future and finds your page, your client's testimonial ("Your friend John *likes* Bob the attorney") will be right there waiting for him. If you represent a children's car seat company, once one happy mommy customer *likes* your product on Facebook, her friends will quickly see her endorsement, and that will be more powerful than any impersonal advertisement.

HOW TO GET THE *LIKE*:
DEVELOP YOUR VALUE PROPOSITION

Before you started reading this book, maybe you already understood the capabilities and importance of Facebook's *like* function. The question you might have now, however, is how do you get people to actually *like* you on Facebook? No matter how well known your brand is currently, you'll need to provide a value proposition to your customers, staff, vendors, and partners, some sort of benefit they will receive from becoming your fans. In other words, don't just tell them to *like* you. Tell them what's in it for them, and tell them in a way that's about them, not you.

Consider the following two different calls to action:

**Like us on Facebook now at
FB.com/LikeableMedia.**
versus
**Ask us your social media questions anytime at
FB.com/LikeableMedia.**

The first one is totally brand-centric. Why would you read that and decide to *like* our company unless you already knew us, loved us, and trusted us? The second call is consumer-centric, and it is likely to generate a lot more action, not only from people who already love us and trust us but also from casual, first-time customers and maybe even prospects. Remember, it's not about you. It's about your customers. Whatever you can do to encourage activity on your Facebook page will in fact encourage *likes*, without actually asking for them. For instance, Oreo asks customers on the company's packaging: "To dunk or not to dunk? Let us know at Facebook.com/Oreo." The company is encouraging people to share their opinions. It is not just telling them to *like* Oreo's online content—yet, more than 42 million people have *liked* the company on Facebook.

The value proposition might be different for each constituency. For example, you may want to invite your own staff to *like* your page with the incentive that they can post questions to the CEO, some of which will receive responses. For customers, however, you may invite them to access a discount.

By giving people a value proposition for joining you and then surrounding your customers with that value proposition, or others, at every opportunity, you'll convert customers into fans, and that's where things begin to get interesting.

Why should people *like* you on Facebook or follow you on Instagram or LinkedIn? What's in it for them that's of value? How can you summarize that value in a short, easy-to-understand call to action? The answer is, it depends on your business or organization. Here are several examples of calls to action to help you think about why people should *like* you:

- Share your feedback with us at FB.com/FedEx.
- Win prizes and join the conversation at FB.com/nickelodeon.
- Get your beauty questions answered at FB.com/livingproofinc.
- Free support for quitting smoking at FB.com/NYCquits.
- Connect with other creatives like you at FB.com/pier1.
- Get some at FB.com/NYCcondom.

It's not about you. It's about your customers (see Table 5.1). In the same way that the Web quickly became too big for you to tell people to visit your website without telling them why, Facebook is too big to tell people—even your customers—to *like* you without telling them why. It's essential to develop that value proposition and then integrate it into your communications with customers and prospects.

TABLE 5.1 **Top Five Reasons Consumers *Like* Fan Pages on Facebook***

1. To interact with brands
2. To feel more connected with the brand
3. Because one of their friends did
4. To get a "freebie" (e.g., free samples, coupons)
5. To be a loyal customer and show support for brand to friends

*Source: Based on a report from https://www.purelybranded.com/insights/why-people-like-and-unlike-brands-on-facebook/.

Getting the *like* approval is essential for everyone, but it is even more important for smaller businesses and new organizations, which can utilize such free social media and word-of-mouth marketing to grow their fledgling companies. Don't be afraid to ask anyone in your organization's circle of influence to *like* you. Just don't do it without creating value for whoever that audience is. You're not going to get *likes* from anyone without giving him or her a valid reason. On the other hand, you're also not going to get *likes* from anyone without reminding him or her to *like* you. Give them value and opportunity, and your vendors, partners, staff, and friends will join you.

Where Should You Tell Customers to *Like* You?

You should provide potential followers and fans with value propositions to *like* you in as many places as possible. Here are a number of places to consider integrating the call to action to your customers:

1. On your website
2. On every email you send out as a company
3. On every staff person's email signature
4. On every business card you hand out
5. On every brochure you print
6. On every receipt you hand out
7. On every piece of snail mail you send out
8. On every inbound phone call to your company
9. On every outbound phone call from your company
10. On all of your packaging (as in the Oreo example)
11. On all of your in-location signage

Some of these more antiquated techniques—snail mail and brochures, for example—are given new vitality and purpose both for you and your consumers if you can connect them directly to your online social network.

Four Ways to Get More Likes and Follows

1. Let your employees create your content. Hilton has built a tribe of internal advocates to power the content found on its employee-led Instagram account, @HiltonCareers. The team sources content from employees directly through a variety of means and allows them to take over for the day, showing Hilton through their points of view. In turn, they end up sharing the posts with their personal networks, growing Hilton's reach and following.

2. Run an Instagram contest or giveaway. In the caption of a photo, ask your followers to tag a friend in the comments to be entered to win a prize (Figure 5.1.). Odds are that tagged friend will also follow your account—and they'll tag another friend to enter too.

3. Use off-social channels to offer an incentive. Instead of including a coupon or call to action to visit a location in its weekly email, Uno Pizzeria & Grill told recipients only to do the following: "Like us on Facebook to earn a free appetizer. Share this with your friends, and when we hit 100,000 fans,

---

FIGURE 5.1   **Hydroflask Instagram Giveaway**

everyone will win a free appetizer on us." Within 24 hours of the email message going out, Uno Pizzeria & Grill had gained more than 10,000 new fans, and within three months, it had reached its goal of 100,000. It didn't get as many sales from that one email as it usually did, but that didn't matter for long. Many thousands of people enjoyed their free appetizer at Uno—and most of them stayed for dinner and dessert.

4. Tap into your network of influencers. These are brand ambassadors who are willing to post about your business or are getting paid to do so. When you're working with influencers on Facebook or Instagram, make sure they don't just push your product, but they also push your brand. By tagging your account in their Stories or posts, more people will be exposed to your account, and more people will hit the follow button.

A NEW INTERNET SALES CYCLE IS BORN

An increased focus on, and ability to measure, every click on the Internet has led to the marketer's obsession with driving subscriptions and sales through Web and email marketing. But if you step back and consider the value of the *like* compared to the immediate sale, you'll see that a long view will yield a better return.

E-commerce: Sales Now or *Likes* Now?

The typical e-commerce site features dozens, hundreds, or thousands of products for sale, many of which are often purchased as gifts. Every piece of text and graphics on such a site has been carefully optimized to drive as many clicks to the shopping cart as possible, attempting to maximize immediate sales. This strategy made sense before the arrival of the social Web, but what if that same e-commerce site were optimized for people to share what they *liked* by clicking the Like button on as many products or categories as possible? This function would create a permanent record of each visitor's interests. Then, friends of the visitor could go to the site, see the exact products their friend indicated he *liked*, and they could then buy it for him for a birthday, holiday, or some other reason. As a company, you'd get fewer immediate sales, but you'd set yourself up to significantly increase your *conversion rate* (the percentage of website visitors who buy your products or take further actions) in the future.

Wouldn't you be more likely to buy something online for your husband or your wife if you saw that he or she had already shown interest in it by *liking* it online?

Professional Services: *Like* as the New Referral

Websites for doctors, dentists, lawyers, accountants, and other service professionals are set up now to convince you to call them—to take action now. But what if these websites were set up to generate *likes* or *follows*? If professionals took the time to say to all of their current clients, "If you are satisfied with our services and would like to let others know about your exceptional experience with our company, please *follow* us on LinkedIn," or "Ask us questions on our Facebook page," these professionals would instantly begin creating a valuable network, not only growing their exposure but also building a clientele who highly trust them.

Ten years ago, if you wanted to find a lawyer or accountant, you might have done a Google search and found those practices that had spent money on search engine marketing so that their site would be the first to pop up on the screen. Now, to find a lawyer or accountant, you can do a Facebook or LinkedIn search of your trusted friends or colleagues and find a practice to which they have given their approval. Are you more likely to pick a lawyer or doctor at random online or rely on the recommendation of a friend?

Dr. Ed Zuckerberg and Aesthetic Family Dentistry (Even Dentists Can Be Likeable)

Edward Zuckerberg, DDS, was a practicing dentist, for many years based in Dobbs Ferry, New York, and now in Palo Alto, California. He also happens to be the father of Mark Zuckerberg, founder and chief executive officer of Facebook. Known as "Painless Dr. Z" by his patients, Dr. Zuckerberg is proof that anyone's business can benefit from utilizing social media. Dentists have always relied on word-of-mouth recommendations and referrals to increase their business—today, social media allows this to happen much more passively and efficiently.

Let's face it, most people don't like going to the dentist (sorry, Dr. Z). If you're anything like me, you consider a dentist appointment more like a tolerable, necessary evil than something you find the least bit enjoyable. Consequently, smart dentists everywhere have gone out of their way to make their practices as tolerable as possible, including friendly front office staff, bright colors on the walls, interesting magazines and other reading material, and toys for children's visits. In addition to these things, which make the physical experience better, Dr. Zuckerberg took the steps necessary to make his practice more likeable on Facebook.

When I first walked into his office, I saw a sign saying, "Like us? Then Like us on Facebook at Facebook.com/PainlessDrZ to join the conversation." This action alone is more effective than the actions taken by 99 percent of all dental practices in the world in driving *likes*. People sitting in the waiting room are a captive audience, and it's the perfect opportunity to convert customers into online fans. However, the conversion opportunities didn't stop there.

Dr. Zuckerberg's email appointment reminders included a call to action to ask questions about your upcoming visit on Facebook, and new patients are invited by phone to "get to know us better before you come in by checking out our bios on our Facebook page." These techniques lead to patients feeling more comfortable on their first visit, but they also lead to more *likes*.

So far, more than 50,000 people have *liked* Dr. Z on Facebook—which led to more than two dozen new patients. I had a Facebook friend whom I don't know that well send me the following message: "Saw you like Dr. Zuckerberg. Is he a good dentist?" To which I replied, "Yes!"

She became a patient the next week of the world's most likeable dentist.

If you own a small business like a dental practice, encourage customers to *like* your page by sharing their pictures on your Facebook or Instagram feeds. Set up a makeshift photo booth in your office with various props and a sign that says, "Tag us in your photos on Facebook and Instagram!" with your company's social handles. You may not catch up with Mark Zuckerberg's dad's likes, but it will help you make great progress.

WHAT IF YOU DON'T CONVERT YOUR CURRENT CUSTOMERS?

There is a risk in focusing on converting your current customers to fans. Seasoned Internet marketers will argue that there's no guaranteed ROI on generating *likes* from your consumers or prospects. They will also claim that by focusing on generating more *likes* on Facebook, you're inherently decreasing your immediate sales.

Every time someone clicks Like, they'll say, that's one less click on *buy now*. This may be true, and you may see a dip initially in online conversions when you first shift some of your marketing strategy to gaining *likes* as compared to *buy nows*, but you don't really have a choice. If you want to grow a social presence, you have to take the time and energy to attract the low-hanging fruit: your current customers and other people who know you. From there, you'll gain other fans and followers who are likely to eventually buy from you. But you have to start with your current customers.

Glossier Turns Its Customers Into Influencers

Glossier, one of the fastest growing beauty startups in the world, was literally born out of social media. In 2010, founder Emily Weiss launched a blog called *Into the Gloss*, where she interviewed celebrities like Karlie Kloss and Bobbi Brown and gave readers an inside look at what was on the "top shelf" of their bathroom cabinets, often demystifying a lot of aspects of the $250-billion beauty industry. After a year, the blog had amassed

10 million page views a month. Weiss took advantage of her incredibly engaged audience, listened to what they liked or didn't like about beauty products, and in 2014, she launched Glossier.

While the brand does share content on its Instagram page from celebrity supporters like Kloss, the ever-growing account relies heavily on "regular" women to endorse the brand. The influencers, referred to as "Glossier girls," closely follow the brand's new product launches and social media posts, then they share them with their followers on social media. One Glossier girl, for example, has just 1,000 followers, but when you add all the girls' followers together, there's a pretty decent sized audience being asked to buy (and follow) Glossier too.

Is there a product you love, but you don't follow the company on Instagram? Probably. It isn't our first instinct to hit the follow button for every brand we encounter, but that doesn't mean your loyal customers aren't sharing. Search hashtags associated with your brand on Instagram and Twitter to see what people are posting about you, then follow them. They'll most likely follow back—but don't stop there; ask them if you can share their content on your page. Now you have a new follower and a new influencer.

ACTION ITEMS

1. Work with your team to create your value proposition, not for a sale but for a *like*. Why should your customers *like* you on Facebook or follow you on Instagram? What's in it for them? How can you craft this value proposition into a short, catchy call to action? What value proposition will you offer employees, vendors, and partners?

2. Brainstorm all of the ways you can integrate this call to action into your current marketing and communications practices. Write down anything and everything. Then, determine which are actionable immediately and which may be actionable over time. Operationalize the *like*.

3. Create a 15-second elevator pitch to tell your customers and anyone you come into contact with why they should *like* you on Facebook and follow you on Twitter. Make sure it's a reason that would resonate with *you as a consumer*.

THE ROAD TO LIKEABLE SOCIAL MEDIA SUCCESS IS PAVED BY YOUR CURRENT CUSTOMERS

Once your current customers have *liked* you, you can begin to earn momentum using content, ads, promotions, and the organic virality of the social graph. But until that happens, you'll be listening and talking in a vacuum. Don't just tell your customers to *like* you. Tell them *why* they should *like* you. Make it about them, not about you, and you'll get the *likes* and follows you're craving to grow your social media network and sales overall.

CHAPTER 6

Engage

Create True Dialogue with, and Between, Your Customers

Do you remember in college when you attended classes held in large lecture halls where professors talked at you for two hours at a time? You also likely had some classes that were a lot smaller and involved a workshop or discussion component. Which type of class did you find more valuable? Which one did you talk about at length, share with friends, and learn from more?

No matter how brilliant the professor of the large lecture was, undoubtedly there were people literally sleeping during the class. And no matter how uninspiring the teacher of the small discussion group was (often, it was a graduate student or teaching assistant in charge), you couldn't help but learn because you were actively engaged in thinking about, talking about, and discussing the subject matter at hand. In fact, you probably learned as much from fellow students and dialogue with others in your class as you did from those professors or instructors who supposedly "held the knowledge."

Just as more engaging classes at a university provide more value to students, the companies and organizations that stand out are those that use social media to meaningfully engage customers and foster dialogue, instead of those who rely on simply, and repeatedly, talking *at* consumers. Companies that can foster communication, not only between organization and consumer but also between consumer and consumer, will reap the greatest benefits of the most connected world we've ever had.

TALKING WITH YOUR CHILDREN INSTEAD OF TALKING TO YOUR BABIES

The twenty-first-century model of truly engaging customers publicly is quite different from marketing and communications models of the past.

Let's say you're a parent. Think about the way you would talk to your children when they are babies versus when they become older. When you speak to a baby, she can't talk back, though she can give you nonverbal cues about how she feels. She won't necessarily understand what you're saying, so as the great parent you are, you'll put on a show to elicit a reaction from her. You make funny faces, talk in a loud or silly voice, and sing to her until you get a laugh or a smile or some other desired result. This situation is like the television commercial of the past (or even present, perhaps). The goal of the commercial is to grab the viewer's attention and produce some sort of response, often using humor, outrageousness, surprise, or song.

When a child gets old enough to talk, as any parent knows, dynamics between the parent and child change. The good news, and bad news, is that the child can talk back to you. Now you get instant verbal feedback on everything you verbally express—you know exactly how well your children understand what you're saying and typically whether they're going to listen to you or not. Of course, sometimes parents don't like what their children say, or how they say it, but as the parent, you have to respond. With the ability to understand what your children are trying to express to you comes greater responsibility and accountability for how you will continue to communicate in the future. Now you're not just talking to your children. You're engaging with them. You're in the conversation for the rest of your life—that's part of your job as a parent.

Consider how this analogy relates to the forms of marketing and advertising that are quickly becoming outdated with the advent of social media. The loudest, costliest advertising formats, such as TV commercials, don't dominate the conversation anymore because, in fact, they no longer own the conversation. The conversation exists on social networks. By engaging the audience directly, you will find that the smartest, most flexible listeners win over the audience. They help create and develop the conversation; they do not attempt to dictate it. Those companies that talk at their customers are less likely to create followers, while those that engage consumers find they will be part of the conversation for life—and that's part of the job of a marketer.

GROWING YOUR CUSTOMER RELATIONSHIPS

So what does "being engaged" really mean?

To be engaged means to be genuinely interested in what your customers have to say. You have to want, even crave, feedback of all kinds because you know it gives you important data to build a better organization. Each individual at your company has to provide his or her full attention, mind, and energy with the customer or task at hand while maintaining the mission and core values of the organization. Anyone can send out an email or a Facebook or Twitter message, but it takes commitment and focus to actually connect with people.

You simply can't "be engaged" on the social Web because it's "the thing to do" now, or you read about it in a book, or you think it will lead to increased sales. You have to authentically believe that being active in growing your social network will lead to deeper, stronger relationships with your customers. You have to be interested in your consumers and prospects, and the creation of a solid bond with them must be your goal.

When two people make a promise to one another that they are to be married, they are said to be "engaged." Similarly, when a company chooses to be engaged with its customers, it commits to being truly concerned about what they say, think, and feel. For many organizations, this connection may be a fundamental shift in how they see and value customers. Instead of creating or outsourcing a customer service department, you want to know firsthand what customers think, how they feel, and what they are looking for from you.

Getting Back to Your Core Values

Most companies, at least when they are first formed, have the best of intentions. Many times, entrepreneurs' original motivation is to create a solution in an attempt to solve a problem. Companies don't necessarily start off by seeing people as dollar signs or statistics. But as organizations grow, they get harder to manage. It becomes easy to lose the initial mindset of authentically wanting to be there, fully present, for your customers and even easier to drift away from your fundamentals and core values.

What is your organization like now? Are you the kind of company that truly cares about its customers and values feedback? Does the marketing arm of your organization act more like an old professor at a large university lecture or like a young, interested teaching assistant leading a group into discovery and learning *together*? It may be hard to honestly and accurately assess yourself and your company, but it's imperative if you plan to survive in the social media age, in which a direct relationship with your customers is becoming the only way to succeed.

If your organization looks like the tired old professor, the good news is that you're certainly not alone. The bad news is that it's going to take a lot of work and a commitment from senior management for the company to get seriously engaged with its constituents and return to the core values of simply being a business catering to the consumers' wants, needs, and desires. You can certainly follow the rules to *look* more engaged, but until you *are* more engaged, you run the risk of being known as only feigning interest in your consumer base. Authenticity is necessary in creating long-lasting connections through the social Web.

Building Communities Around Trust and Loyalty

When you make the commitment to listen to and engage with your customers and prospects, it fosters a genuine sense of trust and loyalty between you and them, and *among them*. Think about the university analogy: In a large lecture, how comfortable would you feel disagreeing with the professor in front of the whole class? How would you feel being the *second* person to speak up, after someone with a dissenting opinion talks? You probably wouldn't feel very comfortable speaking up at all, and neither would others, which is why day after day in that lecture, the professor talks and the students listen and take notes. This setup doesn't really facilitate a valuable relationship or learning experience.

However, if in a smaller discussion class the instructor makes it clear on the first day that the atmosphere is one in which all opinions and comments are respected, where dialogue and dissent is welcomed and even encouraged, and where the teacher hopes to demonstrate that she is as interested in what everyone has to say as they are interested in what she has to say, then the class will become community based around respect and trust. This teacher, whether she's a TA, graduate student, or full-time professor, is seeking to create a discussion, not just lecture at the audience. Students will feel safe and empowered to speak up. They may also continue the dialogue without the instructor and beyond class time.

That smaller discussion class is building a community with value far beyond what the professor may have provided solely by way of imparting knowledge. If you can similarly build and engage an authentic community in this way, your community will bring your brand value beyond what you may see right now. Engaging your customers or prospects and getting them involved in your brand community will create a sense of trust and loyalty between you and your customers. An authentic, engaged brand community can live anywhere online—on a blog, through Twitter, or on YouTube, for instance. However, most brand communities are on Facebook or Instagram, the predominant social media sites. Brand communities are usually started by companies, but when they are run well, they can take off, almost on their own, as more and more customers join the conversation. How well you talk to your fans and stimulate conversation without pushing product will determine how large your community grows and how much they trust and value you.

Customers Solving Customer Service Issues

One example of the benefits of building an engaged community is that customers will help one another out. If you create a place on Facebook or Twitter for people to ask questions, share feedback, and interact with not only you but one another, you will engender trust and loyalty and help the community grow. Customers or prospects will take notice and appreciate when you answer questions on a timely basis and in an authentic way.

If you provide a place for consumers to connect and to gripe, to share information and to learn and to grow, people will realize you are committed to them and the community you are fostering, and they will return that commitment to you. So now when someone unfamiliar with your company comes to the community, a potentially huge new prospect, and posts a question, another member of the community might answer the prospect's question before you have time to. Or when an unsatisfied customer comes to the Facebook page to complain, the community is likely to rally behind you without your even having to ask. How valuable might each of those things be to the bottom line? An engaged community grows your stakeholders in the company way beyond the staff and shareholders. These stakeholders will show support for you throughout their online social network and beyond. Your company's reputation and visibility will grow, and in return, your online, and offline, community will flourish.

ENGAGING: EASIER SAID THAN DONE

Despite the vision of an engaged company, it is far easier to discuss than to actually implement. You will find that unless you are the leader of a small business or organization, the commitment to be engaged cannot happen immediately. Senior managers need to invest themselves fully in the change toward greater customer interaction and community building.

Is it devastating to your organization to not be fully engaged with its customers? The answer to that question is probably not, for a while at least. However, in an increasingly transparent and social world, by not being authentically involved and concerned about your consumers, you risk having one horrible customer experience totally erode your reputation, and eventually your bottom line, regardless of the size of your company. If your senior managers aren't sold on building an engaged community, tell them about "United Breaks Guitars."

In July 2009, country singer Dave Carroll was on a United Airlines flight when his guitar was broken. Dave put a claim in to United, and it not only refused to replace the guitar but also refused to apologize. So he took to YouTube, quickly making the "United Breaks Guitars" video, criticizing the company for its lack of accountability. It was an instant hit. After one day, the video had more than 100,000 views. A United spokesperson called Carroll up and offered to pay for the guitar, but Dave refused the offer, suggesting the company instead give to a charity in his name. United did not respond publicly on YouTube, Facebook, or Twitter. Within four days of the video being posted online, it had more than one million views, and it had received national news coverage. By that time, United Airlines' stock price had fallen 10 percent, costing stockholders about $180 million in value. Four years later, however, the video had more than 20 million views on YouTube, and United never did address the issue through social media. Its brand's reputation remains damaged.

Do you think if United Airlines had engendered an engaged community through social media that the devastating fallout would have happened? If lots of United consumers felt loyal to United, they would have stood by the company when an online crisis developed.

There are countless other examples. Search online for "Motrin Moms" or "Comcast Technician Sleeping" for two great ones. There will certainly be more. You can avoid being *forced* to become engaged by proactively making the commitment to your consumers.

ENGAGEMENT FOR NONPROFITS
AND GOVERNMENTS

As valuable as customer engagement is for companies, it is crucial for nonprofits and governments. Social media is tailor-made for such organizations, and the success of a nonprofit in fulfilling its mission, or a government organization in launching an initiative, is entirely dependent on an engaged constituent base. Nonprofits and governments in the past had to create movements offline, without the luxury of a built-in online community of people ready to support one another and fulfill the mission. Now, a strong nonprofit or local government can build an engaged community using Facebook or Twitter, and it can raise money or effect positive change in faster, more efficient ways than ever before. How can your company replicate this effect? How can your company grow a *movement* online?

New York State Takes Control

The New York State Department of Health (NYSDOH) is a government agency serving the people of New York State, one of the most populated states in the world. The NYSDOH runs many public health initiatives funded by the government, including the Take Control! program, designed to provide New York State teens and young adults with information and local resources to promote positive sexual health. This program is unique because it's about teens connecting with other people like them in a nonjudgmental way. They can get information and have their questions answered without feeling like they're being lectured by adults. So it would make sense that when it came time to build out a marketing strategy for this initiative, the tried-and-true television advertisements, radio spots, subway posters, and online banner ads simply couldn't be at the core of the marketing strategy. That's not where or how teens talk to other teens, so the NYSDOH took to social media where these digital natives spend a lot of their time.

The original objective of the NYSDOH's 2012 launch of the Take Control! Facebook page was to increase awareness of the program, drive traffic to the informational website, and provide teens with content they could relate to and learn from. The DOH agency built the page for the program at Facebook.com/TakeControl, and its staff members worked to create and share daily content, listen to and respond to all questions and posts from New York teens, and build a highly engaged community. Suddenly, humorous content that looked like the images their friends regularly shared—but with a safe sex–healthy relationship spin to it—was getting tens of thousands of comments, *likes*, and shares. Most parents can't get an answer to "How was your day?" from their teens, and these teens were talking about their sexual choices.

But far more important than the conversations and engagement with the program, the Facebook page evolved into a community in which teens could talk to other teens. If a piece of content was posted that didn't resonate with the community, the members let the DOH know. When a question was posed, the community members weren't answering a state government organization. They were answering each other and having conversations with each other. Once a teen spoke up about something, more soon followed. The page became an online forum, a place where friends hung out after school, and the "cool" spot to access funny images about being a teen (and about sex!). Teens began to ask important questions, learn where to get condoms and where to get tested for STDs; and they felt comfortable letting 30,000 of their peers know they were virgins. They received support and guidance not just from the DOH but from each other. What started as a marketing hunch (teens are spending a lot of time on Facebook, so let's build there!) accomplished a seemingly impossible feat—teens voluntarily joined a group and started talking about safe sex. In a time when bullying is running rampant, there is support, humor, education, and acceptance taking place.

No Kid Hungry Gets #Hangry

In 2017, No Kid Hungry, a national campaign run by Share Our Strength, a nonprofit working to solve problems of hunger and poverty in the United States and around the world, went big with its annual Dine Out effort, a national restaurant campaign that raises critical funds and awareness to end childhood hunger in America. With 15 restaurant partners, including Arby's and The Habit Burger Grill, No Kid Hungry wrapped an RV to look like a school bus and drove it from New York City to Los Angeles, stopping in cities along the way to raise awareness of the one in six kids facing hunger.

Millennials are a key target audience for No Kid Hungry because they eat out more often than any other generation and spend a significant portion of their income on food. Taking a word already in the vocab of this target audience, hangry, the campaign inserted No Kid Hungry into the existing conversation. Instead of the traditional definition of hangry, being grumpy or irritable because you are hungry, No Kid Hungry flipped the definition to mean "anger that kids in America are going hungry."

At each "bus stop," they asked for people to rethink the meaning of hangry by recording and sharing videos of themselves telling the world why they are angry that kids are going hungry. "I'm hangry because some children shouldn't have to rely on school lunch as their only meal for the day," one said. "I'm hangry because even though there is so much wealth in America, there are so many hungry children," said another.

More than 272 people recorded videos, which were uploaded to a microsite (hangry.nokidhungry.org) and shared across social media. Along with the 15 national restaurant brands that chose to be a part of the tour, 22 celebrities and chefs, including Kenan Thompson, Eric Dickerson, and Andrew Zimmern, helped spread the word on social media. All told, 92 million people saw the campaign in their feeds.

Starting a movement is easier for a cause, a mission-related nonprofit group, or a government organization, but that doesn't mean your business can't get involved. Never underestimate the potential of any passionate community united around beliefs, commonalities, or shared interests.

ACTION ITEMS

1. Determine what resources you have to put toward a social media program through which your organization can become authentically engaged with its consumers. Based on the size of the company, it may take a long time to foster an online social community—time that will have to come from existing employees, new hires, or outside agencies. Determine who at your company can, and will, make the commitment to authentic engagement, and get those people in a room together to start the conversation.

2. Hire an online community manager if you don't yet have one. This person's main role should be to build and grow an engaged community. If you are a small business owner, figure out a way to devote 10 minutes a day to increasing engagement.

3. Write a list of five ways that your communications could be more engaging than they are right now. How can you be less like the old college lecturer and more like the enthusiastic workshop leader?

THE PROCESS OF GETTING ENGAGED HAS TO START WITH ONE ACTION

Whether your organization is already deeply engaged with its customers or is far from it, the process of becoming further involved starts with one person, and one action. Just because you're not able to turn your company upside down doesn't mean you can't take positive steps toward using social media to foster better dialogue between your brand and your customers and between your customers themselves. Now (at the risk of setting records for corniness) stop stalling, go buy that ring, and get engaged.

CHAPTER 7

Respond Quickly to All Bad Comments

You've worked hard for months with your team and a consulting firm on creating social media best practices, and you've planned how to integrate social media into your business. You've built a Facebook page, an Instagram page, a Twitter account, a LinkedIn company page, and a blog, and you're excited to join the online conversation and foster a burgeoning community. Several coworkers have rallied behind you and your commitment to engaging customers throughout every step of their relationship with your company. Then, the night before the big launch day, you receive a phone call from your frantic chief executive officer:

"Remind me, what the hell are we going to do if people write bad things about us on our Facebook page? We can delete those, right? Because if we can't delete those negative comments, I don't think we're ready for Facebook."

The answer is simple: If you're not ready to respond to negative comments, then no, you're not ready for Facebook yet. If your company is not prepared to embrace the good, the bad, and the ugly, then social media in general isn't right for you now. If you are prepared to handle criticism and respond appropriately, however, then having your own social network community where people post positive and negative comments will be a huge asset.

EMBRACE WHAT YOU CAN'T CONTROL: SOCIAL MEDIA COMMENTS ARE THE NEW COMMENT CARDS

Remember those comment cards every business used to have with a box you could drop them in? Many small businesses and restaurants still have them today. Whether your company officially has comment cards or not, they do exist now in the form of Facebook, Instagram, Twitter, LinkedIn, blogs, and other online social outlets. The good news for the customer is that today's consumer base is the most empowered in history. If you have a negative experience with any company or professional, you can fill out "a comment card" from your smartphone that instant and then immediately share your comment not only with hundreds of friends but also with complete strangers throughout the world.

Of course, if you consider this situation from the standpoint of a company, this is a scary proposition. Just as the aforementioned CEO is freaking out, so are marketers, public relations executives, and small business owners everywhere. For years, it's been the role of communications professionals to control public perception of their companies, and now any kid with a Twitter account or Facebook profile can ruin it all. That said, as a marketer, once you accept and embrace the fact that you cannot control the online posting of negative comments about your company, you can begin to formulate a plan for what you're going to do to respond to criticism.

You could try to ignore it, of course. There are still plenty of organizations that refuse to accept the fact that people are talking negatively about them. You could also try to delete things online—sure, on your own Facebook page, you can delete whatever you want—and perhaps your company's lawyers could write letters to every Web publisher who ever allows negative comments to be published about you, demanding that those comments come down.

But the truth is, there's no way to entirely stop people from making negative posts about your company, whether you have an official Facebook page or not. So, why not prepare yourself and, instead of avoiding it, embrace negative feedback, comments, and criticism? Especially if *you* are the frantic CEO in our example, the following idea might sound like a radical and potentially damaging one—so take a deep breath, and brace yourself.

The Do-Not-Delete Rule

The do-not-delete (DND) rule states that *unless a comment is obscene, profane, or bigoted, or it contains someone's personal and private information, it should never be deleted from a social network site.* It might be best to illustrate the wisdom of the DND rule by first playing out a scenario in which you *don't* follow it.

Johnny Customer posts on Control Freak Inc.'s Facebook page, "I just got a bill for $100 more than I was supposed to. You guys suck!" The frantic CEO insists that the comment be deleted right away so nobody else sees it, and the comment is promptly removed from the page. Johnny Customer logs on later that day to find his comment deleted. He is infuriated that the company has censored his complaint, and he reacts by starting a new Facebook group called "I Hate Control Freak Inc.! Boycott Them!" He also makes a YouTube video singing about his hatred for the company and detailing his bad experience, and he starts a Twitter trend with hashtag #controlfreakincsucks.

As it turns out, Johnny Customer happens to be the captain of the football team at his school and the lead singer for a popular rock band in town. Within 24 hours, thousands of people are posting negative comments on Control Freak Inc.'s wall, and worse yet, customers are canceling orders, and sales are down.

Sure, this is a dramatic rendition of the situation, and it may not be the most likely occurrence, but is it really worth taking the risk (remember "United Breaks Guitars" from the last chapter)? The point is, when you delete someone's comment, it is the ultimate "Screw you." It's like collecting a customer's comment card, reading it in front of the customer, and then ripping it up in his or her face. You wouldn't do that, would you? Plus, the Internet is infinite. Anyone who feels wronged or not heard can turn elsewhere to gripe, finding more energy (and maybe more sympathizers) to vent than he or she had before.

Not Responding Is a Response

The second gut reaction of some executives after wanting to delete the negative comment is to ignore it. "Maybe by ignoring the problem, it will go away," they might think. Or, "We don't want to give this issue credence because it might lead to more negativity from customers."

If deleting a comment is the equivalent of ripping up a comment card in someone's face, ignoring a negative comment is the equivalent of putting a caller on hold and never getting back on the line (with thousands of people watching the phone call!). No, it's not as bad as hanging up on him, but he'll still get the impression that you don't care about him. Worse yet, everyone else who sees the comment and lack of response from the company will conclude that your organization just doesn't care. By not responding, you're actually sending out a strong message: the customer's opinion doesn't matter to you. This is a dangerous message to convey to your current consumers, prospects, and the general public, many of whom would interpret a lack of response in just this way. You don't want to make matters worse, so what's a company to do?

THE SOLUTION: RESPOND QUICKLY AND PUBLICLY, AND THEN TAKE THE ISSUE PRIVATE

In the situation just mentioned, Johnny Customer wants a reply to the apparent $100 discrepancy on his bill. What do you think of the following response?

First, one of your company's representatives publicly posts, "I'm sorry you had an issue, Johnny. Please see the private message we sent you to resolve the matter." Next, this post is followed immediately by a private message sent directly to Johnny, "Sorry you had a bad experience, Johnny. If you email us with your account information to wecare@controlfreakinc.com, we'll try to resolve the issue as quickly as possible."

By responding quickly and publicly, you not only respond to someone's complaint or concern but you also send the message out to the world at large that you're the kind of company that listens to its customers and fixes problems promptly. By taking the individual matter private, you avoid a public back-and-forth between company and customer, which wouldn't help anyone involved but only prolong the negative situation. And when you're apologizing, refer to people by name; it goes a long way toward helping them feel heard and understood. We're all human, and we all make mistakes. Even the angriest of customers will recognize this truth and will be quick to forgive you, but only if you apologize and fix the problem as soon as possible.

Depending on the size of your organization, you'll need to make sure you have enough internal or external resources to handle complaints in a timely manner. You probably already have a sense of just how many complaints you typically receive, maybe from those traditional comment cards if you have them. Of course, comment cards used to get forwarded to a department where someone would read them, write replies, and mail them out a week later. In the online world, things happen a lot faster.

Put on your consumer cap. If you had a complaint or question about something, how quickly would you want to be, or expect to be, answered? Of course you'd like to receive a response almost immediately, so you should answer your customers right away as well. As a rule of thumb, make sure you have the resources in place to answer people's negative comments within 24 hours or sooner if possible. Even if your initial response is, "I'm sorry, and we'll look into that and get back to you with a private message within 72 hours," at least you're immediately telling the customer that you care and you're going to fix the problem as quickly as you can. After all, an angry customer is just like all of us: she wants to feel heard, and understood.

"I'm Sorry" Is Not an Admission of Guilt

Many legal departments are reticent in allowing marketers to say "I'm sorry" on Facebook and Twitter. It's as though lawyers are convinced that apologizing is an admission of guilt and makes a company liable for damages. Some industries are more highly regulated than others, and sometimes, it's just not feasible to apologize. (For instance, as mentioned in Chapter 1, often pharmaceutical companies can't legally apologize in response to online complaints made about their products.) But, in general, the words "I'm sorry" or "We're sorry" can go a long way in helping a customer feel heard and diffusing a potentially hazardous situation. There are lots of ways to put an apology in writing without admitting any wrongdoing:

- "I'm sorry you had this experience."
- "We're sorry you feel this way."
- "I'm so sorry you've had a problem."
- "That sounds so frustrating. Sorry you felt like that."

Responding with a short but genuine apology is a great start, but equally important, *you've got to be able to fix the problem*. For many companies, this means that the marketing and public relations departments have to work closely with the customer service team to resolve people's complaints in a timely manner. Remember, customers don't care about what department you're in—they care only about whether you can solve their problem or not. There's really no difference to customers between a public relations associate and a customer service rep.

Prioritize Your Response Based on the Commenter's Online Influence

It's easy to say, "Respond to every customer who complains," and though this should be the goal, it is not always possible. Some organizations are so vast they don't yet have the resources to answer every single person's complaint. Take online social networks, for instance, such as Facebook and Twitter—that is, the companies themselves. Each has hundreds of millions of users but fewer than 2,500 employees. There's simply no way they have the ability to answer every complaint made. In these situations, and perhaps for your company, you may consider prioritizing how quickly you respond based on the customer's online influence.

Just as you'd probably respond a little faster to celebrities who filled out comment cards years ago, you might consider prioritizing your response time based on how influential the customer is. The harsh reality is that if Johnny Customer has 40,000 followers on Twitter, he can do far more damage to your reputation online than if he has 4. Again, in an ideal world, you could respond to every Johnny Customer's complaint, but you may not have the ideal resources to do so currently.

TURN COMPLAINERS INTO SUPPORTERS

Depending on how efficiently and effectively you can solve a customer's problem, you just might turn a hater into an admirer or even a major brand supporter. Consider if Johnny Customer, from our example, heard back from you immediately, and you were able to address his specific complaint with ease. His mind is likely to be changed about your company, and he might be so impressed and pleased that he recommends you to his peers. Consider the following real-life example of an unsatisfied Verizon customer.

A Foe of FiOS Becomes a Fan

Verizon FiOS is the television, Internet, and phone bundle offered by Fortune 500 company Verizon in select areas across the country. The Fans of FiOS Facebook page has been a marketing, promotions, and customer service asset for Verizon since 2008. When first launched, the page was designed to provide regional support for Verizon FiOS's marketing and promotions initiatives. Customers, however, are typically more concerned about their own service problems than about the marketing and promotional material posted—and they're not afraid to publicly share their issues. The FiOS team always attempts to quickly resolve such customer issues in conjunction with Verizon policies and procedures. My favorite interaction was with Ray Umstot-Einolf, who posted the following on the FiOS fan page on March 22, 2009:

> Hey Verizon why won't you give me my money back!!! I signed up for your Verizon Bundle Pack and I'm paying $300.00 a month and my service is supposed to cost about $120.00. We call you every month and the problem is never fixed. Funny thing is I know of about 10 other people you are doing this to. Telling them one price and billing them another and not refunding when you admit you are wrong. You guys Suck!!! And a lawsuit may be in your near future. Have a great day, you bunch of crooks!!!!

Members of the Verizon team breathed and quickly considered their options. There were admittedly a couple of individuals who suggested the dreaded "delete" tactic, in fear of giving credence to such a complaint. But cooler heads prevailed, and the do-not-delete rule won out. They responded this way:

> So sorry you've had a problem, Ray. We've sent you a private message and someone from Verizon will be in touch with you shortly. —Devin, from the Fans of FiOS

Ray was put directly in touch with the customer support team. A few days passed, and Verizon worried the next post from Ray might be even worse than the first. Then, on March 26, 2009, Ray posted the following on the page:

> I wanna thank Fans of FiOS for fixing my billing Problem. Devin was awesome and I would like to thank her for her help. Had a Regional Manager call us today and went over the bill and corrected our bill. Thank you!!!
>
> And for the Record. I love the FiOS service and the Extreme Internet package makes me jump up and down every time I download anything or play a game. Thank you Verizon FiOS. No more Crookcast for Us.

It was difficult to believe, looking at both posts, that Ray was the same person. And yet there they were, in front of Verizon and thousands of fans on the page. In a few days, Ray went from being a raving hater to being a full-on supporter with an audience of thousands. In this situation, customer service and marketing were blurred together, resulting in a great promotion of the company and an incredibly satisfied consumer.

CONSIDER RESPONDING WITH SURPRISE AND DELIGHT

Responding with an apology and a quick solution to the problem is essential. But remember, unlike the comment card, which is a private matter, social media is of a public nature, so there's more at stake here when replying. Is there a way you can go above and beyond to fix the problem—exceeding the unsatisfied customer's original expectations? Maybe you send a bonus gift in the mail, or you refund the customer's invoice without telling her, or you give her a deep discount on the next month's service. Consider the options, get creative, and the customer's next comment to all of her friends may be raving about the amazing company you are.

1-800-Flowers.com Responds by Surprising

1-800-Flowers.com is the world's leading online and phone service providing and delivering floral and other gifts to customers across the country. It provides services all year long, but its two busiest weeks of the year, as you might expect, are around Valentine's Day and Mother's Day.

While the conversation in its online communities is usually quite positive, occasionally customers post complaints. During the two key holidays, the stakes are raised, as many competitors are advertising in the market. The last thing they want is for complaints to go unanswered at this time. Any complaint could quickly snowball and have a major negative effect on sales.

1-800-Flowers.com decided to staff up its Facebook community 24/7 for key holidays beginning in 2010, and it committed to responding publicly within an hour of any complaint. Further, it resolved to not only fix customers' problems but to also over-deliver, with larger bouquets and orders than the complaining customers had paid for. It was a risk because customers could potentially take advantage of the situation, and profit margins could easily slip. However, the results were great. There were just as many complaints as in the past, but they were responded to quickly, and when the orders did arrive, recipients (and senders!) were surprised and delighted. Many of them ended up posting online again, much more positively this second time. The added spending paid off in keeping the public brand reputation at a high during a critical time.

ACTION ITEMS

1. Determine how you will allocate resources to respond to negative comments posted on social networks. Is it the responsibility of the marketing department, the customer service department, an agency, or all three?
2. Develop a plan to respond swiftly and publicly. Work with your lawyers to develop language that is OK by them and is as customer friendly as possible.
3. Make sure you have enough resources to manage negative comments in a timely manner. Have the resources to not only respond to comments but also to actually fix the problems efficiently.
4. Write a list of five ways you can respond to negative situations positively, turn around customer complaints, and use "surprise and delight" to leverage otherwise negative situations.

ACCEPT THAT COMPLAINTS ARE UNAVOIDABLE, AND REACT QUICKLY: TURN YOUR CUSTOMER CARE INTO A MARKETING ASSET

No human being is perfect, and therefore no organization is either. Your company will surely make errors, and now, thanks to social networks, the whole world can easily find out about these mistakes. But you also have the ability to show the world how responsive a company you are. If you can respond quickly and authentically, with an apology and a solution, you can avoid any damage to your reputation. Further, if you provide an additional reward to your customers when tackling the issue, you can actually turn your response and customer care into a marketing asset. Wouldn't you rather have people like Ray on your side?

CHAPTER 8

Respond to the Good Comments Too

"Excuse me, sir," a well-dressed woman says to you in the aisle of your department store. "I just wanted to take a moment to thank you for everything you and your company have done for me throughout the years. I am a longtime, happy customer—and you've truly brought joy to my life. Thanks, and keep up the great work." You stare at her with a blank expression on your face, then turn and quickly walk away in fear there may be a complaining customer that you need to attend to elsewhere in the store.

This situation is absurd, of course, and it would never happen. You'd never reject a happy customer. Instead, you would welcome her with open arms and invite her to share more. Heck, you'd probably give her a hug or a free T-shirt, or both!

You likely embrace your happiest customers—they remind you of what you're doing well and what your organization is all about. They're also the best unplanned part of your marketing agenda. Word-of-mouth endorsements and conversations with satisfied customers remain the most potentially powerful marketing tools you have.

Yet each day, millions of positive comments to and about brands on social networks go unnoticed or are given no response. Visit the Facebook pages of most big organizations and you'll find people sharing stories, asking questions, and praising products or services—almost always without a response. Do companies not have enough resources to address these posts? Are they so focused on maintaining a defensive posture with regard to all of the negative comments that they decide not to reply to any comments at all? Do companies not see value in responding to positive posts?

Whatever the reasons, they are making a mistake, possibly to your company's advantage. If *your* organization begins to follow not only negative posts and comments but also positive ones, and if it takes action in responding, you are ahead of the game. In fact, if other companies aren't doing a good job interacting with their customers or prospects through online social networking, your company looks even better to consumers when you take the initiative.

Not replying to customers and prospects on social media is like hanging up the phone on them—in the middle of a football field, with a stadium full of people watching. You would never do that, so think twice before you ignore them on social media!

ACKNOWLEDGMENT ALONE GOES A LONG WAY—GET CREATIVE!

Just as the two simple words "I'm sorry" go a long way when a customer complains, so do the words "Thank you" when a customer has something nice to say. "Thank you" says "You matter." "Thank you" says "We're listening." "Thank you" says "We appreciate you." It's best to further personalize your response as well, sharing your brand personality a little bit.

Develop Your Social Personality

Brand personality is formed by giving your brand human traits when presenting your company to the public. Your brand's social personality sets you apart from other brands, giving your company unique features in an attempt to connect more directly, and more humanly, with your consumer. For example, the voice (or wording) you use to respond to posts helps shape your personality. Here are several different ways to say thanks to a positive comment, expressing the personality behind the brand:

- "Thanks a lot, Johnny. You rule!"
- "Thank you for taking the time to share."
- "Thanks for liking us. We like you too."
- "Thanks for your feedback, Johnny. We're listening."
- "Thanks for your comment, and keep spreading the good word!"

Acknowledging your customers' positive feedback is easier today than it has ever been before. With the advent of the social Web, connecting directly to your consumer while showing that, as a brand, you truly care about your public persona ingratiates your company to current and potential customers.

Responding in Your Brand's Voice

Language is a major part of your brand identity. Would a bank talk to its customers face-to-face using the same language that a pizzeria would? Would a pediatrician discuss a medical condition with her patients using the same language an oncologist would with his? Would a major brand target its teenage customers using the same language it uses in its ads for adults? Just as you use different language to talk to different customers face-to-face, or in advertising and marketing, and you choose that language based on who your customers are and what your organization is all about, so too must you consider the language you use on social networks in your responses.

In fact, without the advantage you have in face-to-face conversation to inflect different emotions in your voice or use nonverbal communications, the tone of your written words on Facebook, Instagram, or Twitter is incredibly important. Think about how differently you read these two messages:

Thank you very much for your feedback, sir.
We appreciate your support.
versus
Thanks, man. You rule!

What kind of brand does your organization have? Are you serious or fun? Friendly? Humorous? Outrageous? Warm? More important, what are your customers and prospects like? Are they young, adventurous adults, or are they cautious, serious seniors? Are they teens having fun, or nervous moms, or time-starved business professionals, or another category of people? Depending on the nature of your audience, your words and the way in which you respond, even to positive comments, are integral to the way in which they will be received.

For example, Cumberland Farms Chill Zone is a really popular product for teenagers, and virtually nobody else outside that demographic. So when the company replies to fans in social media, it aims to represent the irreverent teen spirit of its customers. See Figure 8.1 for a great example of its responsiveness in action.

FIGURE 8.1 **Chill Zone Response**

> **Ben** ▓▓▓▓ sometimes, I just lay under the faucet and chug chill zone until i pass out
> November 1 at 3:43pm · Like · Comment
>
> 👍 3 people like this.
>
> > **Cumberland Farms Chill Zone** Hahaha what a baller.
> > November 1 at 3:50pm · Like · 👍 1 person · Flag

GIANT Has Fun with Its Fans

One company whose social media pages take its brand's voice to heart is Giant Food Stores, or GIANT. The company started in 1923 as a small fresh meat market in Carlisle, Pennsylvania, and now operates in Pennsylvania, Maryland, Virginia, and West

Virginia. The brand is very proud of where it came from; as such, its voice is truly local: GIANT is the neighbor you saw at the street fair last weekend—not the big city slicker that eats out every night. The brand is relatable, and it maintains its persona in the messaging it creates.

In 2018, the Philadelphia Eagles won their first Super Bowl. In the days leading up to it, GIANT took to its social channels to engage with the passionate fans and customers in the community. The Likeable team helped by creating and monitoring a series of Eagles-inspired posts: polls on whether Philly prefers pretzels or cheesesteaks (by the way, a Philly pretzel is way different than you think), videos about being an underdog, and, of course, a final victory post—all paired with regional language like "Yo Philly!"

The city loved it. In just two days, the four posts led to over 25,000 reactions across Facebook and Instagram, including over 1,000 comments. Fans took to the pages to share their in-store experiences, their game day food spreads, and their overall love for the team and the grocery store (Figure 8.2). By responding to the comments with an authentic and interested voice, Eagles fans didn't talk to GIANT like customers, they talked to GIANT like friends. The Eagles weren't the only ones to win that weekend—GIANT did too.

KEEP SPREADING THE GOOD WORD

Facebook is the single most viral platform in marketing history. Most marketers are so concerned with squashing or limiting the spread of negative comments that they lose sight of the power of spreading the positive ones. The truth is, people are more likely to buy your products or services if they feel they know you, trust you, and like you (both in general and in an online context). They are therefore much more apt to want to see something positive than negative about your company. If you can authentically amplify and accelerate positive word of mouth about your organization, online social media provides the best tools for accomplishing this on a huge scale.

FIGURE 8.2 **GIANT's Communications with Its Facebook Audience**

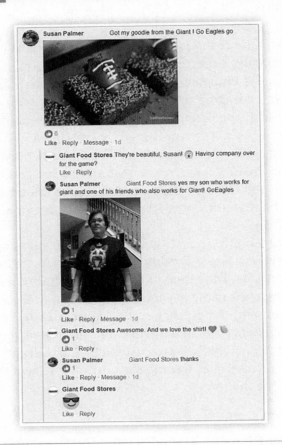

In the offline world, if a customer shares positive feedback with you, it's the perfect time to ask for a referral: "Do you have any friends who would be appropriate for me to talk to?" or more passively, "Thanks. Please let your friends know."

On Facebook, when you receive a compliment, it's the perfect time to say, "Thanks. Please suggest this page to your friends!" The average person on Facebook has about 350 friends, but some people have as many as 5,000! It is likely that your happy customer has more than a few friends who might also be interested in your page and will show their endorsements as well, creating a cycle of approval.

The situation is similar with Twitter. On Twitter, if you receive positive feedback, reply and ask the user to retweet, or share you with his or her followers. The average person on Twitter has 707 followers, and some have as many as *50,000,000* or more. Again, one recommendation on Twitter can go a long way toward building a base of new followers.

None of this can happen, however, if you don't recognize and thank your customers who actively follow and interact with you—each and every one of them.

IT'S A CONVERSATION—KEEP TALKING

In the days of comment cards, organizations responded to complaints, and most good organizations replied to every comment. But then, the communication likely ended there. With social networks, the conversation can continue forever. Once you respond to the first comment, the customer can continue engaging with you. Who knows where things might lead? Think of this process as an ongoing discussion rather than a set of comments to respond to. You want conversations begun by happy customers to go on for as long as possible. How can you keep the conversation going? How can you surprise and delight the *positive* posters?

From a Snap to a Job

A few years ago, Brian Murray, former director of talent and culture at Likeable, started using Snapchat as a tool for recruiting. Yes, you read that correctly. As part of the standard application process, all potential candidates received an email with the following:

> Thank you for your interest in Likeable. We will check out your information and be in touch with any questions! You can always tweet me: @BTMurr. Even better . . . SNAPCHAT me why you belong here (I MAY screenshot): BTMurr.

At Likeable, we are constantly looking at unique ways to use social media for our clients and our own brand. When he started soliciting Snaps, Brian wasn't necessarily looking for the best artist (although there were some amazing ones) or a new life-long friend; the purpose was to give applicants insight into our culture and find people who could use any platform to communicate their message.

What started as an entertaining way to engage with some of the brightest and most creative candidates really led to success. In one case, Brian fast-tracked someone who really grabbed his attention, and less than two weeks later he had an offer in hand. It was for a videographer role, and the Snapchat included "Fingerboarding" and the Likeable logo.

Of course, finding a great candidate didn't happen from just one snap. It happened from a company having a positive attitude about engaging with its audience, going the extra mile, and continuing the conversation. Who knows—your next key hire might be the customer who just tagged you on Instagram.

ACTIVATE YOUR BRAND AMBASSADORS

Every small business knows that handful of customers who are its die-hard fans—the people who swear by your service, who are there all the time, or who consistently refer others to your business. Big brands hopefully have even more of these people—folks I call *brand ambassadors*. Brand ambassadors are those customers who love your organization no matter what. They are happy to tell others about your company without any special incentive, and without you even asking them to. Still, they would be more likely to spread the word if you asked, so why wouldn't you?

Picture Rod Tidwell telling Jerry Maguire (in the movie of the same name): "Jerry Maguire, my agent. You're my ambassador of quan." Tidwell describes "quan" as "the entire package" made up of "love, respect, community, and the dollars too." Come the end of the day, this quality, quan, is what all companies are searching for: a community built of mutual respect resulting in financial growth for the business and satisfied, loyal customers. Brand ambassadors, or so-called ambassadors of quan, want to share the "special sauce" that you've got—all you have to do is tell them to. It helps that you can quickly tell how many online friends people have. Online influence varies greatly from one person to the next, and since all organizations have limited resources, you'll want to find brand ambassadors who not only adore you *but also* have lots of friends, fans, or followers.

Once you've identified your brand ambassadors, you can do much more than just thank them for being customers. You can reward them with incentives, special perks, and exclusive content. For example, provide them with online tools or samples of your product so they can share them with friends or hand the products out at parties they might host with your help. You can give them multimedia content such as pictures and videos and encourage them to create "mashups," adding their own voice and interpretation to your material before passing it along to friends and followers. The goal is to activate your customers who love you enough to regularly share their passion for you publicly.

Full Disclosure

You'll want to amplify your brand ambassadors' voices as much as possible—just make sure you have them disclose their relationship with you. If you end up giving them anything of material value, the Federal Trade Commission requires that reviewers disclose they received something in exchange for posting a review or other comments. For instance, you can't give someone a trip to your resort in exchange for them posting an Instagram Story about their experience, unless they clearly disclose that they received a free trip in exchange for the review. (More on transparency in Chapter 10.)

Word-of-mouth marketing has always been good business practice, but today, the ability to effectively and efficiently utilize it through social networks is unparalleled. In the past, if a celebrity visited your store, you certainly treated him exceptionally well and asked him to spread the word about his experience. Today, it is important to think of every customer as an online celebrity with followers, friends, and, above all, influence. Sure, not everyone who tweets about you or tags you in an Instagram post has as much sway or trendsetting ability as some celebrities, but so-called micro-influencers can certainly spread the word on your behalf—easily and quickly—especially if you thank and encourage them. (Some users probably have more online influence than some so-called celebrities, too!)

A Toast to Responsiveness

One small business in North Carolina takes pride in answering all customer comments and inquiries on Facebook. Toast Café of Cary (now known as Famous Toastery) is a small American breakfast and brunch café that serves food made with the freshest ingredients. During the summer of 2014, Toast Café of Cary was rebuilding its location. The construction was supposed to be quick and painless, but it took much longer than anticipated. The restaurant's employees were anxious to be in business, and the residents were anxious to be served.

In the midst of construction, the owners of Toast Café created their brand values. Authenticity, responsiveness, family, community, and speed were a few of them. Originally, responsiveness pertained to their servers. Dean from the restaurant explained that the whole staff is there to help every customer. "Every server is your server," he said. Dean and his team then took this core value online, incorporating it into their social media strategy (Figure 8.3). This strategy has helped earn Toast Café a nearly five-star rating and over 3,000 likes on Facebook.

Who is better able to defend you against negative posters: you or your thousands of happy customers? What kind of company would you rather do business with as a consumer: a company that publicly answers every single customer, or one that seemingly ignores its customers?

FIGURE 8.3   **Toast Café's Communications with Its Facebook Audience**

ACTION ITEMS

1. Create a social brand bible for responses. Determine what your brand's voice should be like in its responses to customers on social networks. Fun? Serious? Personal? Professional? Write down several different specific ways, based on this brand voice, that you would say "Thank you" to a happy customer.

2. Determine what resources are necessary to enable you to respond to every customer who posts on a social network with a comment or question. Base your estimates on your understanding of the organization's current number of customers, fans, and followers. How will your staff do this? Will you do it internally or use an outside vendor? What about nights and weekends?

3. Determine formal or informal ways you can reward your most loyal and influential customers in order to accelerate the positive word-of-mouth recommendations they will make. What assets can you offer? What expectations will you have? How can you be assured that they are following the laws of the land and disclosing to their friends what they have received from you?

TRULY VALUING ALL YOUR CUSTOMERS

Every company says it cares about its customers, but so many don't actually back up this claim on social networks, let alone elsewhere. You wouldn't hang up the phone on customers or walk away from people you were face-to-face with, so don't ignore them on Facebook, Twitter, or any other online social networking medium either. By valuing each customer at least enough to say, "Thanks," you show the world that you are truly an organization that cares about its customers. By throwing in some surprise and delight and getting your biggest fans to further spread the word, your quan can travel a long way.

CHAPTER 9

Be Authentic

"Thank you for calling us. This is your customer care advocate; how can I be of service to you today?" you hear on the opposite end of the line.

"Great," you think. "This sounds like someone who can help me."

"I'd like to dispute part of my bill that I don't understand," you reply.

"Account number, please," the customer care advocate responds. Though you entered that number into your phone keypad just moments ago when you first called, you proceed to give the representative the information anyhow.

"I'm sorry," the customer care advocate replies. "There's nothing I can do about that problem. You'll have to speak with the billing department, and they're only open Monday through Friday. Can I help you with anything else today?"

The employee is just doing his job, of course, but all his job entails is following a script. Not only does this interaction leave you frustrated at the company's inability to help you with your problem, but it also may leave you scratching your head about the inauthenticity of considering a phone agent a "customer care advocate." In no way does this employee's job seem to involve caring or advocating for you, the customer.

How about "financial counselors"? Have you ever received assistance from a "financial counselor" who in fact is an insurance salesperson concerned little, if at all, with helping you sort out your financial issues?

Not everybody with the job title of customer care advocate or financial counselor is inauthentic. There are likely lots of great folks doing those jobs. But the *job titles* themselves are misleading, intentionally or not. Of course, this inauthenticity does not apply only to job titles: brand promises from slogans, advertisements, and websites are often guilty of the same inaccuracies or false representations.

Many large companies have a hard time being authentic in their interactions with customers. As organizations get larger, it becomes difficult to manage higher volumes of staff and clients. To deal with this growth, managers develop models and processes, and customer service and sales centers create scripts. These attempts at efficiency might cause some aspects of the organization to run smoothly, but in dealing with customers and prospects, they often miss the mark. Models, processes, and scripts will not help you better connect with your consumer. Instead, such impersonal devices create a division between your service or product and your customer because there is a loss of valuable human interaction.

Social media provides an opportunity to reverse this trend for larger organizations and to showcase authenticity for smaller ones. If your company can actually "be human" in dealing with its customers through current social networks, you'll find that your customers will respond positively and appreciate your more personal attitude. Be warned, however, that if you try to deal with huge numbers of customers on social networks in an inauthentic, highly processed way, your actions can and will backfire.

Before going any further, I should point out specifically what I mean when I say that you have to be "authentic" on social networks. Overall, you have to be human and demonstrate a personality. No one wants to feel as if they are talking to a machine or dealing with someone who cannot empathize with their situation. The online social Web is all about human interaction—connecting with one another on some level. As a company, you need to *want* to connect with your consumers or prospects in a personal or individual manner. You also have to be flexible and responsive, with the ability to cater to customers' various or changing needs, wants, opinions, and ideas. Become part of the online conversation and truly seek to understand your consumers and the role your product or service plays, or could play, in their actual lives. While in the context of representing your brand, you, and anyone else connected with your organization, have to be the person you really are—you can't fake it anymore when it comes to dealing with the consumer.

Aaron Sorkin, who wrote the screenplay for the hit movie *The Social Network*, about the founding of Facebook and its early days, told Stephen Colbert in a television interview (aired September 30, 2010) that social networking is more of a performance than a reality.[1] He so glaringly missed the point. On the contrary, social networking, done well, is authentic and real, unlike Sorkin's scripts.

Others have speculated that social network users are narcissists, sharing their every move with the world (think when users post what kind of cereal they had for breakfast this morning). Yes, there are some people, and companies, who use social networks for such self-centered purposes and fail to see the true possibilities of harnessing the online social Web. Such users are shortsighted and in many ways tragic, as the promise of social network communication holds much greater potential. Facebook and Instagram, for example, can in fact be places for people to authentically connect with one another and for companies to build true and long-lasting relationships with customers and prospects.

BE AN IMPROV SHOW, NOT A MUSICAL

Musicals, plays, and operas are all wonderful, traditional forms of entertainment. Theatergoers attend, sit back, and relax, and the performers "put on a show." Performances can be subtle and nuanced but are often loud, larger-than-life productions, especially musicals. Most musicals include lots of color and sound and expensive scenery, props, and costumes in an attempt to dazzle the audience and leave a lasting impression. The same script is performed night after night, and with stellar writing, acting, singing, and directing, the show comes together and wins over the crowd.

Improvisation comedy shows, on the other hand, usually have little to no set and almost nothing scripted. Improv features several performers, who interact with the audience throughout each show by soliciting ideas for skits, then basing their performances on audience suggestions each night. Unlike a musical, every show is different, but as long as the audience brings creative or interesting ideas and high energy and the performers are talented, it makes for an incredible experience.

Your brand, company, or organization can create such an experience for your customers and prospects on social networks. Even better news is that this can be done without the huge budget of a Broadway show or a television commercial. It will, however, require a fundamental shift in the way you see media and marketing, now that social media has enabled a two-way conversation between the company and the consumer. You'll have to think less about "putting on a show" and more about building an excellent team that is flexible, able to go with the flow, responsive, and engaged. And unlike in improv, in which performers are playing different parts every night, your team needs to rely on its own authenticity as unique, individual people.

DEVELOP AN AUTHENTIC VOICE

Advertising has traditionally been more like a Broadway musical than an improv show. The goal has been to create a brilliant distraction to get people's attention, be noticeable, or generate buzz, even if the products or services offered often lack a sense of authenticity.

Consumers, however, have gotten used to talking to each other through social networks with a level of humanity they have come to expect from all users. Now, as an advertiser or company, you need to join in this conversation, and when you do so, your organization must keep your consumers' expectations in mind. You have to be an authentic human being in your interactions. Anything less and your consumers might consider your attempt at conversation nothing more than a marketing ploy, no better than if you repeated a bland corporate mantra. Consider what your brand or organization is really like. How can you convert your mission statement or the About Us page on your website into actual conversations you'll facilitate and be involved in each day on Facebook, Instagram, and Twitter? You need to let the world know about your company's, or brand's, personality while showing that you truly care about your consumers and are willing to put the time in to make a connection with them.

Regulating Discussions

Hopefully, your organization already has protocols for how customer service reps interact with customers, how salespeople pitch prospects, or how public relations executives talk to traditional media reps. With the advent of social networking, all of that "talk" online is a matter of public record *forever*. There is a tendency, especially in large organizations, to carefully regulate that speech, making sure it meets corporate and legal guidelines and that nobody says the "wrong thing." For example, corporate communications and legal departments may be concerned about their employees or representatives going "off message," making negative comments, or admitting liability through an apology.

That attitude is a mistake on social networks, and it renders authentic communication nearly impossible. The more you try to regulate brand conversations, the more impersonal you'll make them, and the less customers will respond. Worse still, the less flexible and authentic you are, the more it will show, and the less you'll be trusted. Remember, online, your trust and reputation with customers are everything.

So what can you do to keep the lawyers happy at your company but maintain that all-important authenticity? The best solution is to develop a set of guidelines for what tone of voice you will use and what you really can't say. Then, make sure that trustworthy people are representing the organization on social networks, whether it's your own staff or an agency's. You need to know that these representatives will make the right choices about what, or what not, to say during social network conversations. You can even put this new set of guidelines in a document and create a "social media policy" (the lawyers will really love that).

Making Mistakes

Will representatives make mistakes when speaking with customers? Of course they will. People mess up at your organization every day in their dealings with customers and prospects, but these mistakes are not a matter of public record the way they are on social networks. The pace of social media is too fast for people to not make mistakes occasionally, and some mistakes are obviously bigger than others. Before social media, many screwups by employees were forgivable, and others cost people and agencies their jobs. The same is true in social media. Remember, though, that it's a conversation. People are forgiving when you admit you were wrong and you fix your mishap quickly.

For example, if you make a typo in an update on Instagram or accidentally share a broken link on Twitter, simply delete it, fix it, and then share it again along with a simple apology. These types of imperfection show vulnerability. This can bring your organization closer to customers and prospects because it helps show them that, hey, you're human too. Instead of attempting to perfectly manicure each status update and tweet you make, concentrate on authenticity in your voice, relationships, and overall presentation of your brand throughout the social Web. People are drawn to what is real, not what is fake or scripted. Be real.

Behind the Curtain: Letting People Know You

A great way to showcase your organization is to take pictures and video of your team and the space where you work and then share them on your Snapchat or Instagram Story. Of course, your customers don't care enough about you to want to see such material every day, but surely they'd appreciate an occasional window into the people and culture at your company. You don't have to hire a professional film crew or write a script. Instead, once a month, you can take your smartphone to a new department, staff person, vendor, or executive, and ask them a few questions about themselves and their roles at the company on camera.

You can also share pictures or video from an organization's summer outing, the opening of a new location, or even an "insider's view" of the chief executive officer or the company's back offices. This slice-of-life video will be effective in humanizing your brand and letting customers get to know the people behind the company, hopefully building their trust in your organization. Just don't go overboard. Remember, on social networks, it's all about your customers—what they want to discuss, see, hear, learn, or understand. It's not about you.

AUTHENTICITY BREEDS TRUST; INAUTHENTICITY BREEDS FEAR

In relationships, with rare exception, we're drawn to people who are able to share their feelings and their true selves, admit their flaws, and be honest and open, or authentic. We feel a connection with such people because we know we can trust in and rely on them.

It's a huge turnoff when people are "fake"—putting on a show or holding something back. People don't want to continue getting to know someone if they think he's being artificial. If you do not feel like there is some type of openness between you and the other person, it is unlikely the relationship will grow. Feelings of inauthenticity breed mistrust and potentially fear, fear that this person is not right for you or that there's someone else out there with whom you would click on an immediate personal level.

The same dynamic takes place in social networks. When an organization shares and connects with customers in an authentic way, it breeds trust and allows customers to feel comfortable deepening their relationships with the organization. Organizations that share highly produced content or that speak in a scripted manner appear inauthentic and breed mistrust. Such situations won't lead to the coveted *likes*, shares, and recommendations your company is trying to attain.

Just as in a relationship between two people, openness and trust helps a connection grow. The goal for your company is to nurture these relationships so customers will have better experiences and even put their personal reputations on the line by sharing and recommending your product or service to friends.

B1Example Puts Teens in Charge

B1Example is a government agency project supported by the Boston Public Health Commission's Division of Violence Prevention and Office of Communications. Its mission is to show positive actions and behaviors that prevent violence while actively influencing and empowering youth to redefine "street cred," earn respect the right way, and feel proud of their communities.

The Boston Public Health Commission (BPHC) felt strongly that the government agency itself not be the voice on social networks for the project. They also thought that Likeable, even as the social media agency providing support, shouldn't be that voice either. We agreed. To preserve authenticity and speak directly to the target audience, we instead recruited and carefully trained a team of 10 Boston teenagers to run the Facebook page and YouTube channels for the project. These teens already had proven themselves as role models and were personally motivated to create an impact in the community. The nature of the objectives necessitated a total surrender of control about messaging—something many companies, and most government agencies, have an incredibly hard time doing. But what urban teenager would trust a local government official telling her to "stay in school" or "stay off the street"? For that matter, what urban teen would trust any adult, as compared to a peer, talking about such issues?

The BPHC paid little attention to the teens' grammar and punctuation. It concentrated on helping them develop the group's voice and their individual voices and to build a process for creating, sharing, and inspiring content. On Facebook you'd see text updates that would frighten English teachers and public relations executives everywhere, who for years have taught that there's a right and wrong way to write things and express yourself. But you'd also see dozens of videos created by kids looking to make a difference and thousands of Boston teenagers interacting with one another in order to prevent youth violence. You'd find kids talking to one another in a way marketers could never duplicate. You'd see the power of authenticity on social networks in action.

Organic Valley Takes Users to the Farm

Organic Valley, a cooperative of family farmers on a mission to produce the world's best organic foods, uses social media to give people a real, authentic look at its farms. On Facebook, it has a program called "Farm Cam," where it shares behind-the-scenes photos and videos of everything from dancing cows to farmer selfies. The company also hosts "ask me anything," or AMA, segments on Facebook Live, letting the community speak directly to its farmers in real time.

On Instagram, Organic Valley puts a twist on traditional takeovers. Instead of having influencers control the account, the farmers do (Figure 9.1). "My name is Peter and I'm an OV farmer. Over the next few weeks I will be visiting other farms in our cooperative and sharing my experience," one farmer writes. Obviously, it's a lot easier to interact with "Peter" than with a nameless, faceless organization. Remember, every post, even from brands, comes from a person, and having the *people behind the brand* responding to and speaking with customers will humanize every interaction.

"There is something so special about getting the information right from the source. Our social accounts allow our customers a unique experience—they are able to speak directly with the people responsible for producing their food," says Leslie Kruempel, mission executive at Organic Valley.

| FIGURE 9.1 | Organic Valley Facebook Live Stream |

BE AN AUTHENTIC CELEBRITY

Social media provides a platform for celebrities, who typically have had to hire marketers or publicists to promote them, to speak directly with consumers and fans. Actors, musicians, athletes, politicians, authors, and other public figures all have excellent opportunities to grow their fan bases, shape public perception, and accomplish their objectives by harnessing online social networking. Authenticity must be a key part of their plan, though. Ideally, all public personas are Snapchatting and Instagramming for themselves, an authenticity that is impossible to top. Keep in mind that mobile phones allow anyone to share information on the run, opening a world of instant communication no matter where you are or what you are doing.

Of course there will be times when fan interaction may not be feasible, and it certainly is not possible for public figures to respond to each and every comment from admirers on their own. Agencies or staffers are commonly hired to help in this process, but they still attempt to make the response as personal as possible, sometimes indicating when they, and not the celebrity, are responding by sharing the initials of their name. Being up front as to who is actually responding on behalf of the public figure maintains authenticity.

Authenticity on Instagram: Busy Phillips

Instagram Story or reality TV show? For *Freaks and Geeks* and *Dawson's Creek* alum Busy Phillips, that line is blurred. The actress has taken to Instagram to chronicle her everyday life— and she's built a huge social following doing so (Figure 9.2). She talks openly and often about her career, social life, and experience as a mother, and she brings her followers behind the scenes for everything from hospital visits to walks down the red carpet.

FIGURE 9.2   **An Instagram Story from Busy Phillips**

Phillips admits that she's struggled to find work since her early television success, but with her honest and entertaining take on Instagram content, she's inadvertently turned herself into a major influencer. "Listen, guys, I'm not above it," Philipps said in one of her Stories. "I just only choose things that I genuinely like and, like, would want to partner with, like, for instance, my Michaels partnership, which, you know, is my favorite thing of all time. And I'm doing one next week, I think, that feels like me." In addition to branded partnerships, Busy's authentic and friendly personality on social media actually landed her a hosting gig for a late-night talk show.

Authenticity on Twitter: Ashton Kutcher

By actor Ashton Kutcher's own admission, he's not a good speller, and he often doesn't use proper grammar in his own tweets. Yet, with more than 18 million followers at Twitter.com/AplusK, he has had one of the leading Twitter accounts for years. The reason for this? Ashton's authenticity, consistency, passion, and value.

Ashton tweets about causes he feels strongly about, such as ending human slavery, but he also tweets interesting and funny video content he discovers online. He's open to tweeting behind-the-scenes footage of his life in Hollywood. Most important, he consistently shares and tweets his actual, authentic self.

A Likeable Star: Lin-Manuel Miranda

Lin-Manuel Miranda is the ultimate multi-hyphenate. A composer-lyricist-playwright-rapper-actor, the man is involved in at least 10 projects at any given moment, but he still makes an effort to wish his two million Twitter followers a good morning and a good night in a new way—every single day. In October 2018, those tweets were turned into a book: *Gmorning, Gnight! Little Pep Talks for Me & You.*

Aside from his creative greetings, Lin uses Twitter to share sneak peeks of his work and stories about his family, but the thing he's best at is truly engaging with his community. He delivers authentic responses to even the simplest comments and questions from fans, and he also uses his platform to advocate for causes he's passionate about, including the recovery of Puerto Rico after Hurricane Maria and #MarchForOurLives.

A Likeable Athlete: Nick Swisher

Professional athletes, similar to actors, have traditionally lacked an easy channel with which to communicate with fans. Athletes are typically represented by agents or occasionally public relations firms. Social media changes this setup. For the first time, athletes now have the ability to directly talk to fans at scale.

Former Major League Baseball player Nick Swisher is a prime example of this new ability to connect with people. He might not have been the best player, but with more than 1.5 million Twitter followers at Twitter.com/NickSwisher, he was one of the top baseball players on Twitter (Figure 9.3). Why? Once again: authenticity. He not only shared photos and videos but also

---

FIGURE 9.3   **Nick Swisher's Twitter Feed**

insights and thoughts directly from the dugout. His popularity comes from his ability to give fans behind-the-scenes access to somewhere they've not been before.

Nick's Twitter use is not just an exercise in ego either. Building huge legions of fans and followers through social media allows athletes to earn better endorsement deals, sell their own merchandise, and eliminate the hiring of middlemen. In 2009, Swisher was in a neck-and-neck race with Kevin Youkilis for the last spot on the American League All-Star team—a spot selected by majority fan vote—and a few tweets to Swisher's 1.5 million followers helped drive him to the top spot, making him an all-star!

ACTION ITEMS

1. If you're a one-person operation or a very small business, write down five things you could say that would seem inauthentic or that would sound like marketing-speak to a customer. Then write five examples of how you could convey the same messages in a more authentic way.

2. If you are part of a large organization, create a plan for how to represent yourself authentically. Recognize that authenticity won't be easy but that it's essential. Meet with key stakeholders and management at your organization to determine how you can make communication more authentic across all channels, especially on social networks.

3. If you already have a social media policy, examine it carefully to ensure that it encourages authentic communication, and tweak it if it doesn't. If you don't yet have a social media policy, draft one now.

4. If many people are responding on Facebook or Twitter on behalf of your organization, have each one sign tweets with his or her own name or initials.

JUST BE REAL

Just as people can usually tell the difference between someone who is being sincere and someone who is being insincere at a cocktail party, they can tell the difference between authentic communication and marketing- and PR-speak or legalese from your organization. If you are robotic or scripted in your social media interactions, despite the best of intentions, you will turn off customers and prospects. If you are real, authentic, and human in your interactions, customers and prospects will trust you, buy from you, and most important, share you with their friends.

CHAPTER 10

Be Honest and Transparent

Eight years ago, I was friended by a New York State senator on Facebook. I accepted, despite not knowing the politician personally, because I admired a public servant using social media to broaden his knowledge and reach. Also, I had nearly run for New York public office myself at one point, and I figured that since I already knew a number of other state senators from that experience, I might eventually run into him in New York City anyway. Who knows, maybe we'd become "real" friends then? So I was surprised, but not necessarily shocked, when one day while logged in on Facebook, a chat bubble popped up from the senator:

"Hey, Dave. What's going on?"

"Not much. How are you, Senator?" I responded via Facebook live chat, now Facebook Messenger.

"I'm good. Hey, can you contribute to my campaign please? Every donation counts, and the next filing deadline is tomorrow, so I could really use your help."

"Maybe," I replied somewhat suspiciously. "Wow, it's great that you're using social media for your own campaign."

"Thanks a lot. We have an event next week too. It would be great if you could come out to support me."

"Maybe," I said once again. Then I thought to ask, "Hey, this is the senator, right? I mean, you're not a staff person or volunteer impersonating the senator on Facebook in order to raise money, are you?"

Silence.

I continued, "As the CEO of a social media firm *and* a constituent, I'd really like you to level with me. If you don't respond at all, I'm going to assume that you're not really the senator."

More silence.

Then, I received the first honest message of the conversation: "I'm the senator's assistant. Sorry about that. The senator, he's not actually on Facebook, so we use this account on his behalf."

In such a situation, immediate and full disclosure is necessary—I shouldn't have had to ask whether or not I was actually speaking with the senator. I'm not sure just how much money that state senator raised through actions such as the one I experienced. Each time the campaign engaged with people under such false pretenses, though, they took the chance of losing that election and tarnishing the reputation of the politician forever. Was it worth that risk just to solicit a few dollars from people on Facebook?

More recently, a Likeable Media employee had a bad experience with a major airline. After a flight full of complications, she finally arrived at her destination. Being a huge social media advocate, she posted an accurate but nonetheless damning account on the airline's Facebook page of what had transpired. Shortly thereafter, she got not one, but two private messages sent to her by users saying how much they love the airline. One user went so far as to say, "How dare you post that horrible comment on the page? What is wrong with you?"

She clicked on the profile of this sender, only to find that the user is an employee of the airline! In fact, the other private message was from another of the airline's employees as well. While the actions were obviously not officially sanctioned by the airline, they reflected poorly on the company, and the lack of disclosure in the messages sent to my employee was foolish and unethical at best and illegal and dangerous to the company's reputation at worst.

BUILDING TRUST: TRANSPARENCY
IS NO LONGER NEGOTIABLE

Traditional marketers have worked for years at shaping people's opinions about brands and organizations using advertising and other linear marketing tactics. While marketers may be tempted to stretch the truth on social networks in order to achieve similar objectives, I can't stress this point any stronger: *You must be as honest and transparent as possible when using social media. Honesty and transparency build a direct relationship between you and the customer, and any deviation from these values can erode brand trust forever.*

In an age when it's virtually impossible to hide the truth, don't bother trying. If you're not ready to face the facts about your products or organization and share them with consumers, don't join the conversation yet. Once you're committed to creating a presence in social media outlets, there's no going back, and you really have no choice but to embrace transparency. If it seems intuitive to you to be honest, that's terrific. But too many marketers have employed dishonest tactics in trying to reach consumers, losing sight of the simple importance of telling the truth. With the advent of social media, consumers expect transparency from companies and organizations more than ever before—including Facebook itself.

In March 2018, *The Guardian* and *The New York Times* released an expose reporting that 50 million Facebook profiles were harvested by Cambridge Analytica, a political data firm hired by Donald Trump's 2016 U.S. presidential election campaign, in a major data scandal. The data included details on users' identities, friend networks, and *likes.* The idea was to use that information to map personality traits and target audiences with digital ads to impact their behavior. The scandal sparked new questions on two major topics: how politicians were using social media to influence voters and the measures Facebook was taking to protect its users' information.

Ten days after the news broke, Facebook shares dropped almost 18 percent, and an online #DeleteFacebook hashtag drew some high-profile support. Since then, Facebook has launched a full transparency movement to try to gain back its users' trust. "We're committed to making Facebook a place that's open and authentic, while safeguarding people's private data and keeping our platform safe for everyone," Facebook's transparency landing page says (transparency.facebook.com). Actions taken since the scandal include the ability for users to see all ads a brand or business is running, including dark posts, via an "Info & Ads" tab, and all election-related and issue ads on Facebook and Instagram must be clearly labeled, including a "paid for by" disclosure from the advertiser at the top of the post.

Disclosure and the ANA Ethics Code

In January 2018, the Association of National Advertisers (ANA) acquired the Word of Mouth Marketing Association (WOMMA). WOMMA was the leading trade organization for word-of-mouth marketing and social media, and it established an ethics code around what language and behavior are appropriate and inappropriate from organizations on social networks. The code is centered around honesty. From WOMMA's former website:

> It's all about the Honesty ROI. Ethical word-of-mouth marketers always strive for transparency and honesty in all communications with consumers, with advocates, and with those people who advocates speak to on behalf of a product:
>
> - **Honesty of Relationship**—you say who you're speaking for
> - **Honesty of Opinion**—you say what you truly believe; you never shill
> - **Honesty of Identity**—you say who you are; you never falsify your identity[1]

It may seem intuitive, but think about how many marketers have broken this code through the years. They may have planted false reviews, pretended to be someone they weren't, paid for positive reviews, or asked employees to write reviews without disclosing their relationship.

All of these things not only violate the WOMMA code but are also generally unethical (and some of them may be illegal in the United States, according to the Federal Trade Commission's 2009 Guidelines, available at Bit.ly//FTC2009). Even if you're not caught by the FTC—which can impose tens of thousands of dollars of fines—right away, the potential damage to your brand reputation is enough reason to never consider violating this code of ethics.

The Golden Rule

This concept is simple and intuitive (as are many areas of social media marketing): put on your consumer hat and do unto others, as a marketer, as you would want done unto you as a consumer. Would you want to be lied to, manipulated, or influenced by untruths? Of course not. So don't even consider these tactics as a marketer. If there's a gray area and you have to wonder whether something is ethical or not, it's probably not—take the high road, and don't do it.

Consider these four guidelines to maintain transparency and avoid potential ethical issues:

1. Insist that anyone you have paid to talk about your company or products online be open and honest and fully disclose the situation.
2. It's OK to ask customers to spread the word about your company, but if you're offering them free products in exchange for their support, you must insist they disclose what they received in any reviews or other material they post about you.
3. If your company or organization is doing something you don't want people to know about, don't think you can cover it up on social networks. Instead, fix the problem.
4. When in doubt, disclose.

Remember, the world is so transparent now that you have to be honest and open from the very start of building your social media platform.

WHEN YOU DON'T KNOW THE
ANSWER TO A QUESTION

Sometime between childhood and now, you were trained to try to answer people's questions honestly. But if you didn't know the answer, or sometimes out of sheer social grace, you may have learned to reply to people's questions with the response you thought they wanted to hear. When utilizing social media, don't tell people simply what they expect in an effort to please them. Instead, if you don't know an answer, just say, "I don't know— but I'll get back to you." People find honesty so refreshing (don't you?) that they may be happier to hear "I don't know" than anything else, especially a faulty response.

Transparent Banking: Educational Employees Credit Union

The Educational Employees Credit Union (EECU) is a medium-sized credit union with several dozen branches, and it is based in Fresno, California. In the highly regulated (and traditionally nontransparent!) financial industry, many institutions are struggling with how to best engage with customers using social media. For big banks using social media, the focus is not on banking itself but on the company's charitable giving or other service initiatives.

The EECU wanted to stand out as a financial institution that really "got" social media and was willing to have an open conversation with its customers. After all, a credit union is by definition owned by its members. They, too, thought the focus of the conversation was better off being based around more interesting topics than banking—therefore much of the conversation on their Facebook and Twitter pages (Facebook.com/myEECU and Twitter.com/myEECU) focused on the Fresno area and exploring the culture and businesses nearby.

However, EECU never shied away from open and honest conversation about rates, customer service experiences, and activities with credit union staff. Take a look at the Facebook discussion in Figure 10.1.

| FIGURE 10.1 | EECU Deftly Handles a Difficult Situation on Its Facebook Wall |

 Melissa ____ Will eecu be helping the state workers that are getting their wages cut to $7.25/hr in some way??
July 8 at 8:15pm · Like · Comment

 Educational Employees Credit Union | EECU Hi Melissa– Yes we will. We are in the process of finalizing the details of our action plan to help members with this hardship. As in the past, we will be able to assist our members with a 0% "emergency" loan to cover pay shortages while the state budget is being finalized. Our plan is to be able to start taking applications by July 15th.
July 9 at 1:32am · Like · 🖒 1 person · Flag

 Melissa ____ thank u so much for the info!! very much appreciated!!
July 9 at 10:40am · Like · Flag

The only topics EECU won't discuss publicly concern the personal financial information of individual customers—information that obviously requires security over transparency. At a time when most financial institutions of all sizes have been unable to create transparent communities for their customers, EECU has established itself as a market leader. Its members are more loyal to a bank they can trust online, and their policies have paid off in increased word of mouth and membership.

JUST LIKE DATING: THE MORE OPEN YOU ARE, THE BETTER . . . TO A POINT

Anyone who has ever dated knows that openness and honesty are key factors in establishing a relationship. When one person has trouble opening up to the other, the potential relationship is threatened—wouldn't you think someone had something to hide if he or she were not completely candid with you? The same situation applies to your company: if you have nothing to hide, only positive outcomes will result from increased transparency.

If a date completely opened up to you the first time you went out and shared his or her innermost secrets in the spirit of transparency, however, it would probably be uncomfortable and strange. Similarly, as a company, just because you're supposed to be transparent doesn't mean you have to share trade secrets, profit margins, or insider information with all of your customers. In fact, a lot of that information would be off-putting, even to the most curious customer.

In general, though, when you share insights into your company's values and culture and encourage an honest discussion of the decisions you've made, your customers will trust you more, feel closer to you, and want to strengthen their relationships with you—just like a dating relationship. Being transparent doesn't mean you have to share everything about your organization, but the more honest insight you provide, the better.

PUBLIC FIGURES, GOVERNMENT, AND DISCLOSURE

In no sector is transparency more important than in government. You, the taxpayers and voters, fund politicians, programs, and agencies. Therefore, they have an obligation to provide public access to honest information. Just as many big companies have been slow to adapt to the social media revolution, governments large and small have taken their time in building a platform or creating any social networking initiatives. But unlike many companies, whose first allegiance must be to shareholders, the government's first allegiance must be to constituents.

The example I began this chapter with is disturbing because the senator's staff person basically impersonated the senator in order to accomplish an objective. The correct way for public figures, such as politicians, actors, authors, and artists, to work with social media is for them to personally use the tools. However, if they think they're too busy to use Facebook and Twitter and instead hire people to represent them, it's best to disclose who is (or isn't) responding to questions, starting conversations, and making posts on their behalf. Entertainer Britney Spears does a great job of transparently letting the world know whether she or someone from her staff is tweeting by signing each tweet with the actual tweeter's initials.

On the political front, we must mention U.S. President Donald Trump, who often says social media is the most effective way to connect with the country without the filter of the traditional media he claims not to trust. "I doubt I would be here if it weren't for social media, to be honest with you," Trump told Fox Business Network's Maria Bartiromo. Since his election, the White House has been obliged to clarify that his tweets also represent presidential statements and should carry the same weight as a comment issued by his press office.

A Transparent Politician: Cory Booker

Former U.S. President Barack Obama set the gold standard for using social media to help win the 2008 election—but it wasn't actually him tweeting and Facebooking his way to the top. While most people understood when it was revealed that Obama wasn't using social media himself, there was a discomfort level among some people due to the lack of complete transparency in the initial stages of his campaign. Cory Booker, a senator from New Jersey and the former mayor of Newark, New Jersey, on the other hand, has set the platinum standard for politicians' honest use of social media.

Despite the many duties of running the largest city in New Jersey, and one plagued by crime, unemployment, and a failing education system when he began as mayor, Booker has done a remarkable job using social media to connect to constituents, the media, and donors. His Twitter account, Twitter.com /CoryBooker, has amassed an amazing 4.08 million followers. In addition, he set up city agencies with social media tools so that they too can connect to Newark residents openly. Though he began the friendship at a conference offline with Facebook CEO Mark Zuckerberg, it was the continued connection online, through Facebook, that culminated in Zuckerberg giving the Newark schools a gift of more than $100 million in September 2010, one of the largest private financial gifts ever made to a city.

However, no story better illustrates the power of elected officials to connect directly to constituents than what happened on December 31, 2009. Newark resident Ravie Rave tweeted during a New Year's Eve snowstorm that she was worried about her 65-year-old dad getting snowed in. Mayor Booker saw the tweet and tweeted back: "Please @BigSixxRaven don't worry bout ur dad. Just talked 2 him & I'll get his Driveway by noon. I've got salt, shovels & great volunteers."

He showed up at her dad's house an hour later and shoveled the snow. Note that Booker didn't care about proper grammar in his tweet. He was too busy listening, engaging, and responding to his constituents.

Booker continues to be an avid Twitter user and proponent of the open Web. We've come a long way from the days when letter-writing campaigns and petitions were the only ways to get the attention of elected officials, and many believe Booker is ushering in a new level of much-needed transparency for future politicians.

ACTION ITEMS

1. Create a social media policy that insists on honesty and transparency as the default expectations. Review with other key stakeholders in your organization what company information, if any, is off-limits and how you can better embrace openness and transparency while still keeping this in mind.

2. If you work at a large organization, determine whether your chief executive officer can effectively use social media tools such as Twitter and Facebook herself to be the ultimate transparent representative of your brand.

3. Closely examine your social media policy to make sure it is aligned with the values of honesty and transparency at its core. If it is not, consider what you could add to help instill these values.

4. Write down three ways you could respond to questions and comments on social networks in a more transparent way in order to further build trust with your customers.

APPLY THE GOLDEN RULE, AND LET YOUR CUSTOMERS FALL IN LOVE WITH YOU

In an age of corporate secrets, a little honesty and transparency go a long way toward building trust with your prospects and long-term commitment from your customers. When in doubt, always disclose your objectives and who you are. Insist that anyone you have paid to talk about your company or products online be open and honest and fully disclose the situation.

Just as we fall in love with people who can listen to us and we can trust, we fall in love with companies that can do the same. Wouldn't it be nice if your customers fell in love with your transparent brand?

CHAPTER 11

Should You Ask a Lot of Questions?

Entenmann's is a baked goods company that started in Brooklyn, New York, around the turn of the twentieth century. The company has since grown to become a national brand, and it has created and discontinued tons of products over the years. It has a passionate fan base, whose loyalties sometimes lie with a specific tasty treat rather than with the brand itself.

Several years ago, an Entenmann's fan asked, "Why won't you bring back the Banana Crumb Cake?" on the Entenmann's Facebook wall. He posted this same question three times in one day. He was so distressed about the Banana Crumb Cake being discontinued, he actually began to rally fans to boycott his previously beloved Entenmann's brand. He wrote letters, created a petition, and posted all over the Facebook wall—where oh where had the Banana Crumb Cake gone?

Entenmann's is a forward-thinking company when it comes to social media, and it realizes that its customers are its most valued assets. Yet, the Banana Crumb Cake had not been selling in great enough volume to continue production, and Entenmann's had to give it the axe. So what's a brand to do? Senior executives at Entenmann's determined that the company would, in fact, resume production *if sales warranted the return* of the Banana Crumb Cake.

They placed a call to the disgruntled fan and let him know that they would be posting a poll on Entenmann's Facebook page so that fans could vote on whether or not to restart production of the cake. If 1,000 or more people voted to "bring back Banana Crumb," well then, he would have his way. This proposal empowered the customer and consumers everywhere, providing them with a stake in Entenmann's product line.

The next day, Entenmann's posted the question on its Facebook page: "Should we bring back the Banana Crumb Cake?" The fan (and anyone else who wanted to) had ample time to rally friends around answering the question. Not only did this provide the Entenmann's brand team with free insight into its current customers, but it also ended up exposing many new people to the brand and its Facebook page.

Wondering what the results of the poll were? It turned out that the Banana Crumb Cake fan was not alone in his love for the product. Many fans voted to bring back the Banana Crumb Cake, and today, it is one of Entenmann's bestselling products. Moreover, Entenmann's has initiated a "Bring It Back" campaign through which Facebook fans vote on new products to bring back to market. Plus, the man continued to be a vocal fan of Entenmann's and enjoy its other products. One public question turned a disgruntled fan into one of the company's most positive and vocal fans today.

WHY ASK A LOT OF QUESTIONS?

People responsible for social media at organizations often lament, "Nobody's responding to our posts on Facebook and Twitter." Especially if you don't have a large organization with many thousands of followers, getting responses to, or comments on, your content can be challenging. To combat this issue, start with the basics. Consider whether *you* would be more likely to respond to a question or a statement in a conversation. Think about your reaction to the following two sentences:

- This book has provided valuable insight to you so far.
- Has this book provided any valuable insight to you so far?

The first statement is likely to elicit a nod, a shake of your head, or the thought to yourself, "Eh? It's alright so far. Let me keep reading." No matter what, it's a light response, if any. The sentence also probably leads you to believe the author is a bit cocky and presumptuous for telling you what he wants you to think.

The second sentence, the question, is likely to yield a more definite response, such as, "Yes, I love it!" or "No, there's nothing here I didn't know already." Furthermore, the question conveys the impression that the author is genuinely interested in learning the answer and doesn't presume to know it.

In a traditional advertising and marketing setting, marketers have limited time and space to get their message out there. They have to tell customers what they want them to think. They can't afford to use that time and space to ask questions. In a social media setting, however, the opposite is true. You can't afford to tell people what you want them to think because they will not respond positively. Now, since you have unlimited time and space to help shape their perception, you can cater directly to them, learn about what they are looking for in a product or service, and understand what they like, dislike, want, and expect from your company. The way to meet this goal is to ask lots of questions—genuine ones, of course—and actually listen to the answers.

FIVE QUESTIONS YOU CAN ASK
YOUR COMMUNITY ANYTIME

1. What would you like to see more of in this community?

2. Who are you inspired by most?

3. Where is the most interesting place you've used our product?

4. When did you first use our service?

5. Why do you like this page?

What Is the Marketing Value of Questions?

Put on your consumer cap, and think about what companies say to you across marketing channels and how it makes you feel. Advertisers have always sought to make an emotional connection with their customers. Consider what better builds an emotional connection: when advertisers tell you about their companies, or when they ask you your opinions about them. Asking questions creates marketing value in these four ways:

1. Helping you guide the social media conversation without appearing forceful
2. Allowing you to become a consumer-centric marketer rather than a brand-centric marketer
3. Demonstrating that you value openness, honesty, and feedback (three values customers and prospects universally hold in high regard)
4. Showing that you care about what your customers have to say

Questions build an emotional connection between you and the consumer, and they generate conversations about your customers' pain points, problems, and needs. As customers have discussions with each other, and with you, you'll gain mindshare, increasing the likelihood that they'll turn to you for your products and services when needed.

What Is the Insight Value of Questions?

Questions on social networks lead to conversations that clearly have marketing value. But even if they didn't have such value, the insight you can glean alone from them is immense. Companies' research and development (R&D) departments routinely spend many thousands or even millions of dollars on programs, such as focus groups, surveys, and customer marketing research, to gain insight into their customers or prospects. Yet, once you've built up a following on Facebook, Twitter, or Instagram, you can tap into these communities on a regular basis without spending a dime! These online networks are living, breathing focus groups. (Instagram Stories is a particularly useful tool for asking questions!) You can ask your customers questions about your products and services, about their perceptions and attitudes, their opinions, their knowledge of competitors, and an infinite number of other topics. Try asking simple questions such as the following to start:

- What can we do better?
- What were your best and worst experiences with us?
- What do you think of our recent advertisement?

Eventually you can also cut or limit the traditional focus group and research activity you do offline, saving money and providing you with a direct, real-time audience whose responses to your questions are almost instant.

In an age of growing transparency, asking questions publicly to gather insight is best. But what if you want to gather insights privately? Even in that case, you can create a private survey online and then solicit people to participate through your social communities. And when you solicit people, in order to generate a better response rate, ask a question! "Who'd like to participate in a survey about us?" will yield a better response than "Click here to participate in a survey about us" every time. Remember, questions have a natural tendency to elicit answers; statements do not.

WHAT DID LIKEABLE MEDIA'S RESEARCH FIND ABOUT QUESTIONS AND FACEBOOK ENGAGEMENT?

Our team at Likeable Media did a study on what makes a Facebook page update worthy of being *liked* by someone and the kinds of posts that generate the highest engagement rates. To find these answers, we looked at a month's worth of Facebook status updates for our clients ranging from independently owned Internet startups to national restaurant chains.

In *90 percent* of all cases, the interaction rate for status updates that posed a question directly to fans was *above the average rate for informational* posts. In *100 percent* of cases, engagement rates for posts that talked exclusively about the company without posing a question were *below the overall average*. In terms of actual numbers, posts that posed a question or otherwise requested immediate feedback were up to *six times* more engaging than straight informational posts. Of course, if you simply post random questions, having nothing to do with your customers or products, those posts won't have much conversational staying power or engagement over the long term. The challenge is to find questions that encourage thought from your fan base. Though daunting, try asking customers what they think of a new product. Even more direct, pose questions inquiring about things consumers *don't* like about your latest products or services—you might get some real feedback you can use, or you still might get people sharing the coveted "I love everything about you" comment. Phrase updates in a way that's relevant to the values of your organization, and don't forget to help facilitate the conversation in a way that is not too sales heavy!

WHAT IS THE POWER OF CROWDSOURCING?

Crowdsourcing is the act of outsourcing tasks that are traditionally performed by employees at an organization to a large group of people or community (a crowd) through an *open call*.

The beauty of crowdsourcing is threefold:

- First, you find great solutions to problems from the people who know you best: your customers.
- Second, you tap into the wisdom of the crowd—as the saying goes, many heads are often better than one.
- Finally, most important, you get vested interest in the outcomes from a potentially huge group of people who are all waiting to potentially become your newest customers.

Crowdsourcing is the ultimate question. It's saying to your community, "We have a challenge. Can you help?"

Who Wants to Choose the Next Auntie Anne's Pretzel?

In 2017, Auntie Anne's, the world's largest hand-rolled soft pretzel franchise, used social media to get its fans involved by crowdsourcing a new flavor. It began with a simple ask to its customers and fans: What new pretzel flavor would you like to see at Auntie Anne's? In just a few weeks, the initial request for flavors on social media generated more than 1,200 fan suggestions, and the 10 most popular flavors became the Pretzel Nation Creation finalists. From there, the public voted on the next pretzel flavor, and Sriracha emerged as the victor with 200,000 more votes than second place S'mores.

The money Auntie Anne's spent was far less than research and development would have cost, and since so many customers were involved throughout the process, when the new flavor launched, it had a built-in audience of more than 1.3 million people who had participated in the process to create it. Who wouldn't want to launch a new product that 1.3 million people already felt they had connected to before it even hit the shelves?

By popular demand, Auntie Anne's brought back Pretzel Nation Creation the following year and themed the flavor finalists in honor of its thirtieth birthday. Unsurprisingly, Birthday Cake came out on top.

Do Lilly Pulitzer Fans Love Avocados?

Involving your community in product development doesn't have to come in the form of a formal contest or large-scale campaign. Sometimes, you just need to validate a hunch.

Lilly Pulitzer is known for its colorful, hand-painted prints that are easy to spot, and to highlight this competitive advantage, the brand started using the same style of art to bring some color into its social feeds. The Instagram community loved it, so in 2013 Lilly Pulitzer launched #Lilly5x5, a content series of original artwork painted exclusively for social media. The social art has since been incorporated into two books that were sent as special gifts with Lilly Pulitzer purchases, and it's been used to inspire accessories that are now part of the collection. But the success doesn't stop there.

At a product development meeting in 2017, the team at Lilly Pulitzer saw a limited offering avocado-themed print they thought its social audience would love. Avocados were a huge trend at the time, and the team wanted to prove that quickly to stress the community's demand. The team asked one of its artists to paint an avocado-themed #Lilly5x5 (Figure 11.1). The *likes* spoke to the love of the print—17,000 *likes*, to be exact. The post also had the second-highest number of comments for the month and the largest reach. The case was made to expand the assortment of the print into Lilly Pulitzer's first "family capsule," or collection of essential items, in years. The print, "Guac & Roll," was offered in styles for women, girls, men, and boys and was a huge success for the company when it launched in October 2017.

FIGURE 11.1   Lilly Pulitzer's Avocado Instagram Post

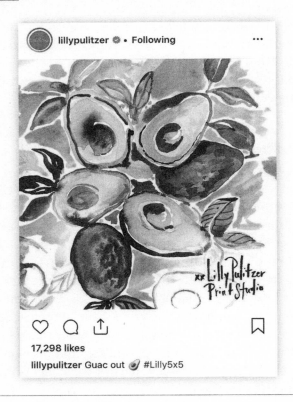

HOW SHOULD YOU ASK DISCUSSION-GENERATING QUESTIONS?

Crowdsourcing might work well when you have the right project and enough of an existing community to make it work, but asking questions through social media outlets on a regular basis can also keep fans interested, engaged, and having fun. It's important to stay creative, innovative even, to keep your customers interested and returning to your Facebook or Instagram page regularly. You need to utilize your customers' growing mindshare and get them involved by posing intriguing questions that can create a full-on discussion.

How Did Redbox Use Facebook Live to Generate Real-Time Engagement?

With 41,500 kiosks across the country, Redbox is in the rare position of being known to almost all. However, the growing popularity of streaming services has made it difficult to remain a first choice for entertainment. To keep the brand top-of-mind before the launch of its new On Demand service, Redbox wanted to find a way to stand out.

Knowing that Facebook prioritizes live video, the dedicated Redbox social audience exceeds five million, and even more millions were tuning in to popular game show app HQ Trivia, the Likeable team worked with Redbox to produce ScreenPLAY Live (Figure 11.2). Hosted by two millennial pop culture junkies, each episode featured a variety of live games where viewers were asked to "Guess the Movie" as popular scenes were drawn, recreated with candy, narrated through emojis, and more. Viewers participated by commenting like crazy, and if they worked together to get all the movies right, the hosts were placed in the hot seat to perform various dares.

Redbox wanted to get people talking—and it's safe to say it did. Despite an average runtime of 23 minutes, the eight live broadcasts averaged one comment per second. And overall, ScreenPLAY Live reached over 1.5 million people, received over 21,500 comments, and garnered over 360,000 video views. The series supported marketing objectives by featuring new release titles, but by gamifying the content first and selling the product second, Redbox was able to generate true fan engagement. Remember, more *likes* or comments on any Facebook content drive that content to the top of people's News Feeds, leading to more impressions, and more top-of-mind awareness for Redbox and millions of fans.

FIGURE 11.2   **Fans "Guess the Movie" on Redbox's ScreenPLAY Live Facebook Show**

ACTION ITEMS

1. Write down a list of the topics of conversation your customers typically talk about. Remember, when you brainstorm, nothing's wrong. Try to write about topics that have something to do with your brand or organization, and also some that have *nothing* to do with your brand. What do your customers like to talk about? What can they have a spirited discussion about?
2. Based on the topics your customers discuss, write a list of questions you could ask them publicly on Facebook, Instagram Stories, or Twitter to stimulate interesting discussion.

3. What questions could you ask your fans to help you glean insight into what they want from you and how you could do a better job serving your customers? If your organization has done marketing research, surveying, or focus group testing in the past, consider how you might insert some of your findings into your social media communications.

4. Do you have any projects that might be well served by crowd-sourcing? Determine whether you have any upcoming design updates, new products or packaging, or other opportunities you could ask your customers and fans to help you with publicly.

WHY SHOULD YOU ASK A LOT OF QUESTIONS, AGAIN?

If social media is a conversation, you can't possibly be an active participant without asking questions. Asking your customers, prospects, and fans questions will get people talking and keep them talking, creating actual dialogue. And, ideally, they'll be talking about you in a positive light.

Asking questions on Facebook and other social networks can help you gain valuable insights about your organization, cut R&D costs, and gain access to ideas you may not have had from the people who know you best—your customers and prospects. Crowdsourcing allows you to ask the ultimate question of your community—"Can you help us?"—and builds a massive number of stakeholders in your success while providing your community with a valuable and often fun activity. Questions demonstrate your organization's fundamental openness to hearing answers, whether you like the answers or not. Can you think of any better way to engage your customers in dialogue online than asking questions?

CHAPTER 12

Provide Value (Yes, for Free!)

"Excuse me, Dave, we've never met, but I wanted to introduce myself," Michael said confidently, as he stopped me at a large social media conference in New York. "I just wanted to thank you for all of the great value you and your company provide," he continued. "I mean, all of the links, resources, and tips your social media agency has shared, all of the articles you've written over the past year—they've just been so helpful that I've recently started my own social media agency with everything I've learned from you. Thanks again, Dave. Keep up the good work. I'll be watching!"

I felt devastated at first. I had always intuitively believed that providing value for free on social networks online was the way to demonstrate expertise and credibility, build a reputation, and become a "thought leader." But here, someone had the nerve (or transparency, at least) to tell me the value Likeable and I had provided for him, for free, was enough for him to start his own business doing what we did. It just seemed so unfair. I questioned my basic assumption that giving away a lot of what we sold built credibility and trust and provided the marketplace with the opportunity to organically spread the word about us. Maybe I had been wrong all along and was just a bad businessperson.

Luckily, only three days after the conference, I received a phone call that helped reaffirm our core beliefs about giving away valuable content online. The call came in from a key decision maker at one of the leading party and tent companies in the country. She was straightforward and to the point:

> Hello, Dave. You don't know me, but I've been following you guys on Facebook, Twitter, and your blog for several months now. I just read another excellent blog article from your staff, and it reminded me that I've been meaning to call you. We need a social media strategy and plan, and we could do an RFP (request for proposal), but honestly, I know we want to work with you because I've seen how you guys think in all these articles you've written and shared over the last few months. I have $250,000 in our budget. When can we get started?

The free value we had provided for months may have allowed competitors to learn from us—heck, it even spawned new competitors. But that same shared content had helped build our reputation and credibility over time so that we were able to attract *inbound* leads and grow exponentially without any outbound sales force. Had we not given away information for free, the $250,000 caller wouldn't even have known about us and certainly wouldn't have contacted us.

PROVIDING FREE VALUE BUILDS TRUST, REPUTATION, AND EVEN SALES

The more valuable content you can share with your fans and followers, the greater the trust and reputation you'll build with them. Share your expertise without expectation or marketing-speak, and you'll create an even better name for yourself.

For example, if you represent an accounting firm, write a blog article such as "Top 10 Tax-Saving Strategies for the Year Ahead" and share it on Facebook, LinkedIn, and Twitter. While it might be tempting to end the article by saying, "For more tax-saving help, call us," it's better to showcase your expertise without asking for anything in return. If a prospect wants more help, she can quickly figure out how to contact you from your website, I promise. If you're worried about not having enough to write about, you can always write shorter, more pointed articles instead. A "top 10" post could just as easily be a 10-part series in which you dive a little deeper into each of the top 10 strategies as well.

You don't need to write articles to showcase your expertise either. In fact, writing articles can be time-consuming and unnecessary. Simply finding helpful articles online and sharing them with your community will provide value that current and prospective customers will appreciate. The material doesn't have to be from you—just credit the source when you share it.

Provide Enough Value to Help People, *Without* Giving Away the Farm

Even if we did give away enough content to inspire others to start their own social media agencies, it's rare that you could ever give away so much information that people could afford to do everything on their own. Accountants can share general tax advice, law firms can present information about the impact of new laws, consultants can describe best practices, and doctors can provide health news and tips. Eventually, however, no matter how valuable people might find your research, tips, and articles, they are not experts, and they'll never know your content areas as well as you do. So when they need help, chances are they'll need *your* products or services—and that's when you can profit from all of the free value you've provided.

By consistently providing great content over time, you won't need to advertise how wonderful you are—your community will already know based on what you've shared. And when they're ready to buy your product or service, they won't need to respond to ads telling them whom to turn to. They won't even need to search Google to find what they're looking for. They'll already feel like they know you—they trust you and like you—so they'll turn to you to solve their problem.

Every Brand Is a Publisher Now

Articles are no longer solely written and shared by professional services firms. Now, every company and brand can post any articles they have written in-house or found elsewhere to their blogs and LinkedIn pages. They can tweet and retweet valuable information throughout their entire community simultaneously. You are essentially able to publish any amount of valuable information with the click of a button, and it has the potential to be seen by millions of users.

Venture capitalist Fred Wilson and many others have said that links are the economy of the social Web. Once you are connected through such links, your audience grows exponentially. Writing and sharing great articles can provide your community with valuable information, no matter what you're responsible for marketing. If it's a food product or restaurant, you can share great recipes. If you're marketing a clothing brand, you can share articles about the latest fashions. If it's a hotel or airline, you can share articles about travel tips. The most important thing is to think about your target audience and provide articles they will find valuable. What would *you* find useful if you were on the receiving end of a status update? What would *you* like to see from your company?

Keep in mind, no matter what your organization sells, you're not selling *that* here. Instead, you're selling your expertise. You're selling your reputation. You're selling your credibility. And, of course, you're not actually trading this content directly for something in return. You're giving it away. But is it worth it to become a thought leader in whatever space you're in? Is it worth it if in the future you never have to *sell* anything because people consider you the top expert in your niche and they come to you to *buy* your product or service before searching elsewhere?

Beyond Articles: Consider Other Ways to Provide Value

Though articles are an effective way to disseminate a plethora of information, other tactics are equally, if not more, helpful. For B2B organizations, for example, perhaps you want to write a white paper or share a research study. For consumer brands, you might want to create a fun augmented reality game to play, a comic that makes people laugh, or a free mobile application, all of which can provide entertainment and practical value. Be warned, however, that the cost of developing your own online game or application can be huge, and therefore it is riskier than writing a quick article.

Another way to provide valuable content is through videos. You may find it easier to create 60- to 120-second-long videos talking about how to do things yourself, top five tips, or any other content you might have traditionally written in an online post or article. For many, filming videos is easier than writing, and videos also have the added benefit of better showcasing your organization's personality than the written word might be able to. Here are a few quick guidelines for creating video content:

1. **Use an inexpensive camera.** There's usually no reason to waste money on high-end expensive equipment.
2. **Keep it short and sweet.** People's attention spans online are short—no longer than two minutes.
3. **Share the videos everywhere.** Share on YouTube and Facebook, and consider using Instagram and Twitter to further spread your word.
4. **Have fun with it.** This shows in your final product. (It also shows if the person on camera is uncomfortable or anxious.)

No matter what medium you decide to use, content and value can be as simple or complex as you want. The main criterion, however, is that you deliver something useful to your customers or communities and truly ask for nothing in return.

THE IMPORTANCE OF CONSISTENCY

Creating and sharing valuable content will provide you with a great reputation and return—but only over time and through consistent effort and commitment. Think about it: The first time you come into contact with a new organization or author, do you trust him or her immediately? No, it takes time and repeated contact for him or her to gain your trust.

The same is true on the social Web. Unfortunately, many organizations try to create valuable content, but when there isn't an immediate return on their investment, they give up. Instead, try using paid ads to remarket new Facebook and Instagram content to those who have watched or engaged with it before. Organizations that make a long-term commitment to regularly delivering value to their communities will succeed; those that put in minimal time and effort will fail.

FIVE PERCENT OFF IS INSULTING: COUPONS, AND THE DIFFERENCE BETWEEN VALUE AND MARKETING

Perhaps because marketers have for years used phrases such as "valuable coupons" and "valuable offers inside," we've grown to associate the words *coupons* and *discounts* with value. Indeed, email marketing as a channel relies heavily on sending discounts on products and services to customers in hopes that the offers arrive in people's inboxes at the moment they want or need whatever the companies are selling. The question is whether or not such emails offer value or whether they are simply marketing ploys. Make no mistake: There is a difference between a *valuable* offer and a *marketing* offer.

Ten percent off is not really a value. It's a marketing offer. Five percent off is insulting. Fifteen percent off may or may not be perceived as valuable—it depends on your audience and product. It's of course OK to offer 5 or 10 percent off—just be aware that you're not really providing much value in the eyes of most consumers.

Can coupons provide real value? Free is always best, of course. No one can argue with the value of a free white paper download, game, sample, or gift with purchase. If you don't ever want to be perceived as a "value" or "discount" brand, a free gift with a purchase is the best compromise. Otherwise, 50 percent off, or greater, tells consumers that you are providing something of actual worth. While many companies won't want to offer any of their products or services at 50 percent off, an increasing number of them are using this model to attract new customers, reward loyal ones, and create buzz on social networks.

Every organization should be providing its fans and followers with valuable content on the social Web, and many are already. The following examples are a few ways companies are providing value on a consistent basis.

Petcube Catches Customers Smiling

Petcube, a tech startup that sells Wi-Fi controlled cameras to monitor your pet while you're away, has used its product to build a highly engaged social media following. Aside from user-initiated video recordings, Petcube cameras are designed to engage with pets and capture video based on major sound and movement. Petcube recently re-Instagrammed a customer's video of a cat rearranging all the clothes in a drawer with the hashtag #caughtonpetcube (Figure 12.1). Check out what else comes up with a quick search of that hashtag on Instagram. Sometimes value comes in the simple form of a smile.

FIGURE 12.1   **Petcube Shares a Video of a Cat Caught on Camera**

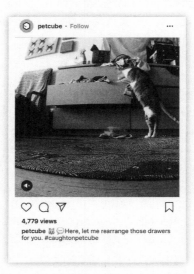

In addition to giving pet owners a glimpse of what goes on when they're not looking, Petcube cameras are used by foster homes, shelters, and local businesses like Lady Dinah's Cat Emporium to drive more social media engagement. The adoption services have found success with Petcube live streams, letting potential animal owners watch, and even play with, the eligible animals before bringing them home.

Gladiator Knows What Works

Gladiator, a garage storage company that sells appliances including cabinets, shelving, wall systems, and workbenches, has a "What-Works" blog where customers share their real-life spaces filled with ideas that the company never even thought possible with the product, and on social, the brand's most engaging posts have been when it asked to see pictures of its customers' spaces. "Our Facebook fans comment on each other's photos and help each other out with solutions sometimes before we've even had a chance to comment. It's great to see the knowledge-sharing and engagement," says Annette Finnigan, senior brand marketing manager.

Gladiator also understands that some customers may need assistance in choosing the products that are right for their gear. That's why the brand has product and installation videos on its YouTube channel to make the selection and assembly process as simple and easy as possible.

Purple Creates Truly Entertaining Videos

If you haven't seen a Purple ad yet and you're by your computer, it's worth putting the book down for a moment and visiting its Facebook page. Purple is a web-only retailer that sells scientifically engineered mattresses, but the brand isn't just great at mattresses, it's great at entertainment, too.

The company's most popular video series to date is called the "Raw Egg Test" (Figure 12.2). In one four-minute video, a woman dressed as Goldilocks demonstrates how traditional mattresses are inferior by dropping a 330-pound sheet of tempered glass on hard, soft, and medium mattresses with raw eggs on them.

In the case of the hard mattress, the eggs break because there isn't enough give. In the case of the soft mattress, the eggs break because it doesn't offer enough support. In the case of the medium mattress, the eggs break because it doesn't offer much of either. And in the case of the Purple mattress, the eggs remain unbroken. The Goldilocks video has more than 138 million views on Facebook and another 166 million views on YouTube.

FIGURE 12.2   **Purple's Raw Egg Test**

The quirky, against-the-grain approach really challenged the category's norms and allowed the brand to stand out, but Purple also did some extra legwork with paid ads behind the scenes. For some videos, Purple tested more than 20 versions before settling on a final cut, and, according to Purple, some of the videos had more than 20 intros and outros tested as well. With social ads, you can see exactly how long users are spending watching your content, which means you can also see when they start to become uninterested. A "test and learn" approach is essential to finding out what resonates with your audience.

A note of caution: of those companies that aren't in the entertainment business who try to create viral videos, 99 percent will fail. If you can truly entertain, that's perfect. If not, figure out another way you can provide value to your community.

Weeks Law Firm Gives Back and Makes More

Weeks Law Firm is a Plano, Texas-based practice devoted to estate planning, special needs trust planning, guardianships and alternatives, and more. The firm hosts a slew of free workshops like "Leaving a Loving Legacy" and "Family Legal Documents 101," and it uses Facebook Events to promote them to the local community. On the event page, users are encouraged to ask questions, download the firm's e-book, and more.

Could people in its target audience take the information and use it without hiring or even contacting Weeks Law Firm? Could competitors take the workshops and repurpose the information for their own use? Of course they could, and some probably do. However, even just a handful of prospects appreciating the information enough to contact the firm has provided Weeks Law Firm with a return on its investments.

A Likeable Blog and Newsletter

Soon after we started our company back in 2007, we wanted to write a blog to share expertise and our point of view and to create and share valuable content about social media and online marketing. To this day, the Likeable team publishes at least one blog post a week, and in 2018, we started distributing a free newsletter. The weekly newsletter, *#TBT: What mattered in social this week*, is equipped with free value, including the following:

- **Know This Number:** An interesting social media statistic or trend
- **Overheard:** A notable quote about social media
- **The Rundown:** News about platform updates and their implications
- **Content Win:** The best piece of social content we saw that week, not done by our company
- **The Latest from Likeable:** Links to our blog posts, podcasts, and white papers

The Likeable blog has become one of the most widely read and shared blogs on social media marketing in the world, and together, the blog and newsletter are consistent sources of new business prospects.

ACTION ITEMS

1. Brainstorm and write down all the ways in which you can provide value to your target audience without focusing on marketing yourself or selling your company to them *at all*. What will help your customers the most: information, entertainment, functionality, or a combination of these?

2. Write down the formats your organization is most capable of using to provide your audience with valuable content on the social Web. Will it be through blog articles you write, videos you create, or a game or application? Or will you comb the Web looking for interesting and useful content based on a particular set of topics and then share your findings?

3. Create several pieces of content you think your customers will find valuable. Before you share the content on Facebook or another social network, share it with two or three friends to test it. Do they find it worthwhile? Equally important, do they see it as pure value or as an advertisement for your organization?

4. Determine the social networks that are most appropriate to house your valuable content. Is it your blog, or Facebook, Twitter, LinkedIn, or somewhere else?

GIVE, AND YOU SHALL RECEIVE

Companies have always sought to provide value for their customers and prospects. In exchange for those efforts, they have wanted *an immediate* return in the form of sales. The challenge on the social Web is to figure out how you can provide valuable content—information, entertainment, and/or applications—without expecting anything back right away. When you give content away for free, there will invariably be people who don't become your customers—but who knows if they would have become your customers anyway? Other prospects will appreciate what you have to offer, share it with their friends, and become customers themselves.

CHAPTER 13

Share Stories
(They're Your Social Currency!)

I was sitting at Andrew's Diner one day in late 2005 with my then-recent fiancée, Carrie, when we began talking about our wedding. I wanted a large one—huge, in fact, as I've always been a public guy, and I hoped to share my big day with as many people as possible. But New York weddings are painfully expensive. We both had extensive experience working in marketing and promotions, however, and Carrie came up with a genius idea: we decided to create a promotion around our wedding.

We're both huge Mets fans, so we called up the Minor League Mets affiliate team, the Brooklyn Cyclones, and we pitched them the idea of getting married at home plate following a game. We'd secure sponsors to cover the costs of the wedding, and each sponsor would have a part in the promotion before and during the game. Sponsors, and the Cyclones, would likely benefit from the amount of buzz that was sure to surround a wedding with 5,000 guests at a baseball game.

The Cyclones thought we were a little crazy, but they loved the proposal and gave us a shot. The florist 1-800-Flowers.com loved it too, and the company gave us flowers for the event. Then Smirnoff got on board, as did David's Bridal, and a dozen other companies. In July 2006, I married my wife at an amazing wedding in front of nearly 500 friends and family and 5,000 strangers (Figure 13.1). We raised $100,000 from sponsors to cover costs and a $20,000 contribution to the Multiple Sclerosis Society.

| FIGURE 13.1 | Carrie and Dave Tie the Knot |

The event generated *a lot* of buzz. Our sponsors and we were featured in the *New York Times*, on CNBC, CBS's *Early Show*, and ABC's *World News Tonight*, as well as hundreds of other linear and new media outlets. We ended up with not only a dream wedding, but a dream promotion.

A few weeks after the event, we began getting calls from our wedding vendors, thanking us for all the promotion and buzz they received and asking what we were going to do next. Since we couldn't get married again, we decided to start a company around the concepts of word-of-mouth marketing—theKbuzz, now known as Likeable Media, was born.

Likeable's origin story hasn't changed for 10 years, but our way of telling it has. Every year on our anniversary, we use social media to honor the day and spread the word—but what was once a status update or a blog post is now a "TBT" video or an Instagram Story.

As the networks grow and evolve, so too can your storytelling tactics. Take a few minutes each day to look at popular marketing publications or the social networks' business blogs. If an update like IGTV (Instagram's competitive product to YouTube) or augmented reality ads makes sense for your brand or business, don't think twice. Sometimes being the first to do something is all you need to get noticed (we're still the only agency ever founded on a wedding day). Creativity and innovation get attention, and using them to tell your story, or write a new one, will ensure you stand out.

STORIES BRING YOUR COMPANY TO LIFE

When you hear the story of how a company was born, or you hear a story about the impact an organization has had on a customer's life, or about the unique experience of a group's staff member or partner, you feel an emotional connection with that company. Social media, especially blogs and online videos, allow you to share your stories with your customers, prospects, and the world, further building powerful connections. In the past, storytelling to the masses was expensive and could be accomplished only through television advertising or a public relations executive pitching a major newspaper. Now, storytelling is free, or nearly free, through social media.

Attorney, entrepreneur, and filmmaker Matt Weiss said, "People love hearing stories. It goes back to primitive tribal times when we used to sit around the campfire. With social media, consumers are in full control the whole time. If you're not captivating, you can lose them at any time. I use storytelling as a vehicle to get people to pay attention and then keep paying attention."

Every company has at least one story to tell, and most companies have lots of them. Ask yourself the following questions to generate some ideas:

- How did our company get started?
- How did we survive the toughest of times?
- Who are some key customers we've had?
- What kinds of funny or interesting things have happened involving customers or staff over the years?
- What employees' lives have been changed as a result of working for us?
- What charitable organizations have we supported?

Stories humanize brands and make them talkable, online and offline. Stories can be told with text, but they are often best told through pictures and videos. They can be told by customers, employees, or managers—they just need to be authentic.

How You Started

No matter how large your company is today, when it started, it was just your founder or founders with a dream and a plan. Every organization has humble beginnings, and by reminding people of this, you connect with your customers, and you keep them from considering your group as a faceless giant, too "corporate" for them to relate to.

You can spend millions of advertising dollars to buy television commercials to tell the story of how you got started, or you can produce gorgeous full-color brochures and mail them out to the world. Or you can tell this story online, using your website, blog, or any social media channels, for little to no cost.

What You Do for Your Customers

If you share stories that are less about you and more about your customers and the emotional experiences they have with your brand, you will create big wins. Consider how your customers have benefited from using your company. How have they grown, and what have you meant to them? How does your product make them feel? Remember, it's not about you. It's about your customers.

At a Word of Mouth Marketing Association conference I attended seven years ago, the topic of discussion was creating buzz-worthy, talkable customer experiences. One woman stood up and said, "My company is a storage company. We're totally boring." I raised my hand, and replied, "Quite honestly, storage has kept my marriage going strong. You see, I keep everything, and my wife usually throws everything out. If it weren't for storage and my ability to keep all of my old baseball cards and Garbage Pail Kids out of sight and mind, things would be a lot tougher for us."

Everyone laughed but took it to heart as well: what's boring to one person might be deeply meaningful to another. Any successful company, no matter what products or services it offers, has lots of stories to share about happy, inspired customers. Whatever your company does or sells, it solves people's problems somehow. You just have to think about what emotional connections your customers make around these problems and how your products or services have truly helped them. By the way, that storage company, Extra Space, soon became our client and now has more than 345,000 fans on Facebook, and it has been successfully using social media to drive leads for years.

Your Key Staff

The third source of great stories is the staff at your company. Maybe it's a senior executive, or maybe it's someone in the mailroom. It could be someone who worked her way up while going back to school and raising a family. Someone who works for you overcame adversity in his personal life to become a productive member of your team. A staff person who always has a smile on her face when serving customers is a story in itself as well. Maybe it's all of the above.

Your organization, no matter what you sell or what service you offer, has people behind it, and each person has a story to tell. You need to find the compelling stories and share them—through social media. In August 2009, a Facebook fan group popped up entitled "I Love Mary @ McDonalds/Chandler" (Figure 13.2).

FIGURE 13.2   Mary at McDonald's

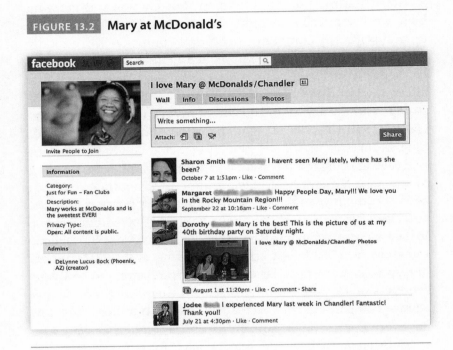

The group featured the description "Mary works at McDonald's and is the sweetest *ever!*" and a picture of Mary. Dozens of wall posts and more than 1,400 fans later, the group featured comments such as, "I just met Mary today! Yep, she is everything everyone says. She complimented my eyes. What a woman. I wish everyone was like her."

A PICTURE IS WORTH A THOUSAND WORDS, AND A VIDEO IS WORTH EVEN MORE

You've heard the saying, "A picture's worth a thousand words." When telling stories online, pictures and photographs are incredibly powerful tools. A huge reason for Facebook's explosive growth since its launch is its addictive Photos product—because people naturally love to view and share photos that have been "tagged" to include themselves and their friends. Pinterest and Instagram have also grown into leading social networks thanks to the popularity of pictures.

As an organization, you should harness this feature on Facebook by tagging and sharing photos of customers, staff, and management. Many Facebook pages recognize a "Fan of the Week," for instance, through which one customer's picture is featured on the page, and his or her story is told. In addition to making the Fan of the Week feel special, many selected fans choose to share the news with their friends, thereby increasing the organic virality of the page.

As valuable as pictures are, there is no better storytelling tool than video. Online videos ranging from 30 seconds to two minutes can captivate audiences in ways that only television advertising could in the past. Start by using your smartphone to film short clips of staff, customers, and senior management sharing their stories. If you capture 30 seconds of video from five people in each of those three categories, you'll quickly have at least a few usable videos to share on Facebook, YouTube, and your blog.

One unique feature of Facebook videos that are shared by company pages is that viewers can click inside the video to *like* the page that originally produced it. When you encounter a great video telling a story you want to share, you do so with your Facebook friends, who then have the opportunity to connect to the company that created the video at any point while watching by clicking *like*.

CREATING A STORY WHEN THERE ISN'T A NATURAL FIT

Drawing from the three categories of how you started, staff experiences, and customer experiences, you'll likely have lots of great stories to share. However, if you're in a highly regulated industry, such as financial or pharmaceutical, or if for whatever reason you can't find stories that you think will build an emotional connection with consumers, you can always use social media to create a new story to tell.

Fannie Mae, a company that provides finances for mortgage lenders, wanted to remind its B2B partners of the impact of their work—that their hours spent working on spreadsheets and the origination process translate to meaningful moments and transformative experiences for millions of Americans. During National Homeownership Month, Likeable helped Fannie Mae create a campaign that celebrated, invigorated, and reignited the passion of its customers, housing industry partners, and employees.

The campaign centered around the idea that Fannie Mae's partners are the *keys* that unlock opportunity; their work opens doors for those who dream of someday owning a home. The key motif was consistent in all social posts throughout the month, including calls to action that asked lenders and real estate agents to share key moments in their careers (generating over 2,540 engagements), a Facebook Canvas about the industry's key innovations, and custom data visualizations that used actual keys to demonstrate statistics about the rise of affordable and sustainable housing.

Each of the campaign assets could have been posted individually throughout the year, but by packaging them together and presenting the partners' hard work through the lens of National Homeownership Month, Fannie Mae was able to unlock a brand story worth talking about.

When you're brainstorming new outlets to share a story, keep in mind that if the story is not core to the customer experience, it's not as valuable. In other words, a bank or large corporation giving away millions of dollars on Facebook won't make up for practices such as excess fees, poor responsiveness, and bad customer service. Like Fannie Mae, think of the impact your brand is already making, and then turn it into a story.

NO MATTER YOUR COMPANY'S SIZE, YOU HAVE STORIES TO TELL

No matter if your company is large or small, new or old, well established or barely known, using stories through the social Web will help garner attention for your organization. Even if your brand has been essentially telling the same story for years, bringing this story online and into the social media conversation breathes new life into it. And if your brand is, well, brand-new, creating a fresh story around your company attracts customers and can invite them to be a part of this narrative. Consider the following two examples.

The Mindtree Journey

Mindtree, a multinational information technology company, got its start in 1999 when its founders took a road trip they refer to as a "7-day, 1000km meeting." That road trip set a precedent for its inspiring origin story: the team wrote its first proposal in the lobby of a Hilton Hotel; the first office desks were upside-down cardboard boxes.

Today, there are 43 offices and over 19,000 employees across the globe. But regardless of how big the company grows, it's always about where the company started. In 2017, the brand launched an employee recruiting campaign on social media that aimed to represent who they are—at every level. Likeable supported the campaign by building out a strategy that positioned the brand as the company next door: a friendly, relatable place where individual voices are heard, collaborative decisions are made, and trust is placed in every employee.

Content was developed within three pillars: The Philosophy of Possible, Mindtree Minds, and The Company Next Door, and social posts included employee origin stories set to mirror Mindtree's own advancement, a look into the company's Corporate Social Responsibility philosophy and mission of empowering and elevating women in STEM, and compilations of employees describing how they've been empowered through the culture and work. By making *who it is* part of *what it does* on social media, Mindtree's employee recruiting campaign drove over 20,000 clicks to the website careers page and influenced 86 hires (and counting).

Dr. Copeland and the Tooth Buggy

Dr. Jerry Copeland is one of the most likeable dentists I've ever met. Dr. Copeland is a pediatric dentist in Tampa, Florida, whose mission is to introduce dentistry to children in a pleasant atmosphere. He and his staff work tirelessly to teach good lifelong dental habits while entertaining their patients. Dr. Copeland doesn't call his patients "patients," however. To Dr. Copeland, they're his friends. Every week, Dr. Copeland tells his friends' stories.

Dr. Copeland gives each of his patients a "Tooth Buggy." The Tooth Buggy is a postcard with his logo on it—a happy red car shining its pearly whites. Dr. Copeland and his staff encourage the children to bring the postcard with them on their family vacations. In August 2014, Dr. Copeland told the story on Facebook of his eight-year-old friend who took the Tooth Buggy on an amazing European vacation. His album *The Tooth Buggy Went to Europe!* read:

> My friend took the Tooth Buggy on an amazing vacation to Europe. I think next year I will have the Tooth Buggy stay in Tampa and work while I go on the same incredible vacation. How many places can you name in this album?

The album got great engagement, and Dr. Copeland inspired more of his friends to share their stories. One of those "friends" even referred a new patient to the office!

ACTION ITEMS

1. Write down your company's founding story. How much do you know offhand about how your organization began? How can you package that story for easy consumption to share on social networks?

2. Research other stories your organization has that would be of interest to your audience. Develop a list of customer experiences, unique staff members, and community involvements that you think the world at large would want to hear about.

3. Determine how you will best share your stories. For instance, will you use a blog or online video? Will you focus on Facebook and Twitter? Is there a niche social network where your stories would be better received?

4. Decide how you can create new stories for your organization. What partnerships or charitable initiatives can you create that will help to drive them?

SO, WHAT'S YOUR STORY?

Do you have a story well articulated yet? You'll need to determine and polish interesting and enjoyable stories about your company. Then, you'll need to figure out the most effective ways to present your stories on the social Web so that others will digest, enjoy, and share them with their friends. If you use a compelling format to share stories and connect with your customers, you can expect your company's story on social networks to have a very happy ending.

CHAPTER 14

Inspire Customers and Influencers to Share Your Stories

It was November 16, 2008. A tweet from Avi Kaplan (Twitter .com/MeshugAvi) led to a phone call, and suddenly, my wife and I were being pitched on participating in a social media fundraiser that was about to launch. The plan was still pretty loosely defined at the time, but it seemed awfully exciting: people would be asked to share on Twitter what they were thankful for around Thanksgiving, and they would have the opportunity to give a donation to the nonprofit behind the event, Epic Change. The nonprofit seemed great. Its mission is to use storytelling to support projects dealing with people in need who can be helped through financial loans. In this Thanksgiving program, the organization's hope was to use money raised to support Mama Lucy, a chicken farmer in Tanzania who had started a school.

But moreover, the project and its leader, Epic Change cofounder Stacey Monk, were oozing with inspiration. So we volunteered to help with word-of-mouth and social media marketing, and we began to figure out the details with Stacey for what we would call TweetsGiving. Epic Change's plan was to launch and execute the program over the 48-hour period leading up to Thanksgiving Day in the United States, which was just seven days from our first discussion with organizers Stacey Monk and Avi Kaplan. They scrambled to get a website together, and they planned to get the word out to influential people on Twitter and Facebook, who would hopefully be as excited about the project as we had been and would not only share their stories of gratitude but also spread the word to their online friends and followers.

TweetsGiving came quickly, and it became one of the first successful fundraisers based on social media. Over that 48-hour period in 2008, thousands of people learned of Mama Lucy's story, and they shared their own stories of thanks through tweets, Facebook messages, blogs, and videos. Participants expressed gratitude for their friends and family, their colleagues and staff, their students and teachers, and anyone and everyone important to them. It was amazing to see so many people share stories in just 140 characters in tweets such as, "Thanks for all you have done for me & given me, mom. RIP, greatest mama ever. #tweetsgiving."

Hundreds of people also donated between $1 and $100 to an organization that, prior to that week, none of them had even heard of. In just 48 hours, TweetsGiving raised more than $11,000 in online donations in what would become one of the first successful Twitter fundraisers. For an organization with no previous database of donors, contacts, or prospects to speak of and for a campaign that was put together from start to finish in seven days, this was an incredible accomplishment.

One of the most successful nonprofits on social media is Charity:Water, an organization bringing clean drinking water to people in developing countries. It was the first charity to have one million followers on Twitter and was also one of the first three brands on Instagram to have over 80,000 followers. Because 70 percent of its contributions come from online donations and online fundraisers, social media is a key component of its strategy.

Scott Harrison started the organization on his thirty-first birthday, asking his friends to donate $31 for clean water efforts instead of giving him a gift. The birthday party ended up generating $15,000 and helped build Charity:Water's first few wells in Uganda. Soon after, social media users were able to initiate their own "MyCharity:Water Birthday" drives to replicate the success. The efforts extended to Charity:Water's website with a wall of those who donated their birthdays, linking to tweets in which they mentioned Charity:Water. The enormous successes of Epic Change and Charity:Water demonstrate the vast power of social media to spread the word quickly about causes, but they also show the unquestionable power of using social media to inspire people to get involved.

THERE'S NOTHING NEW ABOUT THE POWER OF INSPIRATION EXCEPT THE CHANNEL

The only thing that's better than sharing your company's stories on social networks is inspiring your customers and influential fans to share theirs. TweetsGiving wasn't powerful because of its own story, incredible as it was, but because of the thousands of stories it elicited. Inspiring your customers to share their stories is nothing new or unique to social media. In fact, this idea has always been a key component of word-of-mouth marketing. Social media just allows those stories to spread faster and farther than ever before.

Even 15 years ago, if you wanted to tell your friends about an experience you had with a company, you would call one or two of them on the phone and chat with them. Maybe, if you were particularly inspired, you could share your experience with as many as five or six friends. Today, if you want to tell others about an experience you have had with a company or product, you can update your Instagram Story, and with one click, share information with dozens or even hundreds of friends. Essentially, not much has changed from 15 years ago, but in terms of the speed and size of the audience you can disseminate information to, the ante has been upped. *A lot.*

BUILD WORD OF MOUTH INTO YOUR PRODUCTS AND SERVICES

The most effective way of inspiring your customers to tell others about you is to have buzz-worthy, talkable products and services in the first place. These products or features are the types that truly make you say, "Wow!" as a customer or in their very nature create passionate users. Take Facebook itself, for instance. It grew from several hundred users to several hundred million users in just five years, not because of any clever marketing whatsoever but simply because it had built amazing products that people loved and have continued to spread the word about. Even if you're not into Apple products yourself, surely you know a bunch of people who are Apple addicts. They talk about Apple, they write about Apple, they share about Apple, and some of them even sing about Apple. Again, these fans and followers praise the company not because of any marketing initiatives but because its products and features inspire passionate, loyal customers.

It's not always about the products either. Take Amazon, for instance. It started as a website that sold books and grew into a website that sells everything, and despite its transformation into an online retail megagiant, it continues selling amazing customer service. Yes, Amazon sells makeup, electronics, cleaning supplies, and entertainment. But it also sells one-click ordering. It sells free two-day shipping. It sells reliability and convenience. And those are the things that inspire people to share their stories directly or indirectly about Amazon every single day.

Do you have a "wow" factor for any of your company's products and services? Is there any aspect of an experience with your company that really knocks your customers' socks off and moves them to tell a friend, or 350 Facebook friends, about you? If not, what little can you do to increase the likelihood of creating "wow" moments? What about you is talkable right now?

FIND THE CUSTOMERS YOU INSPIRE THE MOST, AND GIVE THEM THE TOOLS TO SHARE

Although most people would argue that it's worth doing, not every company is actually able to inspire all of its customers the way organizations like Facebook, Apple, and Amazon do. The challenge, then, is to find which of your customers are most inspired by you and what you have to offer them. Then you need to give them the tools and opportunities to share their stories. The social networks themselves allow the stories to take off.

Facebook Groups: A Sparkling Way to Engage a Community

Gerolsteiner Sparkling Mineral Water is a wildly popular beverage in Europe, but it faces an awareness challenge in the United States due to limited distribution and strong competition. The brand wanted to use social media to get more Americans to taste the quality of and experience the health benefits of its product, so it launched a U.S.-specific Facebook page. Soon after, it noticed superfans visiting the page week after week to share their photos and positive experiences with the beverage.

Likeable saw an opportunity to engage these fans and give them an exclusive experience by asking them to participate in Gerolsteiner's first U.S. Sparkling Detox Challenge, an annual campaign in Europe where consumers are invited to replace their beverages with Gerolsteiner for five days. With the help of the Likeable team, Gerolsteiner created a Facebook group (Figure 14.1) to host the challenge, and the dedicated fans invited their friends and family to join too. As soon as the challenge kicked off, the group was flooded with health tips, recipe ideas, and words of encouragement and inspiration.

To fuel participation in subsequent years, a sweepstakes element was incorporated and health and wellness influencers were invited to share their tips and tricks with the community, but it all started with the inspiring customers who were already sharing their stories. Today, there are many thousands of members in the Facebook group—and they're already talking about how excited they are for next year's challenge.

FIGURE 14.1   **A Post in Gerolsteiner's Sparkling Detox Facebook Group**

Who Are Your Detoxers?

Who are your most passionate customers? Is it teenagers, perhaps? Or moms? How about hockey fans? Or CEOs? Maybe music-loving baby boomers? Whatever your customer base, there's a subset of them that includes your raving fans. If you can find these fans, connect them, and inspire them, you have the potential to start a powerful word-of-mouth movement. If you haven't found them yet, fortunately, social media provides you with tools and opportunities that were previously unavailable to do so.

First, do a quick search for your company's name or dedicated hashtag on Instagram. If you're a big brand, you might be surprised to find a blogger who is already sharing how your products make his or her life easier. If you're a small business, that person might be the captain of the high school football team or the town's local police chief. Tapping into customers who already have an authentic connection with your product or service will always be more beneficial than paying an "Instagram famous" model to add you to his or her list of contracted posts. But if you are looking to introduce your products to new influencers or brand ambassadors, you'll want to make sure they're the right fit. Try tools like NinjaOutreach, Klear, and GroupHigh to learn more about the demographics of your potential influencers' followers and fanbases, then make sure they align with your target audience.

Once you've identified your most passionate subset of customers or influencers, give them as many tools and opportunities as possible to share their stories about you on social networks. Recognition or encouragement of these customers can go a long way, and once people start seeing other customers posting their stories, it'll remind them of their own experiences that they might want to share. You may also want to consider the influence of this subset of customers and who among *them* is most influential. The reality is that someone with 4,000 Facebook friends sharing a story about you is likely much more valuable to you than someone with 40 friends sharing a similar story about you.

RECOGNITION INSPIRES STORIES

People love rewards and recognition, even when they're not monetary in nature. On Facebook and Instagram, for instance, we've implemented a lot of Fan of the Week or month initiatives for clients based on who shares the best story, picture, or video. For example, Scholastic's "Read to Your Dog, Man" campaign selected fans of the week based on people uploading pictures of their kids reading from *Dog Man*, a series by the creator of the classic *Captain Underpants* children's books, Dav Pilkey.

In general, fans of the week get their pictures added to the sponsoring brand's official pages, which is not only nice recognition for the fans but often leads to those chosen fans sharing the news with *their* friends. With the average number of Facebook friends per user around 350, and often more active users with even more friends than that, you can imagine how quickly communities can grow around this simple form of recognition.

Prizes Can Inspire Stories Too

Recognition is great, but prizes, including cash, really get people talking. If you can reward your customers with cool, out-of-the-box prizes, you will draw out your most enthusiastic customers to share their experiences. Think "a year's supply of . . . ," or, better yet, "a lifetime supply of . . . ," in exchange for the best poem, video, or picture that showcases how someone is using your product.

Unlike contests of old, of course, for which submissions were private and you could showcase top entries only by using them in your advertising campaigns, now, through online social channels, all submissions are public and shareable. If someone uploads an unbelievable or entirely unique video submission to a contest on YouTube, chances are it's going to get a lot of views, and if someone shares a hysterical photo submission on Instagram, it's probably going to generate lots of *likes* and comments.

Likeable recently developed a wildly successful user-generated content campaign for my personal favorite theme park, Great Wolf Lodge, a vacation destination for families with young children. Since the lodge is often seen as a bucket list item that's "one and done," the campaign was designed to start meaningful conversations with previous guests to encourage another visit. With fun, eye-catching photos and a simple prompt, Great Wolf Lodge asked parents to share their child's favorite summer "Tail from Great Wolf Lodge" in the form of a picture or comment for the chance to win a free family vacation for four (Figure 14.2). The campaign generated over 15,000 submissions, many of which will be repurposed into future social content, helping Great Wolf Lodge stretch its creative dollars and resources even further.

FIGURE 14.2   A Facebook Album of "Tails" from Great Wolf Lodge

> **Great Wolf Lodge**
> August 29 at 5:00 PM · 🌐
>
> All of these #TailsFromGreatWolf submissions have been paw-mazing!
> Thank you to everyone who submitted and congratulations to Amy Pummill,
> the lucky winner of a FREE family vacation to Great Wolf Lodge. We've also
> reached out to our 5 second-prize winners as well! 🐾

For big brands looking to give away lots of cash, charitable contests can inspire people to share their stories. PepsiCo diverted a huge chunk of its marketing and advertising budget in 2010 toward Pepsi Refresh, a global giving initiative hosted at PepsiRefresh.com, for instance, asking people to nominate causes they believed in and to share their experiences and stories related to these causes. PepsiCo gave away millions of dollars to community groups throughout the year through Pepsi Refresh, built a huge community of supporters, and created an army of people who associate Pepsi with the idea of not just refreshing your thirst but refreshing the world's neediest and most deserving.

Medtronic Share Your Story

Medtronic Diabetes is a world-leading medical device company dedicated to improving the lives of people with diabetes through its core products: insulin pumps and continuous glucose monitoring devices. Medtronic launched its Facebook and Twitter accounts in 2012. As a highly regulated brand in the pharmaceutical space, the company's presence in social media was revolutionary in many ways. However, because many of its indirect (and in some cases, direct) competitors, that is, bloggers, had been able to grow communities, it was critical that Medtronic launch with a campaign that would make a splash and put its customers in the center of everything.

And so Medtronic, along with Likeable Media, introduced a Facebook application designed to inspire loyalty, increase awareness, and cement the company as the branded diabetes destination on Facebook (Figure 14.3). The Share Your Story photo app (launched as the Let's Build Our Timeline Together app) gave the Facebook community a space for sharing their stories with the brand and with the rest of the community. These personal stories were about memorable moments that were made possible with the help of the types of products Medtronic offers its customers.

FIGURE 14.3   **Medtronic's Let's Build Our Timeline Together App**

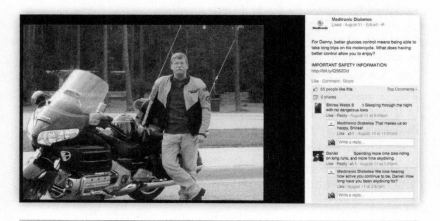

Never before had a brand in the healthcare space opened its Facebook page to the stories of its customers, and Medtronic took it one step further. When users submitted their stories, they were added to the social editorial calendar, and each story was shared with the growing Medtronic community. During launch, the app received over 250 submissions of stories and photos (80 percent of which the submitters allowed the brand to share with the rest of the Facebook community).

The stories that were then shared continued to be some of the highest-performing posts on the network, creating a residual storytelling effect as users have left comments about their own personal stories as well as words of encouragement to the individuals featured. From day one, the Medtronic Facebook community was about building a real community with the company's customers and people affected by diabetes, and the Share Your Story application helped propel them to enormous success.

Uno Pizzeria & Grill Makes a Happy Birthday for One Fan and Inspires Her to Share Her Story

Uno Pizzeria & Grill, mentioned briefly in Chapter 5, is probably best known for its Chicago deep-dish pizza but features a full lunch and dinner menu that can be found at 110 Uno locations across 21 states, the District of Columbia, and several other countries. Uno does, however, have just one location in Southern California, which made the following individual experience a lot easier to pull off successfully.

Kimberly Boynton, Uno's marketing director, ensures that all of the hundreds of monthly comments from more than 134,000 fans are responded to promptly and positively. She looks for interesting stories about customers' experiences and sees on a daily basis how people feel about Uno's services, food, and even online presence and social Web community. One fan posted that she loved Uno so much that she was driving *two hours* to the nearest Uno location in California to celebrate her birthday with family. In addition to responding to the customer with a typical "Thanks for all the Uno love. Have a happy birthday!" message, Kim decided to take the opportunity to further reward the customer for sharing her strong passion with an attempt at surprise and delight.

One phone call to the restaurant and two hours later, when the customer arrived at the Uno location with her family, the staff surprised them *upon entering* the restaurant with a song and cake.

"How in the world? . . ." the woman asked.

"You posted on Facebook," the manager replied with a smile. "Happy birthday."

Said Kim, "You can't always give a cake and song to everyone who posts on Facebook. But if you listen carefully, and respond to everyone, and take advantage of opportunities that come up along the way, it can go miles toward building a brand's reputation."

That night, using their mobile phones, the family shared their story through pictures of their experience at Uno with friends on Facebook. But in the weeks that followed, the return on investment for this small action really began to take form, as the family actively posted on Uno's Facebook page, shared a video, and continued to promote the brand. The customer inspired many others to share their positive experiences and stories as well.

ACTION ITEMS

1. Define your "wow" factor. What aspect of your products or services is truly worth talking about? If there isn't a "wow" factor, what steps can you take to begin to build the "wow" factor into your products, services, or processes?

2. Define your most passionate subset of customers. Who are they, what social networks are they on, how can you reach them, and what tools and opportunities can you give them to encourage them to share their stories?

3. Determine what incentives, if any, might be helpful in order to inspire and accelerate more word of mouth. Will recognition and rewards encourage your customers to share? Will contests, promotions, or giveaways help drive people to share? How about the occasional individual, direct offline interaction?

EMOTIONS GET YOUR CUSTOMERS
TO SHARE THEIR STORIES

If you can connect with your customers on a deeper, more emotional level, you'll be much more likely to inspire them to share their stories about you with their friends, family, and their own fans. Consider your target audience and consumers' tastes. Identify your most passionate subset of followers or customers, then recognize them and provide them with some type of incentive. What will make them want to become the most vocal supporters of your organization? How can you make them really happy, or thankful, or appreciative, or excited? How can you make them say, "Wow!"? How can *you* be a part of *their* stories?

CHAPTER 15

Integrate Social Media into the Entire Customer Experience

I was home with my three-year-old son Seth one day in July 2018 when I saw on Facebook that Build-A-Bear Workshop was having a one-day "Pay Your Àge" promotion. Customers were invited to bring their children to Build-A-Bear locations across the country where they could stuff their own animals for the price of their age (the bears normally start at $25, so it was an excellent deal).

Before making the 30-minute drive the next day, I decided to check out Build-A-Bear's Facebook page to see if there was anything I needed to know. "Please be aware: Based on the unprecedented response to our Pay Your Age Day event in our early opening stores, we are experiencing significantly longer than expected lines and large crowds," a post said. Surely not in Long Island, I thought.

When Seth and I got to the mall I knew it was a mistake. The line was "unbearable." Some parents reported a wait time of over five hours. I immediately opened Twitter to share a photo of the mess when I realized the gravity of this epic failure. Build-A-Bear had issued another statement. "The response to our Pay Your Age Day event has been overwhelming and unprecedented in our 21-year history," the post said. "The safety of our Guests and associates is our top priority." Mobbed with customers and overwhelmed with security issues, Build-A-Bear shut down the event halfway through the day. "We understand our affected Guests may be disappointed, and we are working to address the situation," the company said.

Build-A-Bear handed out $15 vouchers to those who waited in the excessive lines, but that wasn't enough to appease the angry parents. They took to social to voice their complaints, with one mom posting on Twitter, "Thanks @buildabear for ruining my 8 and 2 year olds' day by closing your pay your age event before our mall even opens!" The two cancellation announcements on Facebook racked up over 25,000 comments (mostly negative) and 69,000 shares. Build-A-Bear went from having an interesting, buzz-worthy social media promotion to creating a memorable, negative customer service experience. Their store locations weren't prepared, and whoever planned the social media promotion clearly didn't realize the repercussions of the seemingly great idea. The promotion was so "successful" it failed.

SOCIAL MEDIA IS NOT JUST MARKETING

Social media leveraging is not simply marketing or public relations. There is no way for an organization to use social media successfully if the organization silos the work to marketing or advertising. In order to optimize the results from your social media use, you have to integrate understanding and practice across a diverse group of functions and departments in your organization.

Of course, social media provides great outlets for marketing, public relations, and advertising, but it also involves customer service, customer relationship management, sales, operations, human resources, and research and development. Ideally, *anyone at your company who could possibly ever come into contact with a customer should be trained on the fundamentals of likeable social media*: listening, transparency, responsiveness, and engagement. Furthermore, there are numerous opportunities throughout the customer experience for integration of social networks and social media best practices. The more open and transparent you are with customers throughout the entire customer life cycle, the more comfortable they'll feel about continuing to buy your stuff, hire you, *like* you and your pages, and recommend you to friends.

Put on your consumer cap again, and imagine the following experience. You're at home, logged into Facebook, where you see an ad for a local restaurant your friend has *liked*. You decide to visit for lunch. You enjoy a meal, and your server, along with your printed receipt, encourages you to share feedback about your experience, good or bad, on the restaurant's Facebook page. You post a mostly favorable review that night, but you mention that the dessert was a little disappointing. A manager immediately responds to your post, saying, "I'm sorry," and offers you a gift certificate to come back soon.

Social Media Should Be Integrated Across All Customer-Facing Departments

This type of teamwork, across different roles and departments, is what made the experience so satisfying for you, not social media. Yet everyone you came into contact with had to understand Facebook and be fluent in social media in order for that teamwork to actually function, unlike my experience with Build-A-Bear. If you have a very small operation, you're used to handling many tasks on your own. But assuming you're part of a larger organization, let's review various departments and consider how each one might integrate and encourage social media in order to optimize the customer experience at every corner:

- **Advertising.** Include social media links and value propositions to customers in all paid linear media. For example, television, radio, print, email, websites, and direct mail should all include social media links. The advertising department may also handle social network ads themselves, a growing part of most ad budgets.

- **Marketing.** Determine, create, execute, and measure promotions, contests, giveaways, other marketing programs, and content to be run on Facebook, Instagram, and other social networks. Marketing is where social media typically lives right now, even though it should have a home in every department.
- **Public relations.** Listen to customer comments on social networks and blogs, and respond in a swift manner. Determine the most influential bloggers and other key customers online, and reach out to them to pitch them on participating in programs.
- **Customer service.** Listen to customer complaints and requests across social networks, and respond. Encourage customers who reach out via traditional channels to share their feedback publicly on social networks.
- **Operations.** Create and implement social media policy. Ensure that all staff members are fluent in understanding company social media links and practices and that signage, receipts, and any other customer touchpoints include opportunities to interact and share.
- **Sales.** Listen carefully to prospects online as well as major potential partners and distributors. Leverage listening to create best-value propositions. Have salespeople use LinkedIn to meet and engage prospects.
- **Research and development.** Listen to your customer sentiment and competitors' customer sentiment in order to design new products. Leverage social networks to survey and ask key questions of your customer base.
- **Senior management including the CEO.** Serve as online spokespeople for the brand through Twitter, LinkedIn, video, and blog. Interact publicly with key partners, stakeholders, and media.
- **Information technology.** Ensure that your website is up-to-date with social links, content, retargeting pixels, plug-ins, and applications. Ensure that social media data is secure. Manage Facebook applications and any other social media and mobile applications.

Customers Don't Care What Department You're In

When should a customer's comment on Instagram be answered by customer service versus sales, versus public relations, versus marketing, versus your agency? That's all up to you. The truth is, the key challenge isn't making sure you know exactly who should answer what kind of comment and when. Instead, the issue is making sure that as many people as possible are fluent in social media, are part of the team, and are treating every customer well!

Customers don't care about your job title or what department you're in. If they have problems, then they want solutions. When you're looking for something specific in a supermarket and you find a staff person and ask for help, a good supermarket will have that staff person trained to walk you to the correct aisle. The employee will help you, with a smile, whether he or she happens to be the butcher, the baker, a cashier, or a janitor. The situation applies to the use of social media too. Try thinking of every post on Facebook, Twitter, or your blog as one that could have been written by the most important celebrity customer you've ever had, and you'll be more likely to treat every customer and every post with great care, no matter your official department or role.

DO YOU NEED A WEBSITE ANYMORE?

If you have a small business like a plumbing or a painting company, you can do just about anything with Facebook that you'd want to do with a traditional website, whether you need order forms, sales carts, or secure data, or you need to utilize any other Web content or functionality. With Facebook, however, you have the added advantage of performing all of these processes in a place where two billion or so of your potential customers are hanging out. It's the idea of fishing where the fish are, rather than expecting the fish to come to your boat, or in this case, visit your website.

In 2009, Skittles, the popular candy brand, briefly redirected all traffic from Skittles.com to its Facebook and Twitter presences. This transfer was short-lasting, and it was more of a publicity stunt than an attempt at real engagement. But it proved a point: brands no longer have any control of the Web content people see about their companies. So rather than try to show people a prepackaged view of what you think they should see about your company (on a website that few people will trust anyway), you might consider a total surrender of control and respond to what people are saying, where and when they're saying it. In the meantime, though, you likely do have a website, and it's essential therefore that the website is as integrated with social media as possible. If you have only a tiny link at the bottom of your website to "Join us on Facebook, and follow us on Instagram," you're not leveraging the opportunity to connect to people.

Facebook's social plug-ins, including the Like button and other assorted interactive elements such as Share, are imperative to smoothly and deeply integrating Facebook into your Web presence.

Imagine if, for instance, instead of trying to sell people your product or service, whatever it may be, on your website, all you did was try to convince people to *like* your website's content. You'd get fewer sales at first, of course, but over time, more and more visitors to your website would see how many people *liked* you. More important, you'd increase the likelihood that one of the site's next visitors would see that her friend has already given your site, services, products, or content personal approval. *Is there any sales or promotional content anywhere on the Web more valuable than the honest words, "Your friend* likes *this"?*

HOW CAN YOU MAKE YOUR CONTENT, PRODUCTS, AND SERVICES AS AVAILABLE AS MOBILE FOOD TRUCKS?

New technologies have made it easier than ever for consumers to access what they want. People don't need to go to bookstores to get books, flower stores to get flowers, or shoe stores to get shoes. People also don't need to buy newspapers or magazines to read articles. Thanks to the growth of mobile food trucks, you don't even need to go to restaurants to buy meals anymore in many cities. Now is the best time ever to be a consumer. Just remember, as a marketer, it is necessary that you make it as easy and efficient as possible for people to access your products, services, or content. How can you bring it to them, wherever they are on the Web?

Where in the marketing and communications process can you remind people to engage with you on the social Web? You can integrate your social links and value proposition on your website, in your emails, in your linear media, and on your packaging. You can have salespeople, receptionists, customer service people, and the mailroom all finish their phone calls with, "Ask us questions or leave feedback anytime on our Facebook page." Right now, when you call up any big company and wait on hold, you're told to visit its website. But a website is too often a static environment, so why not consider directing people to an interactive environment where they can quickly get the help they need?

LIKEABLE CUSTOMER SERVICE
IS IMPORTANT TOO

It doesn't matter how good your marketing is if your customer service doesn't make people smile. It doesn't matter how much you spend on advertising to acquire Instagram followers or Facebook likes if you don't respond to people's questions or comments. The bigger and more complicated the world gets, the simpler and more connected and transparent it gets as well. So *before* you spend lots of time and money on likeable social media, you've got to make sure you have likeable customer service, likeable salespeople, likeable products, and likeable processes. Whether you do or not, your customers will notice and share their experiences with others. It is worth training every staff person at your organization now and in the future on your social media presence and best practices for communicating with customers and prospects.

Tragically, many companies still don't even allow computer access to Facebook for employees at work. This is disappointing for two major reasons. First, the reality is that everyone can access Facebook and Twitter now from their mobile phones, so the idea that limiting computer access to social networking sites will keep productivity up simply isn't practical. Second, and more important, not allowing employees to talk to customers through social networks is like telling all of the staff at a supermarket, "You're not allowed to talk to customers walking around looking for help. Unless you're in the marketing department, of course."

Dr. Charles Waisbren: A Likeable Doc

Dr. Charles Waisbren has practiced medicine in Milwaukee, Wisconsin, for nearly 30 years. As a general physician, Dr. Waisbren prides himself on "service like it used to be; medical care how it ought to be." In the age where more and more independent practices are being bought out by larger organizations, Dr. Waisbren works tirelessly to maintain a "family feel."

"You always see the same receptionist when you walk in. You always see the same nurses. You always see the same doctor," Dr. Waisbren said. "Trust is so important in this kind of relationship."

Recently, Dr. Waisbren dove head first into social media. When the patient sits down in his chair, he asks her to take out her smartphone and directs her to *like* the practice on Facebook. "It's not about collecting a ton of *likes*," he adds. "It's about adding another direct line of communication between me and patient." He personally fields questions and concerns on the page regularly. When patients don't have a smartphone, Dr. Waisbren takes out his pad and writes a very important prescription: "*Like* FB.com/drwaisbren and ask questions often" (Figure 15.1).

San Rafael: Launching a Brand and Building a Community

San Rafael is a brand with a long tradition in Mexico, where it got its start in 1948. It was known first and foremost for selling lunch meats and hot dogs, but it expanded over the years to include other delicatessen specialties in countries in Central America and the Caribbean. In 2013, the brand introduced a line of quality Mexican cheese to U.S. consumers—its first foray into the United States. Not only was the company launching a

FIGURE 15.1	Dr. Waisbren: "Ask Questions Often"

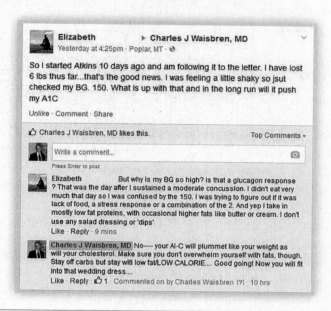

product line, but it was also essentially launching its brand to a group of consumers who didn't know the name San Rafael. The brand simply didn't carry the equity in the United States that it did in Mexico.

San Rafael launched a Facebook page six months prior to the launch of its product. In the midst of planning all the details of a product launch, the company spent a considerable amount of time perfecting its packaging look and feel to ensure that it would resonate with U.S. consumers. Prominently featured on each variety of cheese's package were the social media credentials prompting users to stay connected with the brand and learn the brand's story. In-store displays and product placements, along with special offers, are what got the U.S. consumers to try the cheese. A great product with a great social media community to match is what kept those customers coming back for more. Today, San Rafael has built up a community of Facebook users who have *liked* its page *and* eat its cheese. Launching a product in the age of social media allows you to quickly establish credibility and trust with your new consumers, so making sure they know where to find you from that first interaction needs to be a key part of the launch strategy.

ACTION ITEMS

1. Determine who else besides you at your organization can have a role in using social media to interact with customers. Form a cross-departmental task force to better integrate social media into all of your business practices and operations.
2. Closely examine all of the available inventory, assets, time, and space you have to promote your Facebook and Instagram presence. As you grow your presence, where can you remind people to join the conversation? Where can you share your value proposition for *liking* your company and following you? Have you integrated social media links into your traditional advertising, packaging, and website yet?
3. Integrate Facebook's Like button into as many products and objects on your website as make sense. The easier you make it to be likeable, the more likeable you'll become.

EVERYONE AND EVERYTHING IS A PART OF WORD-OF-MOUTH MARKETING

An argument can be made that every single person at your company who ever talks to a customer or prospect has an opportunity to create a word-of-mouth marketing experience, for better or for worse. And every moment that a customer spends looking at any of your materials online or offline is an opportunity to either be likeable or unlikeable. Create as many advocates for social media at your organization as you can, and get help integrating a social media-friendly culture throughout your company. Ensure that you are using social media as fully and as deeply as possible, and you'll also be as likeable as possible.

CHAPTER 16

Admit When You Screw Up, and Then Leverage Your Mistakes

On June 3, 2010, LOFT, a clothing brand owned by Ann Taylor Inc., posted pictures of a tall, blonde catalog model in the brand's new silk cargo pants on its Facebook page with a click-to-buy link in the caption.

Nothing about the post was uncommon in social media, and it certainly was not uncommon for the fashion industry. But for whatever reason, fans responded particularly negatively to this post. While many fans acknowledged that the pants looked good on the model, they complained that the pants were "not universally flattering" and would "look great if you're 5 foot 10 and a stick like the model in the photo." Fans on the page began demanding that LOFT show the pants on "real women."

Many companies, if not most companies, would have done nothing in response to the fans. The entire fashion industry essentially has been built upon images of super-thin models rather than real women, and few protests have changed anything through the years.

But two days later, LOFT posted an "I'm sorry" on its Facebook page along with pictures of "real women" wearing the pants that had been modeled on the page just days earlier. In fact, the female staff of Ann Taylor posted pictures of *themselves* wearing the pants (Figure 16.1).

FIGURE 16.1 **Loft Staff Models**

LOFT Hi! My name is Julie and I am LOFT's Manager of Digital Programs. Yesterday we received a request to show our new silk cargo pants on real women. Through the day we will be showcasing women at LOFT wearing the pant. To get us started I am posting a gallery showing how I wear the pant at work, at night, and on the weekend.

I am 5'3" and a size 6 and a regular shopper of LOFT's petite collection though I shop regular sizes as well.

How I Wear Our New Silk Cargo Pant

June 17 at 11:53am · Like · Comment · Share

👍 43 people like this.

💬 View all 48 comments

The Facebook community rejoiced. Better yet, word spread quickly about what it had done, and LOFT ended up receiving lots of well-earned media attention from the fashion industry and the online world. Years later, a look at the page still shows mostly pictures of skinny models wearing LOFT clothing, but it also shows quick responses from LOFT staff to all comments and questions from fans—the good, the bad, and the ugly. The page also highlights a community that's grown a great deal since June 2010—up to more than 1.8 million fans today.

What did LOFT do? Quite simply, the company admitted a mistake quickly and fixed it. By sharing pictures on Facebook of themselves, in different shapes and sizes, the staff showed they were willing to open themselves up to vulnerability and "be real" with their customers and audience. Not only did LOFT make up for its mistake almost immediately but it was able to connect on a personal level to those customers it had offended. It was even able to seize an opportunity the mistake gave it to stand out in a good way.

TWO SIMPLE WORDS GO A LONG WAY

Being able to say "I'm sorry" when you make a mistake goes a long way toward making up for your error. Companies are made up of people, and everyone makes mistakes sometimes, so it's inevitable that companies are bound to do something to upset or otherwise anger their customers occasionally. The issue, and what's particularly frustrating, is when companies don't apologize and take care of the problem with speed.

Anyone who's ever dated someone knows, after listening, being able to say "I'm sorry" is the most important ability in a relationship—and it's the same thing for companies. Especially when companies become large, are publicly traded, or have big legal teams, it can be difficult to have someone simply say, "I'm sorry." But it's *always* the right thing to do.

HOW TO SAY YOU'RE SORRY

The best way to tell your consumers you're sorry is to have the highest-ranking person at your organization, that is, your chief executive officer, say it online through a short video that addresses the problem and how it's going to be fixed. Having your organization's leader speak tells customers that your company is taking the matter seriously. Responding on video humanizes your company in a way that no press release or letter ever could. And keeping it short and sweet is respectful of your customers' time. Your CEO should be prepared to be as humble and natural as possible.

If your CEO is not good on camera, consider having another high-ranking leader make the video apology instead. This person should still be someone in senior management, and he or she needs to speak on behalf of your whole team. Also, your CEO could write a note, though this is likely to be less effective. Still, if a note is the best option considering your business leader's on-air personality, then the letter should be as friendly and genuinely written as possible—try to keep the legalese and corporate-speak out of it.

PLAN FOR THE UNPLANNED

You know your company will make mistakes, but you don't know when they will come, what they will be, and whom they will offend. The best thing to do now, then, is to plan for the unplanned. For many years, companies have had public relations firms or internal PR teams develop crisis communications plans. The major difference now is that word spreads much faster online than ever before. The longer it takes your company to respond to an issue, the worse a problem can skyrocket, too. So, before you make the mistakes that you're sure to make, create a cross-departmental team of people who will be able to swiftly handle whatever situation comes up and determine the appropriate social media response.

Teach the Lawyers How to Be Human

Lawyers and corporate communications executives have an uncanny ability to take the words "I'm sorry" and ruin them. And the worst time to argue with your attorneys is in the midst of a crisis. So it's important now that your company plans out what kind of language you will and won't be able to use when a crisis comes. Simple, direct language is almost always better than corporate-speak, *especially* in a social media setting. More relaxed language allows you to be seen as real, vulnerable, and human—and it's way more difficult for customers to be angry at actual vulnerable, real human beings than at an "evil corporation" (as they'd likely see you, even if only at the time of crisis). Just let your lawyers know that in such a situation, you'll want to say, "We're sorry. We screwed up." This alone will make you way more prepared than most companies.

Have Fire Drills

Just as you had fire drills at school so that in the event of a fire, everyone would know what to do, the only way to prepare for inevitable crises is to have your own drills. Imagine the craziest of challenges. For example, a customer dies while eating at your restaurant, or an employee pulls out a rifle at your store's counter (the crazier or more unlikely, the better). Of course, hopefully nothing like this will actually happen, but something else you haven't imagined will.

So what's the plan? Who meets from different teams—and how quickly? What happens if the crisis occurs on a Friday night? What if the vice president of communications is on vacation at the time? Social media is 24/7/365—you'll need a plan to respond quickly, no matter what. How will you communicate with your customers? What about with your employees, partners, and vendors?

It may seem silly to prepare for something that may never happen, but if you don't prepare for a social media crisis, and you're very slow to respond, or simply respond poorly, when one does occur, serious damage can be caused to your brand. Think about British Petroleum's (BP) response to the 2010 Gulf of Mexico oil spill, for instance. If BP had responded faster, more seriously, and more genuinely on Facebook and Twitter, it might have much better protected its reputation—and its stock price.

DON'T STOP AT I'M SORRY

Saying you're sorry is just the beginning of how you'll deal with a crisis. More important than ever before is the ability to listen and respond to what people are saying on social networks. Hopefully, you'll have integrated this process into your regular business practices by the time a serious issue occurs, but if for whatever reason you haven't, you'll need a plan to allocate more resources to online community management because your communities on Facebook and Twitter will surely see more traffic during a time of crisis.

Whenever possible, apologize individually to each person's complaint, and continue to follow up. By swiftly responding and showing you care, you can actually take a serious mistake and end up with an even stronger reputation than you had before it happened. Mistakes and crises will come in different shapes and sizes as well—and you'll want to have different levels of responses. But the most important thing to do, no matter what, is to genuinely care, show you care, apologize quickly, and then fix the problem.

Flying High vs. Flying Low in the Airline Industry

Airlines are among the most hated companies in the United States, and one company that keeps screwing up is United. On April 9, 2017, a Twitter user posted a video showing passenger David Dao being violently pulled from his seat and dragged down the aisle of a plane. Less than 24 hours later, it was one of the biggest news stories in the country. The videos posted across Twitter and Facebook immediately went viral; the Facebook version had more than 19 million views before it was no longer publicly available on the platform.

Around noon the following day, United's chief executive officer issued a statement, which only apologized for the airline needing to "re-accommodate" passengers on the flight—not for the one who was dragged off the plane. The statement was posted across social media, and it infuriated the Internet audience even more. Twitter users instantly started trolling United's approach to customer service, and social feeds were flooded with memes and parody accounts. The incident remains one of the worst public relations crises in history.

JetBlue, however, has a strong brand—one that is well regarded and highly rated by its customers. In February 2007, the company experienced a major crisis when a set of storms and a wide variety of internal challenges over the course of one week saw hundreds of flights canceled and thousands of passengers stranded. What could have been a total disaster for JetBlue's reputation was saved by its fast, appropriate online response. Founder and then-CEO David Neeleman filmed a three-minute YouTube video in which he apologized and made a commitment to customers that nothing like this would ever happen again. The video was shared on Facebook and Twitter, and hundreds of thousands of people saw it. Neeleman followed up the recorded video with traditional media appearances, even including one on the *Late Show with David Letterman*. He was humble and showed that he was committed to fixing things.

Despite one of the worst weeks in any airline's history, this potentially devastating blow to the brand has long been forgotten, and JetBlue quickly was restored as a market leader in customer satisfaction. Over the years, as social media has grown, JetBlue has remained one of the top airlines to use tools such as Facebook and Twitter to engage customers, always flying the extra mile. In 2014, for example, a man tweeted to JetBlue asking why he was charged $50 for taking an earlier flight. Within minutes, a JetBlue employee responded to his tweet and forwarded the interaction to the staff at the airport he was at. After studying the man's Twitter profile picture, the airport staff then went to find the Twitter user so they could follow up with him in person (Figure 16.2).

The Domino's Brand Is Rescued from the Brink of Disaster

In April 2009, two employees of a Domino's Pizza in North Carolina inexplicably filmed a video they shared on YouTube in which they did disgusting things with food they were preparing for customers, including wiping the food against different parts of their bodies. The video had a train-wreck quality to it: since it was so filthy, most people found it hard to eat anything for a while after viewing the footage. Yet hundreds of thousands of people did view the video, and parts of it appeared on national television broadcasts as well.

> **FIGURE 16.2**   **A Tweet from a Delighted JetBlue Customer**

Domino's responded immediately with a letter on its website apologizing. The company fired the employees and committed to prosecute them to the fullest extent allowed under the law. U.S. Domino's president Patrick Doyle also issued a video apology, although it came a full week after the initial incident. But what else is a brand to do to respond to such a literally filthy crisis? As a quick-serve restaurant, its reputation for food quality wasn't the best to begin with, and this was as horrible a situation as the company and its customers could imagine.

What Domino's ended up doing was starting over, launching an ad campaign, supported by a four-minute-long YouTube and Facebook video, in which it showcased customers talking about how little they liked the taste of Domino's. The video actually quoted people saying they thought the crust tasted like cardboard, along with other highly critical comments. Then the video showcased the Domino's staff working together to create a *brand-new, better-tasting pizza* (Figure 16.3). The campaign actually made people feel like Domino's, a corporate giant, was an underdog listening to its customers and trying to become a better company. That's probably because it really was.

FIGURE 16.3   **Domino's Turns It Around**

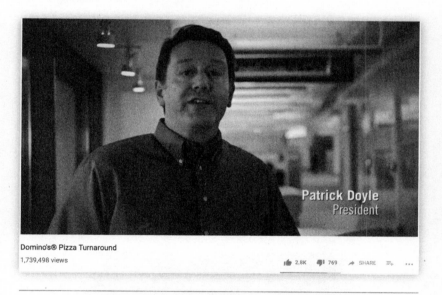

Domino's® Pizza Turnaround
1,739,498 views   👍 2.8K   👎 769   ➔ SHARE   ⋯

The four-minute-long video, too long for television advertising but perfect for YouTube, didn't garner as many views as the disgusting video, of course, but at more than 1.7 million, it came close. Moreover, it humanized the brand and connected it to customers at a time when it was most needed. The story doesn't end there, though. Domino's focus on transparency and technology has not gone unnoticed by investors. In fact, an investment in Domino's at the start of 2010 has grown by more than 2,000 percent to date, leaving the likes of Amazon, Google, Facebook, and Apple in the dust!

McDonald's Sends a Rogue Tweet

On the eve of Black Friday in 2017, McDonald's posted a tweet that seemed to have been scheduled before it was ever complete (Figure 16.4):

> Black Friday **** Need copy and link****

After eight hours, McDonald's responded to its own tweet in the thread with an image of a man drinking coffee, shedding humor on the situation:

> When you tweet before your first cup of McCafé . . . Nothing comes before coffee.

FIGURE 16.4   **McDonald's Saves Itself**

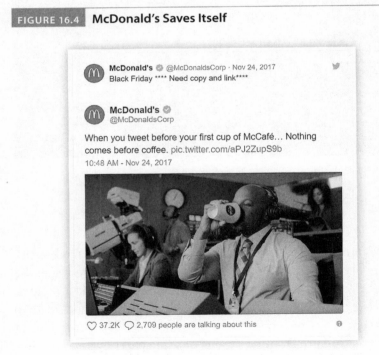

Twitter fans loved the response, one writing, "Please give whoever did that original tweet a break and whoever saved it a raise. If it's the same person—a big breakfast platter." McDonald's knew not to break the "do not delete" rule, but the mistake wasn't significant enough to warrant a formal apology. The calm and humorous reaction is a great example of a brand using creativity to leverage a mistake.

Citizens Bank Shows Humanity

In May 2018, Citizens Bank's online account access went down, and the company immediately turned to Facebook to update its customers:

> For periods of time this morning, access to Citizens Bank accounts via mobile and online banking was unavailable. We've been working to resolve the issue and some users are now able to access their accounts online. We'll continue to work to restore all access for customers, and will post an update as a comment to this message. Sorry for the inconvenience this may have caused.

Angry comments flooded in. If you're in a regulated industry, or if your social pages get so many comments you need a database of approved responses, you know how difficult it can be to give a personalized response to every individual. In this case, the customers caught on. One user commented:

> Any chance we can get a non-canned response from the human running the Citizens Facebook page? We know you're a real live person back there who likes eating pizza and watching movies, hanging with your pals. Can you give us a short 1-sentence statement that will actually convince us that Citizens cares at all about actually connecting with their customers? Doesn't even have to be related to this topic.

In the midst of dealing with all the other frustrated customers, Citizens Bank took a step back to address this person in the most human way possible. Along with a GIF from the popular TV show F.R.I.E.N.D.S., Citizens Bank responded:

You couldn't be more right, Jim, and I'm sorry for going over one sentence but . . . I do love pizza (pepperoni's my fave) and prefer F.R.I.E.N.D.S. at the end of every day. If I couldn't grab a slice for lunch with my own friends, because my accounts were unavailable, I'd feel defeated. That's why it is extremely important to me that I read every message that comes in from each of you, so I can pass your words along and do all I can to make things right. Us pizza-lovers have to stick together! If nothing else, know this: I'll be there for you.

The informal, humble tone of its message told customers that Citizens Bank was listening to them and cared about what they had to say. The quick decision might not have been possible from a less flexible, more traditional executive team. But in times of crisis, quick decisions are more essential than ever. The whole incident improved the Citizens Bank's overall reputation, with other customers engaging positively with the comment.

ACTION ITEMS

1. Create a social media crisis plan. What will you do if a customer shares a negative experience on YouTube, or a promotion goes awry, or a planned communication doesn't go as hoped? Who will respond publicly, and how? Who will be ultimately accountable for decisions?

2. Work with your legal team and corporate communications team now to establish some guidelines so that if and when a situation arises, you can quickly respond using humble, personal language.

3. Once you have a plan established, conduct a fire drill or two to see how well your organization responds.

4. Make sure you are listening in closely and keeping watch on the online conversation about your company—even on weekends and holidays.

AS LONG AS YOU PLAN FOR THE UNEXPECTED AND CAN SAY YOU'RE SORRY . . .

Humans have an amazing ability to forgive one another for mistakes, and they can even forgive companies too (especially when they're reminded that compassionate, understanding, and reasonable people are behind the company in question). The challenge as an organization comes only when you're not prepared or you are inflexible in your ability to respond when mistakes and crises do emerge. As long as you create a plan in advance, and as long as you're able to publicly, quickly, and authentically say you're sorry, you can maintain a strong brand reputation in the face of any social media challenge.

CHAPTER 17

Consistently Deliver Excitement, Surprise, and Delight

I was at a business conference several years ago, tweeting some of the things I was learning throughout, as I always do. One of the speakers recommended the book *Built to Last*, by Jim Collins, as a must-read. I had heard of it before, and I wanted to remember to buy it while also sharing some of the speaker's wisdom, so I tweeted, "Recommended Biz Book: *Built to Last*. Anyone read it?"

I got a few responses, but my favorite was from Jesse Landry, someone who was following me on Twitter and whom I'd never met, who responded, "I'd be happy to overnight my copy to you if you do not have a copy already."

Not "Great book, Dave, you should check it out," or even "I'd be happy to loan that to you." He offered to overnight it to me. I was immediately wowed. I responded that I certainly didn't need it sent overnight, but that sure, thanks, I would take it, and I gave him my address. Of course, he still overnighted it to me. *Double* wow.

I looked at Jesse's profile and found out he was a consultant for Administaff (now known as Insperity), a company that provides human resources support for small- to medium-size businesses. Jesse didn't pitch me on ever working with him. If he had, I probably would have said, "Thanks, but no thanks," and I would have assumed that he had overnighted the book in order to win my business. Instead, I got excited to see what he did for a living, investigated his company, and determined if he could provide services that I might need someday.

Jesse sent me the book "just because" and received nothing directly in return. As it turns out, of course, months later, I explored the potential of outsourcing Likeable Media's human resources work. Naturally, I turned to Jesse and Administaff to perhaps help solve my problem. But Jesse had no way of knowing I would consider using his services when he sent me the book. *He just sent it.*

If you can figure out ways to do little things for your customers and your online communities, to surprise and delight them, to provide unexpected value, or to add a smile to an individual consumer's face, you will always stand out, be remembered, and win the community's business. If it was important to be remarkable *before* the age of online social media, it's essential to stand out today, when word can spread lightning fast. How can you be remarkable on social networks?

YOU ARE ALREADY AHEAD
OF THE COMPETITION

The good news is, simply by doing the basics of likeable social media, such as listening and responding with transparency to everyone's comments about you on Facebook, you're way ahead of so many companies that still maintain a broadcast mentality when using social networks. But eventually the world, and your competition, will catch up and understand social media best practices. On social media now, you're not just competing with your real-life competitors for attention. You're competing with all of your customers' friends and the brands that they are already attached and connected to. You're competing with pictures and video of your cousin's new baby!

So it's your job to figure out not how you can be better but *how you can be different.* Everything you've read in this book up until now has been about meeting the standards for excellence on social networks. But how do you exceed expectations? How can you do the little things (and the big things) to stand out from your competition? How can you use social networks to be different, to truly create as many "wow" moments as possible? How can you operationalize "surprise and delight"?

The Little Things Matter

Many times it's the little extra things that matter the most. In this chapter's opening story, Jesse definitely didn't need to overnight the book to me—in fact, I hope he got a good deal on it because the shipment may have been more expensive than the book itself. But this action stood out. What little things can you do to separate your company from the pack and have consumers and prospects take notice? The truth is, a lot will depend on the specific nature of your business and your online communities.

One thing you can do is "listen" to conversations that are not necessarily about your company and respond to questions that aren't directly aimed at you. Become part of these conversations, and get involved in the community related to your company or industry, but don't try to push your organization or a sales pitch onto consumers. Listening is particularly easy to do on Twitter, where conversation with strangers is the norm. So if you're a real estate agent, for example, you could listen for people asking questions about getting bank loans for down payments in your town and answer these questions with links to helpful online articles. Or if you're a local bed and breakfast, you might listen for people asking questions about great vacation spots and recommend a few colleagues in exotic locations whom you met at a trade show.

If you can provide unexpected value to people on Twitter and LinkedIn and expect nothing in return, you can create "wow" moments that collectively will have an impact on your business. Those vacation spots you recommended to others on Twitter will eventually have an opportunity to recommend you to their followers, for instance. Or if the articles you've supplied about loans are extremely helpful, these potential buyers may seek your assistance when purchasing a home.

Best Buy was the first large company to begin delivering unexpected value on Twitter in the form of answering people's questions. It developed the Twelpforce, a group of nearly a thousand employees who were trained to respond to people's questions on Twitter about electronics products. When one of these hundreds of staff people wasn't on the store floor helping an in-person customer, he or she was helping online customers or prospects—and answering any questions about electronics products, *including products not sold at Best Buy.*

The Big Things Matter Too

In April 2017, 16-year-old Carter Wilkerson tweeted at fast-food chain Wendy's asking how many retweets it would take to get free chicken nuggets for a year. "18 million," Wendy's replied. One month later, Carter's rally cry on Twitter surpassed Ellen DeGeneres's famous Oscars selfie and became the most retweeted tweet of all time. The 3.42 million retweets may not have satisfied the original agreement, but it was enough for Wendy's. Not only did the company give Carter a year of free chicken nuggets, it made a $100,000 donation in his name to the Dave Thomas Foundation for Adoption. Carter continues to raise money on his website, NuggsforCarter.com.

What started as a silly response on Twitter turned into a major win for Wendy's. It could easily have ignored Carter's initial request, but by giving attention to one excited fan, it built an energized community of 3.42 million in the process—and the hundreds of millions of people who saw those retweets in their feeds!

Cisco, the worldwide leader in networking, is a huge technology company, but it realizes the importance of delighting customers through social media. It's managing to find ways to integrate social media into all of its business practices. In 2013, I talked with Petra Neiger, then social media marketing manager at Cisco, and she told me this:

> We believe engagement needs to happen on multiple levels—from sharing information to conversing, and finding ways to excite, inspire, and nurture our customers and partners. Each approach has its purpose. For example, excitement through special offers and sweepstakes can increase virality, lead to more sales, or increase engagement with your brand. Our Facebook sweepstakes are great examples. Nurturing, if done right, can help take customer and influencer relationships to the next level where they become your ambassadors or ideation team. Our ambassadors are our loyal advocates who, amongst other things, help spread the word, initiate and participate in conversations pertaining to Cisco, correct incorrect information, or even bring important information to our attention. Our engagement efforts so far have also enabled us to tap into the collective wisdom of our target audience and create new opportunities for Cisco.

Cisco understands the need to incorporate both large and small tactics in its social media platform, always focusing on cultivating relationships with customers and partners by standing out and providing something extra. It's also done one thing differently from any company I've seen on social networks: it actually let customers become the administrators of its Cisco Networking Academy fan page on Facebook (Facebook.com /CiscoNetworkingAcademy), essentially giving them control of the content that went out to over 1.2 million fans along with Cisco's brand reputation. While the move was an extremely risky one, especially for a company of Cisco's size, it paid off. The company delighted the group of customers it trusted with its brand's reputation, and it found resources from an unlikely source (customers!) to scale the work of community management.

WHEN EVERYONE WINS SOMETHING, YOU WIN EVERYTHING: SHARED PRIZES FOR COMMUNITY GROWTH

Contests and sweepstakes definitely create excitement, but nothing generates more excitement than opportunities for everyone in an audience to win something. Shared opportunity can drive an entire fan page to work together in promoting the growth of its community. The first time we at Likeable Media saw this was with the Cumberland Farms Chill Zone page (Facebook .com/ChillZone). Cumberland Farms wanted to capture some of the passion it knew teenagers throughout New England had for its Chill Zone product. Using Facebook social ads, group outreach, and weekly Chill Zone giveaways, the Chill Zone page on Facebook soared to more than 10,000 fans in its first month. To incentivize fans to spread the word and share the fan page with others, it presented a challenge: help us reach 50,000 fans by August 21, 2009, and we'll hold a Free Chill Zone Day (Figure 17.1).

FIGURE 17.1   **Free Chill Zone Promotion**

Less than three months after the launch, the fan base surpassed this goal by more than 20,000 additional fans.

The results were incredible in terms of the numbers of fans joining the community, but the sentiment of people in the community was even more incredible. People posted things like, "I've invited my whole school to become fans," and "I won't rest until we have 50,000 fans. Chill Zone rules!"

The sales results were excellent as well. The first Free Chill Zone Day on June 5, 2009, led to redemptions of 27,000 more units over previous years (Figure 17.2). The second Free Chill Zone Day as a result of the Free Chill Zone Day Challenge in August increased sales by 23 percent from the previous Friday, and 50 percent of the total sales were attributed directly to Facebook.

FIGURE 17.2 | **Chill Zone Fans**

COMBINE AUTOMATION WITH THE HUMAN TOUCH

As valuable as it is to have tools to manage large groups of *likers*, followers, and conversation, there is no replacement for the human, personalized element of social media. Social network promotions, contests, giveaways, and sweepstakes can entertain and delight thousands or even millions of people at once. But wouldn't a personal, unique response from a real person at a big company really wow you even more than even the coolest contest ever?

Unique Words Have Unique Impact

Sometimes, just recognizing people publicly is enough surprise and delight to make someone's day. Giant Food, a supermarket chain in Delaware, Maryland, Pennsylvania, Virginia, and Washington, D.C., has a focus on connecting with its local community both inside and outside the store. Knowing people love sharing photos of their pets (anyone who has a social media account can attest to this), we created a video for National Pet Month to promote Giant's line of Nature's Promise dog and cat treats—and we told fans we wanted to see their pets' "treat faces" in return.

The Likeable community management team reached out to a few of the users who participated and asked for permission to share their photos on Giant's Instagram Story. We followed up by getting their home addresses and sending them a Giant gift card with a handwritten note.

"Thank you! Will be sure Waffles and Susha get some treats," one fan said, "Can't wait to see my girls smile on your page!" The fan submitted without expecting anything in return, but recognition, a gift card, and a story will surely get her back in-store soon, and the user-generated content shared in Giant's Instagram Story continues to serve as a subtle reminder that the brand is committed and connected to its community.

Shinesty, an irreverent clothing company for themed parties and general ridiculousness, uses Facebook to uniquely engage with its users, giving responses such as "Walk on the wild side with us, Amy. No guarantees you'll go back." and "Check out the double wide [sunglasses] fo your big ole head." Recently, it responded to an Internet troll dissing its American flag–themed boxer briefs with a link to purchase a three-pack of Fruit of the Loom tighty-whities on Amazon. "Ok mad props. That's [expletive] awesome," the user responded. No matter what kind of day you're having, you're sure to smile if you're on the receiving end of such a comment (Figure 17.3). And you'll probably tell a few friends. Imagine if an accountant always tweeted to new followers, "Hope your day isn't too taxing," or an attorney thanked new LinkedIn connections by sharing, "May the law be with you." What can you say that's even a little different, and yet remarkable?

FIGURE 17.3 **A Facebook Response from Shinesty**

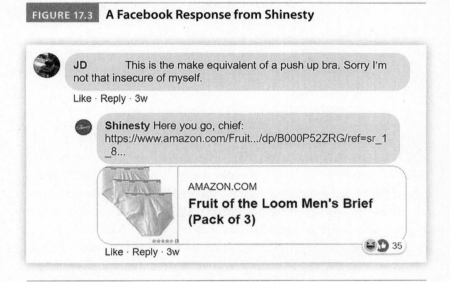

JD   This is the make equivalent of a push up bra. Sorry I'm not that insecure of myself.

Like · Reply · 3w

Shinesty Here you go, chief: https://www.amazon.com/Fruit.../dp/B000P52ZRG/ref=sr_1_8...

AMAZON.COM
Fruit of the Loom Men's Brief (Pack of 3)

Like · Reply · 3w   35

Surprise Conversations with Condoms— for Better or for Worse

The New York City Department of Health wanted to create buzz around its NYC Condom campaign in late 2009. The NYC Condom is the first municipally branded condom in the United States. The government program gives away more than 10 million free condoms per year in efforts to promote safer sex throughout New York.

The department wanted to use Twitter to surprise New Yorkers and make them take pause before acting foolishly. So, it created a Twitter account (https://Twitter.com/NYCcondom)

that actually tweeted *in the voice of the condom itself.* It began conducting nightly searches on Twitter for people who were talking about going out partying and for New Yorkers who, based on their conversations, were likely to need a condom. It searched using keywords such as "getting laid," "looking to hook up," and "partying all night."

Then, it would respond to people each night with funny tweets from the condom, such as these:

"Pick me up. I'll keep you covered."

"Don't leave home without me."

"If you need me, make sure to wear me tonight."

"Going out in NYC? Pick me up. I'm easy."

People weren't just surprised. They were shocked. Most people responded, surprised but happy to have had an unexpected "direct conversation" with a condom. Some users actually indicated that they would be picking up an NYC Condom, and they thanked the condom for the reminder. Others shared the health department's wit and wisdom by retweeting @NYCcondom.

A few people also felt surprised in a bad way. Conversation on Twitter is public, but when a government agency operating a Twitter account tweeted back, it reminded them they had been talking online to actual individuals about planning to have sex, and that probably led to a feeling of discomfort. Still, the campaign definitely led to increased buzz, surprised a lot of New Yorkers in the health department's target audience, and affected some people's behaviors. The tweeting condom may have even saved some lives.

ACTION ITEMS

1. Develop a strategy for how you can exceed customers' expectations on social networks to surprise and delight them. To start, write down five ways you, as a consumer, could be surprised, in a good way, by your company's actions.

2. Determine what budget you have for dedicated promotions, contests, giveaways, and sweepstakes on Facebook, Instagram, and Twitter. Depending on your products and services, decide what you can give away to everyone who *likes* you or what you can give away to all of your *likers* if you achieve certain milestones.

3. Create a social network communications plan that includes unique language about talking to your customers and prospects. No matter what your budget, a unique catchphrase can differentiate you, make people smile—and make people spread the word.

OPERATIONALIZE SURPRISE, FOR A GOOD RISE

How can you build systems and processes around making people smile, while generating surprise? How can you encourage a culture of conversation that differentiates you from the growing number of competitors on social networks? If you can truly reward all of your fans and followers, you'll be able to energize a huge group of online advocates. Consistently up the ante for what it means to bring value and delight to your customers and prospects, and not only will they remember you when they need you, but they'll also recommend you when others need you.

CHAPTER 18

Don't Sell! Just Make It Easy and Compelling for Customers to Buy

It was early December 2009, and my wife and I were cuddled up on the couch, laptops in hand, as any other social-media-happy couple might be. Carrie was logged in to Facebook, checking out all the latest updates from her friends and pages she *liked*, when she saw one about a new scarf from The Limited "as seen on *Oprah*." She thought the update was interesting enough to click, and when she did, the seemingly typical "shopping cart" appeared, with options to purchase the scarf in a wide variety of colors.

One thing that was quite different, though, from other online shopping carts she or I had clicked on before was that the cart was inside the Facebook News Feed, not on The Limited's website. Out of curiosity alone (though the scarf was nice, and it had in fact appeared on *Oprah*), she clicked through the entire shopping process, eventually entering her credit card securely and purchasing the scarf without leaving Facebook. The scarf arrived at our doorstep two days later, but not before my wife had shared with hundreds of Facebook friends how easy it had been to purchase the beautiful scarf.

Carrie *bought* that scarf from The Limited, but it wasn't aggressively *sold* to her. In one of the first business transactions involving physical items within the Facebook platform, The Limited had made the process straightforward and attractive to its thousands of fans. The Limited had created an application through which customers could browse and buy merchandise without ever leaving Facebook, had built up trust in its fan base over several months, and had the credibility of a recent mention on *The Oprah Winfrey Show*. All of those aspects added up, providing The Limited with the opportunity to temporarily turn a social channel into a sales channel, resulting in many thousands of dollars' worth of immediate revenue.

SALES IS NOT A DIRTY WORD, BUT MAKE IT SIMPLE AND EASY (AND EASY DOES IT)

Facebook, Instagram, Pinterest, and other social networks have grown immensely in a few short years, and, by definition, they are primarily social channels, not sales channels. However, *that doesn't mean you can't use Facebook, Instagram, or Pinterest to directly sell, market, or grow your business*. It does mean that the expectation most people have when they're on Facebook or LinkedIn or another social network is that they are there to socialize and connect with others, not to shop. In order to effectively change a social network into a sales channel, you have to make the buying process as effortless and satisfying as possible. You also have to tread carefully. If you push too hard to market or sell, you will erode the all-important trust and likeability you've worked hard to achieve.

The big question on every marketer's mind is how to make money using social media. What is the real return on investment of all the time and money spent in the space? The ROI comes in many forms, of course: brand reputation and credibility, increased loyalty and frequency of purchase, increased recommendations, and decreased need for advertising, to name a few. *But what about direct sales?* The answer is, if you follow all of the strategies presented in Chapters 1 through 17 of this book, it's OK, even advisable, to sell to people across social networks. Make the sales process as easy, fun, and shareable as possible, and *never get too pushy.*

Think about the situation this way: If you engage your prospects online, have a great product or service targeted toward the right people, and make it painless and compelling to buy whatever you're offering, then you don't really have to do any selling at all. Selling and marketing are usually disruptive, unwanted experiences, while buying is normally considered a fun, rewarding, and sometimes even exciting experience. So how can you create social buying opportunities instead of social sales and marketing opportunities?

Facebook Turns the News Feed Into a Dressing Room

In addition to the advertising capabilities mentioned in Chapter 3, Facebook has a few other ad units made just for shopping. One of my favorites is augmented reality ads. Augmented reality, or AR, alters or enhances a person's immediate surroundings with computer-generated information. Unlike virtual reality, which requires a specific device, AR lets users experience content on a deeper level using just their smartphones. Say you're scrolling through your News Feed and you see an ad for a piece of Pottery Barn furniture. What if you could hold your phone camera up to your living room wall and visualize that furniture in your space? With Facebook's augmented reality ads, you can. These ads have great implications for beauty, fashion, and home decor brands, and you can expect to see more augmented reality on social media in the coming years.

Instagram Lets Users "Shop the Look"

If you connect your product catalog to your Instagram account, you can tag those products in your photos. When users tap the post, a bubble will appear telling them the name of the product pictured and its price (Figure 18.1). If they follow the user journey, after a couple taps they'll be taken directly to your mobile site to shop. When you're creating "shoppable posts," you'll want to ensure you're not thinking product-first. Instead, consider how your customers use the products, then photograph them in those environments to ensure the photos feel true to the feed. Remember, your posts will be among your customers' connections' posts (think: friends, family, animals, and nature), so you don't want to come off as "spammy."

FIGURE 18.1   **A "Shoppable" Instagram Post**

TWEET Doesn't Include Selling—or Does It?

At Likeable, we suggest our clients follow a brief set of guidelines when using Twitter, based around an acronym we came up with for TWEET:

- Trust building. Build relationships.
- Wisdom. Learn from industry leaders and your customers.
- Ears open. Listen to the conversation.

- Establish your brand. Create a strong presence.
- Teach. Tell the world about what you do.

Of course, there's nothing in this mnemonic device about selling. There's nothing even there about marketing. But if you do a great job listening, learning, and building trust with the right people, if you establish your brand with the right fan base, and if you share what it is you and your organization do, you won't have to sell. People will already know your product and service, and they will come to you when they are ready to buy. The less friction in the buying process, the better, and the clearer and simpler the checkout or order process, the more likely your customer will be satisfied.

Ultimately, you still have to make sure your fans and followers know what you do or sell and give the customer a buying opportunity. You could be the most engaging, transparent, responsive, and attentive company in the world, but if you never actually educate people about what you sell and, without hitting them over the head, tell them how to buy, you won't be optimizing your social network presence.

THE FACEBOOK SALES FUNNEL DOES INCLUDE SALES

The traditional sales funnel includes awareness, intent, trigger, and then purchase. The Facebook or social media sales funnel still includes purchase—it's just a longer path to get there (Figure 18.2). First, you must generate awareness, and a *like*. Then, you'll take the prospects through a series of interactions, engaging them and providing them with interesting, educational, or valuable content. When the customers are ready to buy, as long as you have given them a clear, simple path to purchase, the sale can be triggered.

But the best part of the Facebook sales funnel, as compared to the traditional sales funnel, is that it doesn't end in one sale. The customer, still a *liker*, is eternally connected to you, unless he or she *unlikes* you. And with Facebook advertising, you can remarket to those who made a purchase even if they never *liked* you at all. So after the sale, you can still engage with the customer, giving him or her value outside of directly purchasing your product. Staying connected with your customers on social networks after an initial sale also gives you a huge new advantage—the power of leveraging your customers' social graph and introducing yourself passively to *their* friends and followers via social endorsements of *likes* or shares. While the sales process through Facebook is clearly a longer one, it also yields greater frequency of purchase and increased awareness of you among your customers' networks.

USE SOCIAL NETWORKS AND INVENTORY MANAGEMENT TO SELL OUT

When you have a limited supply of inventory and a need to sell it quickly at a discount, there is no faster or more efficient way to do so than through social media. Airlines, hotels, and theaters are examples of industries that can particularly benefit from this use of social networks, especially right before the plane takes off, the rooms are booked, or the curtain rises. In general, though, any type of company or business can benefit from careful inventory management, price control, and distribution, utilizing the large social network community they've tapped into or helped grow.

Dell Sells on Twitter with Likeable Results

One company that has had great success using Twitter to sell inventory is Dell. Through its @DellOutlet Twitter account, with more than one million followers, it has sold millions worth of refurbished computer and other electronic equipment.

How has Dell done this? When it has excess inventory of products, it deeply discounts the items, then shares a timed offer on Twitter with a coupon code and link to purchase. This setup results in immediate sales but also creates word of mouth about the great deals. In turn, more Twitter users become Dell followers, and therefore, more sales opportunities are created the next time the company shares an offer.

Have you ever wondered why last-minute flights get expensive instead of cheaper? Last-minute travelers either pay an extraordinary amount to fly, or they are forced to make other travel arrangements, typically leading to lots of empty seats or half-empty flights. JetBlue was the first airline to solve this "empty seats" problem using social media. It created @JetBlueCheeps, a Twitter account dedicated solely to sharing great limited-inventory, last-minute deals on airfares. While earning $39 to $89 a ticket is not a tremendous amount of revenue for JetBlue, it's better than flying with empty seats. Customers who can be flexible about waiting for deals on Twitter can also leverage this to the fullest degree.

Do you have inventory you could deeply discount to give away quickly? Remember, in addition to driving immediate sales, you'd gain the advantage of creating a buzz on a medium in which word spreads lightning fast. You are also likely to generate returning, and new, customers.

Keds Puts Its Fans First

In 2012, Keds repositioned itself as a brand for teenage girls, tapping stars such as Taylor Swift for campaigns such as "Ladies First" and "Be Brave." Knowing that young women love posting photos of what they're wearing while traveling, attending concerts or festivals, or hanging out with friends, Keds decided to take advantage of the visual content its customers were already creating.

What the brand did was simple. It made all of its own Instagram posts shoppable on its website's homepage, and it let users submit content through hashtag #KedsStyle. When a photo is clicked on the website homepage, customers can see the product details and price tag, and then they can "Shop Now" (Figure 18.3).

FIGURE 18.3 **Keds Lets Customers Shop UGC on Its Website**

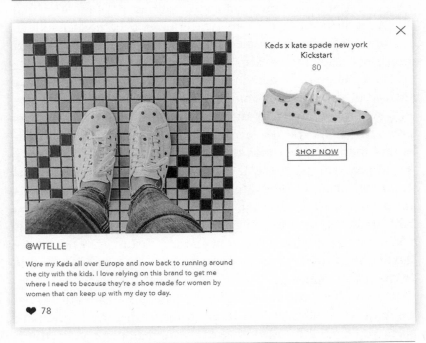

@WTELLE

Wore my Keds all over Europe and now back to running around the city with the kids. I love relying on this brand to get me where I need to because they're a shoe made for women by women that can keep up with my day to day.

♥ 78

You know when you see someone on the street and you think, "Nice watch"? You weren't in the market for a watch, and you'd never seen yourself wearing that style of watch, but now you can't stop thinking about it. That's basically what Keds did by linking its Instagram to its website. By allowing potential customers who visited the page to see the shoes in the real world, those shoppers were able to visualize more than just a product on a shelf. They were able to visualize the product on the street, at the movies, in the park—and in their closets. Instead of telling its community to go out and buy its products, Keds reminded them of the great products that were a click away—and ended up increasing its sales because of that reminder!

BUYING OPPORTUNITIES + ENGAGING SOCIAL MEDIA UPDATES = GREATER SALES SUCCESS

If the object of the social media game is to create engaging, valuable, and likeable content and experiences for your community and if the object of the business game is to create compelling buying opportunities for your prospects, consider pairing those two objectives via one Facebook update. For instance, let's say you're responsible for marketing and selling shoes. An example of an engaging Facebook update to your community might be this: "What do you think the most common women's shoe size is in the United States?" An example of a compelling sales update could be this: "Click here to enjoy 50 percent off on our newest line of women's shoes [link]."

Remember, though, that Facebook's News Feed algorithm is such that updates need to generate comments and *likes* in order to remain at the top of people's feeds. So in order for people to even *see* the 50 percent discount offer, you'll have to be at the top of people's News Feeds. Hitting people over the head on Facebook with offers will not lead to sales, but it may very well lead to people *unliking* you or unsubscribing from your feed. Thus, try combining the two objectives to create a best-of-both-worlds scenario: "What do you think is the most common women's shoe size? After you guess, click the link to find out the answer, and enjoy 50 percent off select shoes [link]."

By engaging your community, you're creating value and optimizing for people's Facebook feeds (and other social networks with similar algorithms such as LinkedIn and Instagram). Combining this engagement with a compelling offer, you give your followers a great buying opportunity, and thus you provide your company with an equally great sales opportunity.

1-800-Flowers.com Will Win Because It "Gets" Likeable, Social Sales

The company 1-800-Flowers.com won the national floral space when it became the first florist to have a memorable 1-800 phone number. It then continued to win the space by establishing a strong e-commerce platform through its website before any other flower company. Now, 1-800-Flowers.com will continue to dominate the national floral space because it understands the conjunction of e-commerce and social media.

Through third-party technology company 8thBridge, 1-800-Flowers.com was the first major retailer in the world to establish a Facebook store, in 2009. Today, commerce, from start to finish, can take place directly through the Facebook platform at Facebook.com/1800Flowers, creating an easy, compelling buying experience. More important, the company has grown a sizable fan base of more than one million customers on Facebook. It offers weekly promotions and contests, asks questions, and listens to the feedback it receives. The company is responsive and transparent about customer inquiries, it inspires customers' stories, and it surprises and delights random fans. It engages!

It's the combination of positive social media practices and easy, compelling buying opportunities that will help 1-800-Flowers.com continue to thrive in business. How can you model your practices after it, Keds, Dell, and JetBlue? How can you create the most likeable buying process online?

ACTION ITEMS

1. Conduct an assessment of your current online buying processes. How simple and compelling is your online sales cart? How interested and capable would you be as a consumer in buying from your company?
2. Depending on your business, research whether or not your product catalog can be uploaded to Facebook, and start thinking of organic ways to feature tagged products in your feed.
3. Write five sample Facebook or LinkedIn updates that combine an engaging question or valuable content with an irresistible offer, and link to your website to buy or learn more. Test, track, and measure the results in order to optimize them for future ROI.

KEEP ON YOUR CONSUMER CAP, THINK BUYING, NOT SELLING, AND THE SALES WILL COME

The days of push-marketing tactics are quickly coming to an end, ushering in better times for consumers everywhere. Always think the way your consumer does, create buying opportunities that you yourself would want to leverage, and make purchasing simple and easy. Be patient, and continue to provide value for your communities. Develop simple, user-friendly opportunities for customers to buy from you, wherever and whenever they choose to. The sales *will* come.

Just Be Likeable

The last 10 years have brought about a major paradigm shift in marketing, media, and communications. Social networks such as Facebook, Instagram, and Twitter have ushered in a new era marked by increased transparency and the most empowered consumers of all time. There is no doubt that this shift creates massive opportunities for the organizations that are most able to adapt their thinking and strategies to successfully implement plans via social media.

All of the new social networking tools and sites can be overwhelming, and so-called experts, sharing opposing information or telling you to emphasize different priorities, have made it even more challenging. In your company or organization, you're driven and measured by results. Since the results of leveraging social media are often not immediately apparent, it is tempting to rely on traditional marketing tactics that have been proven to generate immediate results instead of utilizing social media. Resist that temptation.

KEY CONCEPTS TO REMEMBER

An understanding of the 18 concepts outlined in this book will guide you in your conceptualization, creation, and implementation of a social media plan. Familiarizing yourself with Facebook,

LinkedIn, and the other social networks that your customers use can help guide your decisions about where and how to allocate your resources. And knowing the tools available through social media will make your job easier. But the process can be overwhelming. The contents of this book alone may be difficult to digest and implement, so I suggest that when you first explore all the possibilities social media has to offer, you concentrate on these five key concepts: listen up, pay up, be transparent, be responsive, and be likeable.

Listen Up

The biggest paradigm shift of all that social media represents is that it gives you the ability to listen to what your customers and prospects are saying publicly. You can start listening today for free, and your ability to do so will inform and prepare you to best accomplish all of your social media marketing and advertising objectives. Acknowledging to your customers that you're listening can endear you to them forever. Before you talk, be sure to listen, and once you start talking, never stop listening.

Pay Up

In the last several years, social media has gone from a time expense only to a hard cost. The reality is, content worth creating and sharing is now content worth advertising. Determine which social networks matter to you and your business, and develop an advertising plan to reach the right people with your content and offers. Monitor your advertising spend and continually make adjustments to make sure your money is well spent.

Be Transparent

Transparency is the new default. People like it when others are honest and transparent. You like it when other people are honest and transparent. Yet somehow, so many companies and industries are secretive, even dishonest, about aspects of their business. Embrace transparency and openness. Be honest when you mess up and when things don't go as planned. The Internet becomes more transparent with every day that goes by. For you as a consumer, this situation is incredibly beneficial, and it can also be a great thing for you as a marketer, if you can embrace it.

Be Responsive

The world is talking about you and to you. People everywhere are discussing their problems that you can solve better than your competitors. They are telling you about their wants and needs that your organization can help them with.

Every time a customer or prospect talks publicly on a social network, it's an opportunity for you to respond and engage. Whenever you don't respond, you either make a negative impression or you give a competitor an opportunity to reply. Whenever you do respond, you have an opportunity to make a positive impression on customers, prospects, and on all of their friends.

Just Be Likeable

In the end, succeeding on social networks amounts to your ability to be likeable. There are two fundamental aspects to this term: likeable business practices and likeable content. Adopting *likeable business practices* means treating customers the way you'd like to be treated. Follow the Golden Rule in each decision you make affecting your customers. Posting *likeable content* means that you share only those updates on Instagram or Twitter that would make you click the Like button if you were on the receiving end. Create and share stories, text, photos, videos, links, and applications that you as a consumer would want to *like*, comment on, and share. To be likeable, always respect and add value to your community.

THIS ISN'T THE END; IT'S THE START

Now it's time to get out there and apply the contents of this book. Use social media to grow your company and meet your organization's objectives. And I really meant what I wrote at the beginning of this book: if you have questions, suggestions, compliments, or complaints:

1. Connect with me on LinkedIn at https://www.linkedin.com /in/DaveKerpen.
2. Tweet to me anytime at https://twitter.com/DaveKerpen.
3. Send me a direct message on Instagram at https://www .instagram.com/davekerpen.
4. Facebook private message me at https://Facebook.com /DKerpen.

I hope to have the opportunity to prove to you that I'm as transparent, responsive, and likeable as I know you will be.

Be amazing, and be likeable.
I'll see you on social media!

A Refresher Guide to the Social Networks That Matter Most

My wife, Carrie, and I bought a new home a few years ago and have since made several renovations. As I watched Carrie fall down the rabbit hole of home renovations, decorating, and furniture shopping, I got to observe how she, as a consumer, used social media to investigate and make purchase decisions, what networks affected her choices, and how.

Every social media user has his or her own pattern, or "social DNA," for how to use each network. My wife (and now more than 2.23 billion others!) uses Facebook for her actual friends, past and present. If you've met Carrie in "real life," chances are she'll friend you on Facebook. She uses Twitter, however, to connect with celebrities (her guilty pleasure is reading the tweets of Justin Bieber, Ashton Kutcher, and Heidi Montag!) and with people she doesn't know but with whom she shares commonalities: moms, social media agency leaders, fellow female authors, and people who live in our town. She also connects with brands she loves through Twitter. LinkedIn acts as a Rolodex of every professional contact she's ever had, and Instagram serves as her photo album of her favorite moments with our family, friends, and employees. Pinterest is where she gets ideas for home projects and crafts and cooking with the kids. YouTube is a place where she can learn how to do things she's never done before. As an active Internet and social media user, she also uses other social sites and tools as needed.

Now that you've got Carrie's social DNA, let's look at it in action. Her first step in our new home renovation was to find contractors who would do the physical work on our house. Three big things happened here.

First, she Googled. Through her search, she found ServiceMagic (now called HomeAdvisor), a social review site for home services providers, where she was able to check reviews on contractors.

Second, she posted to her Facebook friends, asking if anyone knew anything about repairing a roof (or if they knew anyone who knew anything about repairing a roof and could make any recommendations).

Third, she threw the same question out to her followers on Twitter. When she got her replies, she cross-referenced the comments she had received from her Facebook friends (which she viewed as the most valuable) with the comments from her Twitter followers. She then looked up the recommended contractors on HomeAdvisor to check their reviews. Carrie would end up posting her own review about the wonderful work the contractor performed, and, thanks to the Facebook integration on HomeAdvisor, she was able to share the review with her Facebook friends. The post received 10 *likes*.

Now, on to decorating. My wife and I have a ton of books, and we were fortunate to purchase a home with a traditional parlor that has floor to ceiling bookshelves. In Googling ideas for creating the perfect library, Carrie stumbled upon a website called Houzz, a small niche social network where decorators and designers create slideshows of their suggestions, categorized by subject. She found about six slideshows devoted entirely to libraries, and she tweeted each image to her friends, asking for feedback. She even got to know some of the other folks in the Houzz network.

Later, as Carrie was on Facebook, socializing away, she saw an interesting post come into her News Feed from a furniture store she had previously liked, Raymour & Flanigan: "Want to create a dream library in your home? Click here for perfect accents for your quiet space." The status linked to pieces that worked for a library or study, including the electric fireplace that now sits in our home in Port Washington.

Was it luck that Raymour & Flanigan decided to place that post right at the time that Carrie was making purchasing decisions about buying home accessories? No. Carrie had decided to become a fan of Raymour & Flanigan's Facebook page weeks before simply because she knew that the company sold furniture and that she was moving.

Raymour & Flanigan used smart marketing to engage with Carrie—the same way any designer who was searching for tweets about furnishing a library could engage with her on Twitter or any Houzz designer could have asked to evaluate her empty space and offer suggestions. These networks are ripe for connecting with consumers; you just need to figure out how your customers and target audience are using these sites, and then connect with them in the way that's most natural.

Once we moved in, Carrie used YouTube to learn how to arrange the perfect bookshelves—and I have to admit, we had a lot of fun that night, drinking wine, going through our books, and creating a useful and picturesque arrangement. Thanks, YouTube, for a romantic evening at home. In the years since then, Carrie and I have made several more renovations to the home, and we have Pinterest and Facebook to thank for all of Carrie's ideas (and the bills).

Seven years since the first edition and four since the second, I have the opportunity to demonstrate just how fast-moving social networks are. We recently moved and just completed another round of extensive renovations on our new home, including a tree house, new patio, and outdoor fireplace. The inspiration for my wife's latest decision? Pinterest, of course—a network that didn't even exist when I wrote the first edition of this book.

THE NETWORKS
AND THEIR USES

As our home furnishing stories demonstrate, the integration of many social networks is now commonplace in our lives. Surely, you and your friends use social networks each day to influence your own behavior and decisions as a consumer. But to utilize them effectively for your own marketing and advertising purposes, you must first fully understand the tools at your disposal.

Each person uses social media and social networks in different ways—we all have our own specific social DNA. Though some believe Facebook is the most important social network for companies to consider, at the end of the day, every user is looking for the same thing—to connect and to engage, to be heard and to listen. It's just that they choose different networks for different engagements. There are dozens of niche social networks, so it's worth looking at what communities might exist around the needs *your* company or organization serves.

Since we can't look into all of those niche networks, I provide the following information as a refresher about the major ones that have emerged, their basic uses, and some advice on how marketers can get started in incorporating social media networks into their plans. Whatever networks you choose, you should consider integrating them with Facebook and using it as a hub for your social strategy. Your Facebook presence will be infinitely richer, and your results that much stronger. If pictures and videos are the best way to promote your business, then Instagram should be your main platform. If you're in B2B, consider using LinkedIn as the hub for your social networking activities.

This primer for social media newcomers and refresher for social media veterans will help you better understand the 18 concepts outlined throughout the book. Take a close look at the information and statistics that follow because even social network veterans may find some likeable content to help them further understand the abilities, tools, and powers of harnessing online social media.

FACEBOOK: TWO BILLION PEOPLE CAN'T BE WRONG

BEST USES: Connecting with and engaging your target audience

Facebook is the number one social network in the world, with more than 2.23 billion people using the service and 1.47 billion daily active users. This is a growth rate of roughly 11 percent year over year. Facebook features three main entities: individual profiles, groups, and pages.

- **Profiles.** This entity is how individuals sign up for the service, identify themselves, and interact with others. When two people who have written individual profiles "friend" one another, they have equal access to each other's streams of information. When two individuals connect on Facebook, they are considered "friends."

- **Groups.** Groups can be started and joined by any individual around any topic or interest. Some groups are more serious and functional in nature (for example, the "Port Washington Moms and Dads" group is busy every single day), many groups are less serious, and some are downright silly (for example, "Join this group and I'll quit smoking," or "Mean people suck," or "I love my Pop-Pop"). You can also use Facebook groups for businesses, which can be a great way to connect with your target customers. Business pages can create and monitor both public and private groups. One great use for Facebook groups is for internal communication among employees, departments, clubs, or other groups of people. Likeable Media uses a Facebook group to communicate during and after work hours. Groups can be public, private, or even secret so that no activity whatsoever is shared outside of the group.

- **Pages.** Also commonly referred to as "company pages" or "business pages," pages are intended to be the official representation and voice of companies, nonprofits, brands, governments, and celebrities and other public figures. Within the Facebook platform, it is through pages that you will have the most opportunities to build a responsive, transparent, engaging brand for your customers and prospects. Facebook pages operate similarly to individual profiles, with a few notable exceptions. First, pages are one-way connections—when an individual connects to a company page, he or she gains access to the business's stream, but the business doesn't have complete access to the individual's profile. A business page can only message individuals in response to their comments or posts. Second, pages have increased Web functionality—Facebook applications can be added to a business's page to replicate just about anything a business would want on its own website. Third, and arguably most important, the terminology is different for pages. When individuals connect to a page on Facebook, they *like* the business, public figure, or other entity represented by the page, as compared to becoming "friends" with the individual.

As fellow wordsmiths would agree, language is important, and it hasn't always been this way for Facebook or other social networks' use of different terminologies. Myspace, for instance, didn't differentiate between individuals and non-individuals, calling all connections "friends." This terminology ultimately makes little sense. You are friends with people you know, but no matter how much you love your favorite cereal brand, it's not your friend. Even Facebook originally differentiated between individuals and organizations by asking people to "become a fan" of pages. While this setup worked for certain categories (you may be a "fan" of the New York Mets, Conan O'Brien, and Ashton Kutcher), again, you'd be a lot less likely to become a fan of Cheerios than to *like* Cheerios. When Facebook changed the terminology from "become a fan" to "*like*," millions more clicked Like. Today there are tens of millions of pages representing companies and organizations, and 60 percent of Facebook users *like* at least one brand's page, with the average person *liking* around 50 pages.

In Figure A.1 we can see a screenshot of Likeable Media's official page.

FIGURE A.1   **Likeable Media's Official Facebook Page**

Liking Content: Pages and Friends

In February 2009, Facebook added the function to *like* any content your friends or business pages shared. This lightweight action allows people to express approval of or endorse content without having to type a full comment to say, "I like this." In an increasingly time-starved world, adding the Like button to all content on Facebook encourages a greater deal of interactivity and, with every click on Like, it gives your friends, and Facebook, a better picture of who you are and what content you find valuable.

Beyond *Likes*: Reactions

In February 2016, Facebook added *reactions* for users to respond to posts. Facebook users can press and hold down on the Like button to then select from five other predetermined emotions: "Love," "Haha," "Wow," "Sad," and "Angry." By the spring of 2017, Facebook expanded reactions to be available for comments. Reactions give your users the opportunity to engage in a fun and unique way.

A Lot More to Like

Since 2012, Facebook has expanded three more key features—video, events, and Messenger—in its quest to reorganize the social Web:

- **Video: Native, Live, and Watch.** Since the second edition of the book, video content has made a massive surge across all social media platforms, and Facebook is no different. Native video is when a user posts the video directly on Facebook. This is completely different than posting the link to a video on YouTube or Vimeo. Facebook rewards the native video in numerous ways including increasing its organic reach and automatically starting the video when a user scrolls past it. In order to post a native video, the video must previously be recorded and saved as a file on your device. A very important note is that over 75 percent of Facebook videos are played without sound. This means that it is essential to add closed captions or text to your videos. Luckily, in 2017 Facebook released a feature that will help you automatically caption videos.

  In April of 2016, Facebook released *Facebook Live* to all of its users, which allows everyone with a smartphone to broadcast live. This directly competed with Twitter's Periscope. Facebook Live is a great way to have direct conversations with your audience or to share breaking news.

  Following the success of the video content, in September 2017, Facebook launched *Facebook Watch* for produced original content. Along with a Facebook Watch show, there are Show Pages that act as a homepage for the shows. For now, Facebook Watch shows must be approved and supported by Facebook. Facebook has announced plans to increase its budget for original video content over the next several years. Following are some suggestions to help you with video, whether on Facebook or other social networks.

A FEW HINTS ABOUT ONLINE VIDEO

1. Content is more important than production quality. Any smartphone will do.

2. Short and sweet is almost always better. A good rule of thumb is 30 to 90 seconds per video.

3. Have fun. Video is a great way to showcase your brand's personality.

4. Don't just post it on Facebook. Post your video on Instagram, LinkedIn, YouTube, and other sites as well.

5. Engage with your followers and respond to all comments.

- **Events.** Regardless of the size of your business, events are an excellent opportunity to directly engage with your consumers and audience. For example, if you are a small retail business, you could use a Facebook event to announce the launch of a new line of clothing or to promote a sale. If you're an author, you can create an event for a book signing. Events can not only help you connect with your most dedicated followers but also reach new ones.
- **Messenger.** Facebook Messenger has over 1.3 billion users per month. In the past, Messenger was a place that was pretty much limited to friends talking to each other. However, that is quickly changing! In the newest version of Messenger there is a feature, Discover, that allows users to directly connect with brands. Studies have shown that after speaking with a brand through Messenger, around 70 percent of consumers feel more confident about the brand. Messenger is a fantastic tool for personal interactions with your audience. One of the newest and hottest trends within Messenger is the use of Facebook Chatbots. Chatbots can be programmed to automatically respond to questions and provide customers with key information. This allows your brand to efficiently and directly communicate with its audience.

Facebook's News Feed

The News Feed is the way users see content. Essentially, it is the flow of information when one scrolls down Facebook. Following the controversial 2016 U.S. election, Facebook was in hot water about the spread of misinformation. In response to this, CEO Mark Zuckerberg announced that the algorithm would be changed to prioritize "meaningful social interactions." This emphasis on community engagement is a huge shift from the former support of promotional content. In practice, this means that your brand has to actively engage with your followers and that picture and video content must be key elements of your strategy. That is why it is as important, if not more, than ever to be likeable on Facebook.

Web Integration: Social Plug-Ins

In April 2010, Facebook released what it called *social plug-ins*, allowing websites to add buttons to layer people's Facebook information into their own website experience, using very simple lines of code. Social plug-ins have become an essential element of any website. This feature took Facebook from being an enormous social network to being the body reorganizing the entire Internet around your social graph. The Like button is by far the most prominent example of these buttons, and more than 150 million distinct websites have added it to their websites. (You can do it too—at Developers.Facebook.com.) The Like button allows people to endorse a website, product, article, picture, or video to all of their Facebook friends with one click. Future visitors to the website see how many people have *liked* this page or object before, but more important, they see if any of their friends have *liked* it. Other great plug-ins to add to your website are the *share* and *messenger* buttons. The *share* button allows users to share information from your website directly to their Facebook feeds, and *messenger* gives visitors the opportunity to directly message your company. Facebook continues to make aggressive changes to keep up with other growing social networks.

With the addition of these features, this personalized Web is much more appealing than the impersonal, link-driven Web that Google had previously organized. And it's very powerful. The best way to fully understand *like*'s potential is to pay attention the next time you're on your computer or smartphone. Many websites have added a deep integration of the Facebook social plug-ins, what Facebook calls instant personalization. As long as you're logged into Facebook, you'll see all the *likes* and comments from your Facebook friends. Would you rather see reviews from critics or from your own friends, family, and connections, many of whom share your interests and tastes?

The implications of the Like button are vast, as billions of people are now publicly *liking* their favorite brands, companies, celebrities, and ideas. We can all agree that word of mouth among friends is the strongest form of marketing, and now, Facebook has made it easier than ever to see what your friends recommend and have to say about anything you'd search for on the Web. As more people continue to join Facebook, and a greater number of website owners integrate the Facebook plug-ins into their user experiences, the Web will become even more personalized, and it will be easier to find people, places, and things your friends have already *liked*.

The two most important features to consider on Facebook are your business page and the implementation of Facebook's social plug-ins on your company's website. On your business page, you can share so much information where visitors land and are introduced to your page. Check out a few examples in Table A.1.

TABLE A.1   Ten Great Brand Pages on Facebook

BRAND	FACEBOOK SITE
Taco Bell	https://www.facebook.com/tacobell
FedEx	https://www.facebook.com/FedEx
Dunkin' Donuts	https://www.facebook.com/DunkinDonutsUS
Auntie Anne's	https://www.facebook.com/auntieannespretzels
Nutella	https://www.facebook.com/nutellausa
NHL	https://www.facebook.com/NHL
Keds	https://www.facebook.com/keds
Nickelodeon	https://www.facebook.com/nickelodeon
SoulCycle	https://www.facebook.com/SoulCycleInc
AMC Theatres	https://www.facebook.com/amctheatres

Once people *like* your page, it's all about engaging your community—through videos, pictures, status updates, links, and applications like virtual gifts, contests, and promotions (see Table A.2).

TABLE A.2 The Five Most Engaging Facebook Status Updates
Videos
Photos
GIFs
Links with images
Interactive applications (polls and quizzes)

The best tools and tactics for Facebook change a lot, as Facebook is constantly innovating, and companies are always working hard at better optimizing the tools available. Keeping up is hard work, but take a look at Table A.3 to check out five blogs worth reading to stay as current as possible on Facebook and to learn how to best leverage Facebook's changes to your advantage.

TABLE A.3 Five Blogs to Read to Keep up with Facebook Changes	
BLOG	WEBSITE
Facebook Blog	Blog.facebook.com
Social Media Today	SocialMediaToday.com
Likeable Media	Likeable.com/blog
Adweek	Adweek.Com/SocialTimes/Category/Facebook
Mashable	Mashable.com/social-media/Facebook

Facebook is certainly the biggest game in town, and it likely will be for a long time to come. But it's not the only game in town.

INSTAGRAM: TURNING EVERYONE WITH A SMARTPHONE INTO AN EXCELLENT PHOTOGRAPHER

BEST USES: Bringing your brand to life through photos and live video; social networking from your smartphone

Instagram is a free photo-sharing app that launched in October 2010. The platform allows users to take a photo, apply a digital filter to it, and then share it on a variety of social networking services, including Instagram's own. The service grew quickly to 200 million users. In April 2012, Facebook purchased Instagram, with its 13 employees, for approximately $1 billion in cash and stock before it had earned a single dollar in revenue.

At the time this was a massive risk. Maybe Facebook CEO Mark Zuckerberg realized that the future of the social Web is the mobile Web, and Instagram had conquered the mobile Web better than anyone. In 2017, there were 95 million photos posted on Instagram daily. During the summer of 2018, Instagram reached a whopping one billion active users. Out of these users, 80 percent follow at least one brand on Instagram, and 30 percent of users have purchased a product that they first discovered on Instagram. Instagram has even added Shoppable Posts, a feature that allows a business to tag a product in its post (if it's in your product catalog that's connected to the account). The user can then see the price and purchase the product seamlessly. Instagram has quickly ascended to being an essential platform for businesses, with roughly three out of four businesses using Instagram.

Hashtags

It's essential that your brand's Instagram account is public. This will allow users that are not following your account to see your posts. Hashtags (#) are the single best way to both organically reach new followers and increase engagement. Posts with at least one hashtag had nearly 13 percent more engagement than posts without hashtags. Hashtags allow new users to find your posts through their Search & Explore page. For example, if you run a food blog and you post a picture with several hashtags such as "#foodie #foodblog #yummy #cleaneating," users that like similar content will easily be able to find your post.

Stories

During the summer of 2016, Instagram added *Stories*. Stories are series of pictures and/or videos that disappear 24 hours after being posted. While they are not automatically saved on the profile, they can be pinned to your profile using the Highlights feature. And Stories have done an amazing job of increasing reach to daily active users. By the summer of 2018 there were 400 million daily active users of Instagram Stories. For brands and businesses, these Stories provide an excellent way to share creative content and connect with your audience. On average, one in five Stories gets at least one direct message in response.

Video

When Instagram first released video capabilities in 2013, the videos had a 15-second limit. In March 2016, this limit was extended to 60 seconds. In November 2016, Instagram launched live video. This allows users to broadcast live on Instagram for up to one hour. Live video is a great way to interact with your audience as you can read and then respond to their comments while the video is live.

In June 2018, Instagram announced the launch of *IGTV*. IGTV is a video platform that Instagram hopes will compete with YouTube. All users can now upload videos that are up to 10 minutes long, and some creators and high-profile users can upload videos that are an hour long. Table A.4 shows five brands that are doing a great job on IGTV.

TABLE A.4	Five Amazing Brands Maximizing IGTV
BRANDS	**VINE SITE**
Netflix	@netflix
Bacardi	@bacardi
Warby Parker	@warbyparker
Louis Vuitton	@louisvuitton
West Elm	@westelm

For Instagram users, it's all about sharing "on the go"—taking pictures around you, applying a filter to make the pictures look as likeable as possible, and then sharing those pictures.

For business users, Instagram is best when you have something beautiful to share, so industry categories that are excellent candidates for Instagram include fashion, food, and travel. For busy small business owners, it's exciting as well because you do not need a computer to use it. In fact, you can't post on Instagram from your computer! While you can now scroll, *like*, and comment on your computer, for posting it's all about your iPhone or Android device, snapping photos, selecting a filter, and sharing.

Similar to Twitter, Instagram uses the @ symbol to tag other users, and the # hashtag symbol to tag categories and keep track of them for later. Table A.5 shows seven noteworthy brands using Instagram and lessons you can apply to your business.

TABLE A.5 Seven Noteworthy Brands Using Instagram Well

BRAND	ON INSTAGRAM	WHAT YOU CAN LEARN FROM THEM
Shake Shack	@shakeshack	Vary how you share your product and include fun pictures with customers
Saturday Night Live	@nbcsnl	Give fans sneak peeks and behind-the-scenes looks
Ben & Jerry's	@benandjerrys	Develop a strong brand personality
Airbnb	@airbnb	Share more value than just your product
TikTok	@tiktok	Share user-generated content
National Geographic	@natgeo	Capture high-quality content and write thoughtful captions
Sharpie	@sharpie	Inspire passion from otherwise boring products

TWITTER: REAL-TIME CONSUMER ENGAGEMENT FOR BETTER OR FOR WORSE

BEST USES: Consumer insight, customer service, real-time communication

You've heard before of the giant cocktail party that is social media. If Facebook is a consumer's high school reunion, her book club, and her playgroup—well, Twitter is her rave, a flashy, trippy sort of place where you can talk to anyone about anything at any time, connected through a series of 280-character exchanges. Twitter was born in 2006, and media and celebrities have helped drive the network to more than 335 million monthly active users and over a billion accounts worldwide in slightly more than 10 years. Twitter still suffers from what I call "cereal syndrome"—if you're like many people, you may think Twitter is a bunch of celebrities and narcissists running around, inundating people with the minutiae of their lives, such as what they had for breakfast. While Twitter surely has its share of such people, many others are there to learn, share, and grow, just as they might at a cocktail party.

Here are five types of ways to share on Twitter: updates, @replies, direct messages, polls, and multimedia:

- **Updates.** Also known as "tweets," these messages go out into the stream of everyone who's signed up to follow your account. Tweets are a great way to share any industry-relevant information, news, and links. This isn't limited to just your company's blog. Sharing information from an assortment of sources builds credibility, trust, and thought leadership. One really effective way to share information and curate content is to retweet relevant articles and updates from the accounts you follow.
- **@Replies.** Such messages are meant to get the attention of one or more accounts on Twitter without bothering other users. For instance, if you begin a tweet with @DaveKerpen (my "Twitter handle"), the only people who will see your tweet are me and anyone who's following both you and me. This arrangement keeps noise to a minimum and allows you to effectively tweet an unlimited amount of times without annoying others not directly involved in the conversation, as long as most of your messages are directed @ individuals. Therefore, tweeting @ individuals keeps your Twitter stream relevant. Many people don't realize the difference between starting a tweet with @DaveKerpen (just the people who follow both of us and I will see your tweet) and .@DaveKerpen (starting with the dot means all of your followers will see the tweet).
- **Direct messages.** These updates are private messages between two accounts, similar to text messages or private messages on Facebook. This comes in handy if you need to share or solicit private information, such as an account number or a phone number.
- **Polls.** Asking questions is a fantastic way to interact with your audience. Running polls is a great tool for generating a conversation and learning about your audience's thoughts on a particular topic.

- **Multimedia.** The same is true for Twitter as is for almost every platform: posts with multimedia have better engagement than those without it. On Twitter, you can post videos, GIFs, and pictures. You can upload videos that are shorter than two minutes and 20 seconds (140 seconds). When posting a tweet, you can search Twitter for the perfect GIF to convey the message. A GIF is essentially an animated picture and typically is either funny or cute. You can share up to four images in the same tweet.

One of the main distinctions of Twitter versus Facebook is that Twitter's conversations are typically much more public. While people on Facebook mostly share with friends they know, only 10 percent of all Twitter users keep their updates private since most of them opt for all-inclusive, completely open conversations. Because of this, marketers are able to conduct a search on Twitter and see all the conversations currently taking place. Twitter search is like the Google of conversation and provides insight to countless companies.

Before you even think about a social media strategy, you should head to Twitter to find out what your current social media presence actually is. Don't think you have one? Whether they're mentioning your brand by name or they're mentioning experiences related to using your brand, consumers are talking about interactions with your company or other companies like it, and you need to know what they're saying before you begin your specific strategy. What words do people use when describing the problems your company solves? These are the words worth searching. Use "advanced search" to look only at specific geographic areas if only certain places apply to you.

Twitter is also an incredible customer service tool. You can, as a brand, send a direct message to someone who's following you on Twitter. The other reason that Twitter works for customer service is simply because the customer has decided it does. Customers increasingly expect you to provide customer service on Twitter, and that expectation will only grow over time. Check out five companies listed in Table A.6 that are using Twitter well for customer service.

TABLE A.6 **Five Prominent Companies Utilizing Twitter**

COMPANY	TWITTER HANDLE
Target	@Target
Apple	@Apple
Lyft	@Lyft
Forrester	@Forrester
Starbucks News	@StarbucksNews

You might consider using Twitter during live offline events or when hosting live chats. Twitter works well for conversations in which people want to address specific individuals and a general group at once. For example, if you are to tweet someone directly, addressing a message to one person's Twitter handle, only this specific user will receive the tweet. If you use someone's Twitter handle in the text of a tweet you are sending out to a group, for example, congratulating a user, then both the entire group and the individual will receive the message.

You can also use Twitter to host contests and promotions. Twitter can get overwhelming quickly to the novice user, so I suggest using a wide variety of applications to make your Twitter experience easier and richer. See the list in Table A.7.

TABLE A.7 **Five Twitter Applications**

APPLICATIONS	WEBSITE
Hootsuite	Hootsuite.com
Tweetbot	TapBots.Com/Tweetbot
Plume	MyPlume.com
Social Mention	SocialMention.com
Twitterrific	Twitterrific.com/ios

The best way you can learn about Twitter and all of its potential, though, is to join today, or if you've already joined, to commit to spending more time using the platform.

Try the following:

- Spend 30 minutes per day on Twitter from your computer or phone.
- Follow 20 to 30 accounts from people and organizations you like and want to interact with.

Within two weeks, you'll understand Twitter for business far better than you do today.

LINKEDIN: FROM ONE PROFESSIONAL TO ANOTHER, TO 550 MILLION MORE

BEST USES: Recruitment, retention, industry collaboration, B2B business development, thought leadership

You may not be the most organized professional on the planet. And I'll be the first to admit that people have looked at my business card holder and cringed. It's stuffed to the brim with cards, exploding out of every angle. This mess used to be my bible—one of the things I'd grab first if my office were on fire. Although you may keep your business card book, it's quickly becoming irrelevant thanks to LinkedIn. The largest social network that's "strictly" professional, LinkedIn boasts more than 550 million users, in a space that's not for sharing pictures of your kids or talking about sports or music.

A business card doesn't tell someone when her former colleague left financial planning to become a singer and songwriter. Nor does a business card tell you when a former assistant at your first job made partner at a top law firm. LinkedIn does. That's what's appealing about it to users. What's appealing about it to businesses? Well, essentially the same thing.

LinkedIn, when used properly, is a recruiter's dream. Every individual is no further than about six degrees away from any person who would be a good candidate to recruit to join her team, or to talk with about a business deal or partnership. In addition, LinkedIn can be used to position your company as the single best place to work in the industry. Consider working with your HR department to create a dynamic company profile, with videos about the corporate culture of your organization. More recently, LinkedIn added Showcase Pages, which allow you to highlight any specific aspect of your brand or company. This is a great tool if you're trying to promote a new initiative.

LinkedIn is especially useful for marketers in the business-to-business space. Executives and prospective customers, vendors, and partners feel safer networking on a website created just for business than they feel about networking on Facebook. Consider creating a space for your company to be the thought leader in your field. Do you run an accounting firm? Create a LinkedIn group where CPAs can connect and collaborate about new tax laws. Own a chain of restaurants? Create a LinkedIn community for restaurant management professionals. In 2011, LinkedIn launched LinkedIn Today, then called Pulse, which now is your home page feed, a curated news product that allows users to see what articles are resonating most with their LinkedIn connections. As the product has grown, it's made LinkedIn a place where people spend more time, making it more appealing to marketers.

In 2013, LinkedIn launched the LinkedIn Influencer program where business and world leaders published articles on a weekly or monthly basis. I was fortunate enough to slip into the program, and I've been blessed to write alongside Richard Branson, Bill Gates, and Barack Obama. In fact, I've generated over 25 million page views with my posts, more than just about any other Influencer. Even though I'm much less famous, accomplished, or smart than the other Influencers, I've been more successful—proving that content itself is more important than the person writing the content on LinkedIn. In the spring of 2014, LinkedIn opened up its publishing platform to all of its users. Now, you too can publish your content and articles on LinkedIn. It's similar to a blog—only there are 550 million fellow professionals who can potentially read any article you publish on LinkedIn, and they're all connected by varying degrees to your own network. To date, I've published four articles with over one million views each!

Over the last couple of years, the combination of blogging on LinkedIn and the addition of the home page feed have really helped LinkedIn take off. LinkedIn is no longer just a way to store electronic business cards, but rather the perfect space for professional social content. What I mean by "professional social" is that users are now sharing much more content than ever before, but all of the content is professional. If you're going to share a picture of you with your family, most likely, that would be better on Instagram or Facebook. However, if you want to share a really interesting journal article that's relevant to your industry, then LinkedIn is the perfect place to go. This is an exciting and interesting evolution as it gives everyone a chance to demonstrate their knowledge and thought leadership.

The newest addition to LinkedIn is native video, which was added in the fall of 2017. This means that all users can now upload video content directly to the site, instead of just sharing a link to YouTube or Vimeo. Video is a great resource as it allows you to share a more personal message and build trust with your audience in ways that you can't through writing. Some of the most popular video content on LinkedIn includes behind-the-scenes footage at an event or the office, messages from high-level executives, and regularly shared series. Now, of course, you can use Facebook in many of these ways, but remember, you want to engage others in ways that are consistent with a target's DNA. Many potential job candidates won't take kindly to your posting on their Facebook wall about an upcoming position at your company—especially if they are Facebook friends with their boss. Many senior executives, even if they're on Facebook, might consider Facebook only for personal use and stick to LinkedIn for all of their business networking, business activity, and decision making. It's simply a matter of the users applying the tools in the ways that work best for them.

SLIDESHARE: THE INSTAGRAM OF LINKEDIN

Founded in 2006, Slideshare is a presentation-focused social media network for businesses. Slideshare was initially meant to host strictly business presentations, but it has exploded as a fun, interactive social marketing platform in recent years and has become a lead driver. Presentations posted to Slideshare entertain, inspire, and educate. In 2012, LinkedIn acquired Slideshare for $118.75 million.

From small businesses to major brands, and every business in between, marketers have a unique opportunity to share beautiful PowerPoint presentations, webinars, and videos on Slideshare. There are over 80 million Slideshare users, and a vast majority of the traffic on Slideshare comes from search. This shows that Slideshare is a fantastic opportunity to expand your audience and demonstrate thought leadership. If you're focused on selling and marketing to other business professionals, you should definitely take a look at Slideshare.

YOUTUBE: IF A PICTURE'S WORTH A THOUSAND WORDS, HOW MANY IS A VIDEO WORTH?

BEST USES: Demonstrating corporate culture or product uses

YouTube, owned by Google, is one of the largest search engines in the world in its own right. It is the largest video-sharing website in the world by far, with over five billion videos watched each day and 400 hours of video being uploaded per minute. Use YouTube to showcase your corporate culture and your coolest products, services, and expertise so that when people search for keywords related to your business, your videos will appear.

There is no better way to tell a story than through video. While television has dominated the video space for decades, through YouTube and other online video channels your videos can be seen for a lot less money than what you would spend for traditional television advertising. While videos that are short and sweet perform the best on social media platforms such as Facebook and Instagram, YouTube is a great place to share longer form (8–12 minutes) content. The average time a user will spend on YouTube is 40 minutes per session. When people are on YouTube, they are more likely to be ready to watch a longer video than when they are scrolling around on Facebook or Instagram.

Are you a trusted advisor to your audience, creating valuable how-to videos? Are you completely customer focused, capturing video of users and allowing them to speak about your products or services? Whoever you are, consider taking the things your fans love most about you and bringing them to life on YouTube. See Table A.8 for a list of five companies that have been able to harness the power of YouTube in creating their own video content and channels.

TABLE A.8 **Five Amazing YouTube Channels**

COMPANY	YOUTUBE SITE
GoPro	https://www.youtube.com/GoProCamera
BMW	https://www.youtube.com/BMW
Nintendo	https://www.youtube.com/Nintendo
LEGO	https://www.youtube.com/LEGO
Red Bull	https://www.youtube.com/redbull

In addition to creating your own content on YouTube, many brands look to vloggers, or video influencers, to talk about them in their videos. There are thousands of popular vloggers across dozens of categories. Just a few examples are Casey Neistat, Tanner Fox, and Zoe Sugg. The idea here is to find YouTubers who not only have large followings but would be inclined to talk about you, and send them free stuff! Who knows, they might just vlog about you to millions.

Think about why you search online. It's usually because you want to know something—how to do something or where to find something. Consider creating videos that answer those questions relating to your products or customer experiences.

Also, forget the notion that YouTube is about creating "viral videos" and getting millions of views. Is it possible to create videos on YouTube that will go viral? Sure. But think of the last 10 viral videos you've seen on YouTube. Chances are few of them, if any, were created by or for a business. Most of these videos take off organically. Videos that are "produced" don't tend to go viral. What makes content viral is that very thing that often can't be produced: the spontaneity of human experience. Even parody videos are based on an initial experience that was captured on video and released to the world, then deemed "viral."

You will receive far more relevant views answering questions focused on your customers or prospective customers than if you try and force virality. Remember, it's not about reaching the most people with your video. It's about reaching the right people.

PINTEREST: CONTENT CURATION AT ITS BEST

BEST USES: Curating visual content, driving e-commerce

Pinterest is a pinboard-esque social network that allows users to curate images and videos around categories based on interests, themes, hobbies, and so on. Cofounded by CEO Ben Silbermann, Pinterest's mission is to "connect everyone in the world through the things they find interesting." The platform launched in March 2010, but it experienced a heavy spike in popularity in January 2012, reaching 11.7 million unique users and becoming the fastest site in Internet history to reach the 10 million mark. In March 2012, it became the fourth largest social network in the United States. At the start of 2018, there were over 200 million monthly active users on the platform. Among the key demographic of Pinterest users are females ages 25 to 34, and popular interests are crafts, cooking, gifts, fashion, and interior design.

On Pinterest, users are able to easily curate by "pinning" images and videos that interest them from other websites (hence the name: pin + interest = Pinterest). Images can be pinned via a "Save" button or on the mobile app. A user can share an image pinned by another user in an action called *repinning*. Pins can be organized by topics called *boards*. As with Twitter, users can follow fellow users and see their interests in a feed.

But this social network isn't just for millions of women to pin designer shoes—a majority of users who visit the network are doing so with intent to buy. Pinterest is the planning network. When you post or advertise on Pinterest, you're reaching consumers who are actively looking for goods and services. For instance, if you're a painting company, consider targeting Pinterest users who are searching for wall color inspiration. Many brands use Pinterest to link images to product pages on their websites and drive direct sales through the growing social network. Consumers are very visual, and brands have an opportunity with Pinterest's emphasis on the visual to inspire current and potential customers to make a purchase. The platform has even developed a price display feature to generate a price tag banner across the image of a product. Online marketplace Etsy has taken advantage of this feature to make it easier for its more than one million followers to buy what they see and like. Check out Table A.9 for six other brands thriving on Pinterest.

TABLE A.9 **Six Brands Thriving on Pinterest**

BRAND	PINTEREST
L.L.Bean	Pinterest.com/LLBean
StubHub	Pinterest.com/StubHub
Nordstrom	Pinterest.com/Nordstrom
Lululemon	Pinterest.com/Lululemon
Target	Pinterest.com/Target
DIY Network	Pinterest.com/DIYnetwork

As a brand, the first step is to begin following and repinning others' relevant content. Build your audience, and figure out what interests them. From there, explore these Pinterest strategies.

Create Boards Beyond Your Products or Services

Successful brands expand their Pinterest board horizons beyond just pinning images of their own products. Create boards with unexpected themes, and curate content that is still relevant to your brand but more relevant to your customers. Take Chobani's "Fit With It" board, for instance. Chobani is able to connect with over 44,500 followers and customers on another level and show off an extra dimension of personality with its board dedicated to fitness and motivation.

Go Behind the Scenes

Give your followers a more intimate connection with your brand by offering a behind-the-scenes look. For example, *The Today Show* shares exclusive shots of the show on its "Anchor Antics" board to over 171,000 followers.

Humanize

Pinned pictures have the ability to reveal the human side to your brand. With images and videos sharing the stories of its 1,200 farm families, Cabot Cheese's Pinterest board "Farmers and Farms" reveals the people behind the brand to over 12,000 followers and more.

Crowdsource

You will be able to better understand your customers' wants and needs if you crowdsource your curated content. Ask your customers to pin relevant pictures and tag your brand. From there, you can repin content on a special board—for example,

Starbucks' "Starbucks Cup Art" board shows customers' artwork on Starbucks cups.

SNAPCHAT: SPONTANEOUSLY AND INSTANTANEOUSLY CONNECT TO CONSUMERS

BEST USES: Directly share pictures and videos with your audience

Snapchat launched in 2011 as a platform to instantly share pictures with friends, and by the end of 2012, users could share videos. Unless the pictures and videos are saved (via screenshot), they are deleted after the allotted amount of time. In October 2013, Snapchat added *Stories*, which allows users to share a picture or video with all of their friends on Snapchat. In January 2015, Snapchat launched the *Discover* feature, which gave major brands and networks a way to advertise and reach users through the platform. Snapchat now has over 191 million active daily users. However, Snapchat's main demographic is very young, with 71 percent of users under 34 years old and 45 percent of Snapchat users between 18 and 24 years old.

Should You Use Snapchat?

As with every social media platform, the answer is: it depends. If you are a brand that markets to millennials, then absolutely. Also, if you have, or are trying to build, a strong personal brand that you want to appeal to young people, then Snapchat is a great platform to use. The instantaneity and impermanence of Snapchat allows for content to be incredibly authentic. As long as you are sharing valuable content, your following will grow.

In Table A.10 are five brands that use Snapchat effectively to share fun and engaging content with their audiences.

TABLE A.10	Five Brands Using Snapchat Effectively
BRAND	**TUMBLR SITE**
General Electric	@generalelectric
Sour Patch Kids	@sourpatchsnaps
Warby Parker	@warbyparker
The New York Times	@thenytimes
Cisco	@wearecisco

TUMBLR: SHARING IN HYPERDRIVE

BEST USES: Expanding content, reaching a specific demographic, strengthening relationships

Tumblr is a microblogging platform that allows users to create text, audio, image, and video content in a short-form blog. Launched by David Karp in February 2007, the platform became popular with teenagers and young adults. As of February 2018, Tumblr was host to 396.8 million blogs and more than 158.1 billion total posts. Today, it is owned by Web giant Yahoo!, and it continues to grow by 120,000 sign-ups per day.

Tumblr is an incredibly user-friendly blogging platform that makes it easy to start building a community. Users are given a Dashboard that, similar to Facebook's News Feed, allows them to see recent posts from Tumblr blogs they follow. Posts can then be reblogged or *liked*.

Businesses, especially in retail or media, can use this microblogging platform as a sort of social media hub, facilitating content curation and enabling them to expand their Facebook and Twitter content by feeding it into the vast Tumblr ecosystem. Brands can also build content directly onto Tumblr, offering unique content to help build a strong following. Vans does an incredible job of creating a sense of community while showcasing its products. Even if your brand isn't image based, you have the opportunity to post or reblog relevant photos. Matt

Silverman of Mashable described to me that Tumblr is "sharing in hyperdrive," with a multitude of recycled content being churned daily. Make sure to highlight your products using high-quality photos that don't sell aggressively to consumers. Denny's does a great job of letting its Tumblr images speak for themselves (Figure A.2).

FIGURE A.2   **The Denny's Tumblr Page**

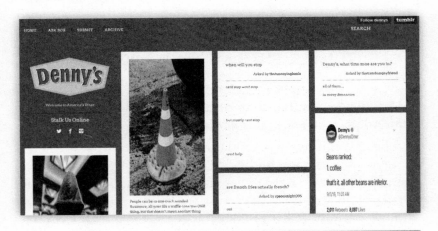

Another strategy is to give users an inside look into your brand to strengthen your relationship and foster loyalty. For example, in its "NBA Through the Lens," the NBA shows games from different angles and allows followers to view scenes ranging from the locker room to historic pictures. With Tumblr, brands can reach a young demographic, expand the reach of their content, and reinforce their relationships with consumers.

THE BLOGOSPHERE: EVERY BLOGGER IS "THE MEDIA" NOW

BEST USES: Connecting more deeply to your target audience; positioning yourself as a thought leader in your industry

A *blog* is a website, or part of a website, that features articles or entries displayed in reverse chronological order. There are more than 450 million blogs in the world,[1] and two million new blog articles are published daily. In order to be successful with a blog, you need to provide valuable content for your target audience, write consistently (at least twice a week), and provide a truly interactive atmosphere. Table A.11 provides a list of the best blogging platforms for you to get started.

TABLE A.11 **Four Best Blogging Platforms**

PLATFORM	WEBSITE	PROS
WordPress	Wordpress.com	Variety of themes and plug-ins on your own or as a WordPress-hosted blog
LinkedIn	LinkedIn.com	Automatically connect your network with your blog
Medium	Medium.com	Built-in audience introduces your content to others like you
Blogger	Blogger.com	Easy-to-use instantaneous setup

Many company blogs are unsuccessful because they are updated infrequently, and too often they're updated with broadcast materials that read like press releases, rather than being valuable resources or content. With a blog, you have the opportunity to include longer text updates than you're able to through Facebook or Twitter. A blog also allows you to incorporate photos, videos, polls, and other multimedia. You can also tell stories at your own pace and on your own terms.

Building a successful blogging strategy is twofold. It includes both the creation and growth of your own blog as well as interaction with other bloggers writing for your target audience and/or about similar topics. By solidifying a large audience for your blog, you can, in effect, become your own publisher or media network and cut out or reduce the so-called media middleman. Many blogs today have larger audiences than a great deal of newspapers, for instance, so you can use blog content to grow your own media outlet.

Five Reasons Your Company Should Be Blogging

Of the many reasons your company should be utilizing blogs, the following five are the strongest and will provide you with ideas on how to start, and continue, the blogging process:

1. **Extend the conversation.** A corporate blog is the perfect outlet for long-form communication with your audience and/or clients. Twitter and Facebook are ideal platforms for quick, short-form messaging—and they are incredibly important—but a blog allows you to really dive into the topics and trends that matter in your industry.

   Also, blogging aids you in being transparent and providing the "insider look" your audience craves. Someone researching your company will be able to glean more information from the company blog than is available in the standard website "About" section and from social media updates. While these forms of communication heavily involve proactive response to questions and concerns, a blog stands as a channel for sharing in-depth ideas, practices, and stories that make your company unique . . . and amazing. You can even use your blog as a platform for crowdsourced information.

   Developing a new product? Ask your blog audience for input and ideas, getting the targeted consumers involved in the development process!

2. **Attract future customers.** Blogs influence purchasing decisions—whether you are giving your readers a behind-the-scenes look at how a product was conceptualized and made

or showing your products in action, consumers will have an added reinforcement as to why your products rock. In this sense, a product can be literal, such as a camera, or figurative, if your company provides services rather than tangible goods. You can think of your company's blog as a cost-effective extension of your sales calls or advertisements. In reality, twenty-first-century consumers have come to expect the brands they purchase from to be available to them in the online social world, and having a corporate blog where they can research and interact with you is one of the first steps to take in meeting that expectation.

3. **Attract future employees.** A company or brand is only as good as the talent it recruits to represent it. By providing potential employees a look into your corporate structure—life at the company, how ideas are formed, and the exciting things that are happening—you are essentially dangling the carrot. Let your target employee base know why working for you would be an amazing opportunity, and they will come to you.

4. **Position yourself as a leader.** As a brand, you want to be seen as innovative—a thought leader in your industry. To see how competitive companies in your industry are getting involved in the blogosphere, check out the resources listed in Table A.12.

TABLE A.12	**Four Great Resources to Find Blogs in Your Industry**
RESOURCE	**WEBSITE**
BlogDash	BlogDash.com
On Top List	OnTopList.com
Google Blogs	BlogSearch.Google.com
Blog Lovin	BlogLovin.com

Blogging allows you to share your company's best ideas and intelligent commentary for what's happening in your space. Having a well-written blog will help you stand out from, or above, your competitors. By allowing multiple people to contribute either posts or simply ideas for the posts, everyone in your company has a voice—and I'm sure they have a lot of great things to say.

5. **Search engine optimization (SEO).** Ideally, blogs are updated regularly, which inherently lends itself to great SEO. HubSpot has reported that companies that have active blogs receive up to 55 percent more traffic[2]—including higher rates of both organic search and referral traffic. HubSpot also found that companies with an active blog earn up to 97 percent more inbound links. By utilizing appropriate keywords, sharing "link love" with others, and submitting your blog to directories, you will help drive more eyes to your page. Once you post the content on your blog, it will live there indefinitely. Someone searching for a specific topic can stumble upon a post from months, or even years, ago. Blog content continues to work for you long after it's been published. And of course, more eyes on your company's blog and website ultimately will lead to higher customer conversions down the road.

TWITCH, FLICKR, SOUNDCLOUD, YELP, AND THE HUNDREDS OF OTHER NICHE SOCIAL NETWORKS

BEST USES: Connecting to a highly targeted audience

You know your audience. That's your job—as a marketer. If you don't, it's time to go back to step one and start listening and understanding your customer. If you do, then it's definitely in your best interest to do a little research on niche networks for your heavy-user group. While most of your customers are probably using Facebook, Instagram, LinkedIn, and YouTube, some of your most passionate customers might be using smaller, niche social networks. There is literally a community for every interest, so if you know what your customers are into, you can build a presence in the niche community that makes the most sense.

Twitch is a live streaming social network for video game players that grew so quickly Amazon purchased it in 2016. Frozen pizza product brand Totino's knew video gamers were a huge part of its audience, so in 2016 it hosted a three-and-a-half-hour gaming competition on Twitch where one gamer sat on a regular couch and the other on the "Bucking Couch," which would spin, roll, and buck based on chat commands sent in by viewers. Pizza rolls were obviously on the set for players to munch on during the battle.

SoundCloud is another very popular niche social network. It is a great place to share music and connect with fellow artists. Is your brand all about vampires? Try VampireFreaks.com. All about dogs? Dogster.com. There's even a rumor about a site for secret agents in the United States called A-Space. It's all about finding the best group for your brand.

Yelp, a review site for restaurants and other local service providers, and TripAdvisor, a review site for travel, are just two of dozens of review sites for different niches and topics. User reviews are still one of the most trusted forms of marketing, with more than 70 percent of Web users trusting this form of consumer engagement.[3] Whether you should devote your resources to any of these niche sites depends on what you're marketing and who your audience is.

As a marketer, you have a responsibility to ensure that any reviews you solicit are honest and come from real customers. The best way to receive such reviews is simply to ask for them. When I get a receipt that asks me to fill out a survey about my experience for a chance to win a $10 gift card, I am perplexed. Why not ask me to share my review on Yelp, or TripAdvisor, or some other appropriate review site? If the review is good, it helps the brand infinitely more. If the review is bad, it's echoing what many are feeling, and it gives the opportunity for the brand to respond publicly.

Niche networks aren't always as brand friendly as Facebook, Instagram, or Twitter, but they are worthwhile nonetheless. Begin by researching how the community works, and ask community leaders about how to best get involved. It's a smaller net you're casting, but an incredibly valuable one if you engage in a way that works for the group. Remember, your goal is to find your audience, wherever they are, listen to them, engage them, and join them.

CHAPTER 2

1. http://Investor.FB.com, accessed January 12, 2015.
2. http://internetlivestats.com/twitter-statistics, accessed January 12, 2015.

CHAPTER 8

1. Aaron Sorkin, interview with Stephen Colbert, The Colbert Report, Comedy Central, September 30, 2010, available at http://thecolbertreport.cc.com/videos/h7gmgz/aaron-sorkin, accessed January 12, 2015.

CHAPTER 9

1. https://archive.ama.org/archive/ResourceLibrary/documents/Ethics%20Code.pdf.

APPENDIX

1. http://www.wpvirtuoso.com/how-many-blogs-are-on-the-internet/, accessed January 12, 2015.
2. http://blog.hubspot.com/blog/tabid/6307/bid/5014/Study-Shows-Business-Blogging-Leads-to-55-More-Website-Visitors.aspx, accessed January 12, 2015.
3. http://www.nielsen.com/us/en/insights/news/2012/consumer-trust-in-online-social-and-mobile-advertising-grows.html, accessed January 12, 2015.

Dave Kerpen is the founder and chairman of Likeable Local, a social media software company serving thousands of small businesses, as well as the cofounder and chairman of Likeable Media, an award-winning social media and content marketing agency. He is the *New York Times* bestselling author of four books and a frequently requested global keynote speaker.

Following Dave's sponsored wedding that raised over $100,000, including $20,000 for charity, he and his wife Carrie started and transformed theKBuzz (founded in 2007) into Likeable Media, the only three-time WOMMY Award winner for excellence from the Word of Mouth Marketing Association (WOMMA) and one of the 500 fastest growing private companies in the United States, according to *Inc.* magazine, for both 2011 and 2012.

Named by *Entrepreneur* magazine as one of 10 up-and-coming leaders, Dave has been featured on BBC, CNBC's *On the Money*, ABC's *World News Tonight*, CBS's *The Early Show*, in the *New York Times*, and in countless blogs. Dave has also keynoted at dozens of conferences across the globe including Singapore, Athens, Dubai, San Francisco, and Mexico City.

Likeable Social Media: How to Delight Your Customers, Create an Irresistible Brand, and Be Generally Amazing on Facebook and Other Social Networks was Dave's first *New York Times* bestselling book. Dave followed *Likeable Social Media* with three more books: *Likeable Business*, *Likeable Leadership*, and *The Art of People.* Dave lives in Port Washington, New York, with his wife Carrie and three children, Charlotte, Kate, and Seth.

Dave Kerpen

—

International
Keynote Speaker
including Greece, Singapore,
Mexico, and Thailand

New York Times
bestselling author of 3 books

#1 LinkedIn Influencer
of all time in page views with over
20 million ahead of Bill Gates, Richard
Branson, Jack Welch, and Barack Obama

You read about likeable brands.

Now it's time to become one.

To learn more about working with Likeable the agency, visit www.likeable.com.

 likeable